Arms at Rest

Recent Titles in
Contributions in American History
Series Editor: Jon L. Wakelyn

The Whiskey Rebellion: Past and Present Perspectives
Steven R. Boyd, editor

Law, Alcohol, and Order: Perspectives on National Prohibition
David E. Kyvig, editor

The Line of Duty: Maverick Congressmen and the Development of
American Political Culture, 1836–1860
Johanna Nicol Shields

Propaganda in an Open Society: The Roosevelt Administration and the
Media, 1933–1941
Richard W. Steele

Congress, Courts, and Criminals: The Development of Federal Criminal
Law, 1801–1829
Dwight F. Henderson

Radical Beginnings: Richard Hofstadter and the 1930s
Susan Stout Baker

Organize or Perish: America's Independent Progressives, 1913–1933
Eugene M. Tobin

The Absent Marx: Class Analysis and Liberal History in Twentieth-
Century America
Ian Tyrrell

"Co-operation with Like-minded Peoples": British Influences on
American Security Policy, 1945–1949
Richard A. Best, Jr.

The Antislavery Rank and File: A Social Profile of the Abolitionists'
Constituency
Edward Magdol

The Paradox of Professionalism: Reform and Public Service in Urban
America, 1900–1940
Don S. Kirschner

American Frontier and Western Issues: A Historiographical Review
Roger L. Nichols, editor

Continuity and Change in Electoral Politics, 1893–1928
Paul Kleppner

ARMS AT REST

Peacemaking and Peacekeeping in American History

EDITED BY

JOAN R. CHALLINOR
AND
ROBERT L. BEISNER

CONTRIBUTIONS IN AMERICAN HISTORY,
NUMBER 121

GREENWOOD PRESS
NEW YORK · WESTPORT, CONNECTICUT · LONDON

This book is dedicated to all those willing to work for peace.

Library of Congress Cataloging-in-Publication Data

Arms at Rest.

(Contributions in American history, 0084–9219 ;
no. 121)
Bibliography: p.
Includes index.
1. United States—Foreign relations—1783–1865.
2. United States—History—Revolution, 1775–1783—
Peace. 3. United States—Foreign relations. 4. Peace.
I. Challinor, Joan R. II. Beisner, Robert L.
III. Series.
E183.7.A75 1987   327.73′009   86–14954
ISBN 0–313–24642–4 (lib. bdg. : alk. paper)

Library of Congress Catalog Card Number: 86–14954
ISBN: 0–313–24642–4
ISSN: 0084–9219

First published in 1987

Greenwood Press, Inc.
88 Post Road West, Westport, Connecticut 06881

Printed in the United States of America

The paper used in this book complies with the
Permanent Paper Standard issued by the National
Information Standards Organization (Z39.48–1984).

10 9 8 7 6 5 4 3 2 1

Contents

INTRODUCTION   vii

PART I:

   WAR, PEACE, AND AMERICAN CULTURE
   AND SOCIETY IN THE REVOLUTIONARY
   ERA   xv

1. "May all our Citizens be Soldiers, and all our
   Soldiers Citizens": The Ambiguities of Female
   Citizenship in the New Nation
   Linda K. Kerber   1

2. The Problem of Dependency after America Became
   Independent
   David F. Musto   23

PART II:

   PEACE AND EXPANSION THROUGH
   COMMERCE, COOPERATION, AND
   SINGULAR INITIATIVE   37

3. Trade as a Precursor of Diplomacy: The Beginnings
   of American Commercial Relations with the
   Pacific and Indian Ocean Areas, 1782–1815
   Harold D. Langley   39

4. Winning the Peace: The New Diplomacy in a
   World of Change
   James A. Field, Jr.   75

PART III:

   THE VARIED PATHS TO PEACE IN THE
   NINETEENTH AND TWENTIETH
   CENTURIES   99

5. United States Expansionism and the British North
   American Provinces, 1783–1871
   Reginald C. Stuart   101

6. The Anglo-American Armies and Peace, 1783–1868
   Russell F. Weigley   133

7. The Precarious Peace: China, the United States,
   and the Quemoy-Matsu Crisis, 1954–1955, 1958
   Michael A. Lutzker   161

PART IV:

   PEACE THROUGH THE OBSOLESCENCE
   OF WAR?   187

8. The Evolution of Battle and the Prospects of Peace
   John Keegan   189

BIBLIOGRAPHICAL ESSAY   203

INDEX   213

ABOUT THE CONTRIBUTORS   223

Introduction

In May of 1783, five months after the negotiators for the United States and Great Britain signed the Preliminary Treaty of Peace, Frederick II of Prussia shared his thoughts on the treaty with Frederick William von Thulmeier, his minister plenipotentiary at The Hague. "I am very much persuaded," the king wrote, "that this so-called independence of the American colonies will not amount to much . . . little by little, colony by colony, province by province will rejoin England on their former footing." Fortunately for the United States, Frederick's view, widely shared in Europe, proved mistaken. Two hundred years later, in 1983, the nation he predicted would revert to colonial status observed the bicentennial of its first peace treaty, now called the Treaty of Paris.

By 1983 the United States had celebrated three bicentennials: independence, with typical American exuberance in 1976; victory on the redoubts of Yorktown, with military pomp in 1981; and the Treaty of Paris, with a diplomatic emphasis in 1983. This book of essays is the result of one of the events sponsored by the National Committee for the Bicentennial of the Treaty of Paris: a symposim on peacemaking and peacekeeping held in Washington, D.C. in September 1983, organized jointly by the Smithsonian Institution and The American University.

No achievement of the Revolutionary War was more important

than the signing of the peace treaty between Great Britain and the United States on 3 September 1783. This agreement, aptly described by Samuel F. Bemis as "the greatest victory in the annals of American diplomacy," was crucial to the birth of the United States. It ended the American Revolution, acknowledged the independence of the United States, more than doubled America's territory, and ushered the fledgling nation into the world of sovereign states.

For contemporary Europeans, 3 September 1783 was the day on which the United States won its independence. The fourth of July, 1776, was merely the day on which the colonies *declared* their independence from Great Britain; it did not signify that freedom had actually been attained. No matter that John Adams, Thomas Jefferson, and all of America dated the independence of the colonies from 4 July—in European eyes, American independence could be achieved only when George III acknowledged their freedom by treaty. After seven long years of struggle, the British king did reluctantly recognize the independence of the United States of America. The first article of the peace treaty declared: "His Britannic Majesty acknowledges the said United States to be free Sovereign and independent states," and the states were then enumerated one by one.

The treaty's importance is far greater than its fame; the Treaty of Paris has become America's "forgotten treaty," long relegated to the back room of history. In 1883, its centennial passed unnoticed, and as 1983 approached its bicentennial seemed headed for a similar fate. Not even a bicentennial nod was planned by the U.S. government. Other bicentennial events—commemoration of the Declaration of Independence and the battle of Yorktown, and the upcoming celebration of the framing of the Constitution—have been assigned generously funded, well-staffed presidential commissions. But for America's first peace treaty there were no government plans, no commission, no appropriated funds—in short, no national recognition for the Treaty of Paris.

There *are* valid reasons why this treaty is so easily forgotten. First and foremost, the winners write the history of any war, and to the victors belong the date of the birth of the new nation. The American Revolution is no exception. Thus July fourth, not September third, is our "independence day." Second, the beautiful language of the

Declaration of Independence has convinced Americans that their independence was achieved instantly by the sheer majesty of that document. Third, the military drama of Yorktown and the import of its being the last Revolutionary battle have persuaded most Americans that the war ended not at a peace table in Paris, but on that Virginia battlefield in 1781. Surely our government cannot be faulted for failing to celebrate an event unknown to most Americans and hardly mentioned in United States history textbooks.

By default, then, the observance of the bicentennial of the Treaty of Paris in 1983–84 was a private effort. Dismayed by the oversight, struck by the value of commemorating our first great peace treaty in an age when peace seemed tenuous at best, and encouraged by President Ronald Reagan's statement that if government fails to act, private citizens should step forward to fill the need, a group of civic-minded citizens organized the National Committee for the Bicentennial of the Treaty of Paris.

Composed of noted historians, past and present ambassadors and other diplomats, three senators, churchmen, and men and women prominent in civic affairs, the Committee began its work in the spring of 1982. The Honorary Committee consisted of Her Majesty Queen Elizabeth II, President Ronald Reagan, and Vice-President George H. W. Bush. The aims of the Committee were four-fold: to organize a national observance and increase public knowledge of this historic treaty; to mark the abiding friendship between Great Britain and the United States; to celebrate our friendship with France and remember that without the help of our first ally, independence could not have been won; and most significantly, to call attention to peace and historic peacemaking while emphasizing the importance of the too-often neglected topic of diplomatic negotiations.

It was this last objective that provided the focus for the bicentennial celebration. The Committee decided that a heightened regard for diplomacy and diplomats in the search for peace—the diplomacy and diplomats of 1783 and of 1983—would be a worthy theme for the Treaty's observance.

The phrase used to embody the diplomatic thrust of this observance was "the work of peace." Benjamin Franklin in 1785 first used these words to describe diplomacy when, on leaving Europe for the last time, he described peacemakng to the British negotiator, David

Hartley: "We have long been fellow labourers in the best of all work, the work of peace." "The work of peace" became the theme of the bicentennial, emphasizing both the labor and the tenacity that peacemaking requires. Peace requires long, arduous effort—it is not easily attained. Diplomats are intimately concerned with peace, afforded little recognition, and given even less thanks for their difficult and tireless labor.

A recognition of the talents required for successful diplomacy and a heightened regard for the skills of international negotiation were the centerpieces of the observance. The United States, the committee suggested, should put negotiators on an equal footing with its martial heroes, putting diplomats in their rightful place beside warriors in the American pantheon. The Committee encouraged the United States to be about the work of peace with the same concentration of effort it has summoned up when going to war. Durable peace, the events of 1783 demonstrated, required struggle, mutual trust, and the will to achieve peace.

The committee's task was both educational and celebratory. Its greatest educational problem was Americans' lack of knowledge about both the Treaty of Paris and its negotiators. Five peace commissioners were appointed by Congress in 1781; three actually carried out the work. Thomas Jefferson remained in America because of his wife's illness, and Henry Laurens was captured on the high seas by the British and sent to the Tower, where he languished, unable to take part in the negotiations. The three active negotiators—Benjamin Franklin, John Jay, and John Adams—are well-known today, but not for their negotiating triumphs. They are mainly remembered for other achievements: Franklin as writer and scientist, Jay as the first chief justice of the United States, and Adams as its second president. Other than historians, many Americans were surprised to learn that these men had also served their country as diplomats. The narrative of the negotiations leading to the Treaty of Paris is as dramatic as the story of Yorktown, yet it is practically unknown to the general public.

To bring the treaty to the attention of the public, the National Committee sponsored a number of educational events in 1983 and 1984. A half-hour movie and an accompanying teachers' guide on the treaty negotiations were made in conjunction with the Smithsonian Institution and disseminated throughout the high schools of seven eastern states. The Committee also created and distributed a poster exhibit for schools, historical societies, and libraries. The Smithsonian's National Portrait Gallery mounted a major exhibit on the treaty. The exhibit placed the treaty squarely into its world context, using both portraits and captions to explain how the war between England and America widened into a major European conflict, eventually contested in the Caribbean, India, Gibraltar, and America.

Music played a part in the celebration. The Committee persuaded over twelve symphony orchestras to play concerts in honor of the treaty, and commissioned a short composition entitled "Fanfare for Peace" from Stephen D. Burton. This new composition was played by the National Symphony Orchestra on the steps of the Capitol in Washington, D.C., one day after the actual bicentennial of the treaty signing. A ballet entitled "Signatures" was commissioned for the San Francisco Ballet by friends of the Committee.

The Committee's specially designed "Treaty of Paris" balloon flew in France, Great Britain, and in more than a dozen meets in the United States. A flyer, designed to resemble an eighteenth-century broadside and distributed free to the public at launch sites, explained the relationship between the treaty and the first balloon flights in 1783, which were enthusiastically witnessed by America's three negotiators: they saw both the new science of ballooning and the newly independent United States as the wave of the future.

The French government organized a four-day celebration of the treaty and its European counterpart, the 1783 Treaty of Versailles. Reconstructed American revolutionary war units took a leading part in these festivities, held both at Paris and Versailles.

Several religious commemorations also took place. The committee helped organize special church services in three great cathedrals: St. Paul's in London, Notre Dame in Paris, and the National Cathedral in Washington.

The people of the United States received a gift from Great Britain in honor of the treaty. Sir David Wills gave a splendid gift of bells, replicas of those in Westminster Abbey, that were accepted by the United States Congress and now hang in the Old Post Office Building in Washington, D.C. In return, the committee donated a set of new iron gates for Grosvenor Square, London, designating them "The Diplomatic Gates" and dedicating them to all British and

American diplomats who for two centuries have labored for peace and understanding between their countries.

Although the United States government fell short of a proper observance, the academic community enthusiastically turned its attention to the treaty, without prodding by the committee. Many academic gatherings had been scheduled long before the committee came into existence. To mention but a few of these scholarly meetings, the Franklin Guild in Bloomington, Indiana sponsored a four-day symposium on French-American relations over the last two centuries and explored the importance of the treaty to the Midwest; Princeton University offered a symposium on "The Treaty of Paris and American Independence"; and Georgetown University's Institute for the Study of Diplomacy held a seminar on "The Modern Ambassador." The Smithsonian's Woodrow Wilson International Center for Scholars and the Folger Institute's Center for the History of British Political Thought jointly sponsored a two-day symposium. It addressed the effect of the successful revolt of the American colonies on relations among the nations of Europe between the early 1780s and the outbreak of the Napoleonic Wars.

Soon after organizing, the committee decided to sponsor a symposium on peacemaking and peacekeeping. Aware that the treaty itself would be fully considered in other symposia, the committee strove to widen the discussion to include peacemaking not only in the eighteenth century but the nineteenth and twentieth centuries as well. Thus the committee joined with the Smithsonian's Office of Symposia and Seminars and with the Department of History of The American University to sponsor a symposium appropriately entitled, "The Work of Peace."

This symposium on historic peacemaking and peacekeeping formed an important part of the bicentennial observance. One of the benefits of centennials and bicentennials is that the historical profession's scrutiny of a single event results in a "state-of-the-art" report both for historians and for the general public. Further, bringing a single event to the forefront of historical studies can stimulate future scholarship.

Unfortunately, there was little in the way of "state-of-the-art" studies on peacemaking and peacekeeping. As General Omar Bradley remarked in 1949: "Ours is a world of nuclear giants and ethical infants. We know more about war than we know about peace, more about killing than about living." Wilton Dillon of the Smithsonian's Office of Symposia and Seminars and the editors of this volume— Joan R. Challinor, chair of the National Committee for the Bicentennial of the Treaty of Paris, and Robert L. Beisner, chair of The American University History Department—sought to help correct this problem by asking the authors of the following chapters to turn their attention, not to the times when society's fabric had been rent by war but rather when it had been kept intact through the preservation of peace.

Linda K. Kerber, aware that rising social classes often gain status through participation in war and revolution, examines the meaning of the American revolutionary war, and the peace that followed, for American women. David F. Musto explores the psychological adjustments required among Americans during the same period, as Britain's role changed from parent to enemy, and then to former enemy. Harold D. Langley, focusing on the extent to which Americans saw peace after the Revolution as an opportunity for profit and as a private rather than government-dictated political issue, depicts the mercantile community's vigorous and confident outward thrust into the Far East. James A. Field, Jr., also emphasizing the role of private citizens, discusses the extraordinary energy with which merchants, missionaries, and many others hoped to secure the peace of 1783 through the worldwide conveyance of American commodities, including those of republicanism and Christianity. Reginald C. Stuart and Russell F. Weigley both explore why peace was maintained between Canada and the United States after the War of 1812, arriving at remarkably different (but not incompatible) explanations. Moving to our own century, Michael A. Lutzker offers a rare analysis of a war that didn't happen, when in the 1950's the United States and the People's Republic of China maintained a formal state of peace during the recurring Quemoy-Matsu crisis, though several times approaching the brink of war. Finally, John Keegan, insisting that war must be identified with battle itself, speculates on the possibility that war has become obsolescent in our own era because man "has made battle more than flesh and blood can bear. . . . "

As a whole, the chapters—written by leading scholars from the United States, Great Britain, and Canada—do not present a simple or unified vision of peace. They show, on the contrary, that "peace" for one nation sometimes means defeat or frustration for another. They reflect an understanding that peace is a dearly-purchased commodity, sometimes achieved through means of force or the threat of force; and certainly that peace must be sought through active effort rather than passive hope. A novel theme that appears in some of the works that follow is that amicable ties among nations often have as much do with the actions and thoughts of private citizens as with the maneuverings of ambassadors or the campaigns of generals. Thus, from varying angles and perspectives, the authors suggest some of the most important prerequisites—and consequences—of peace.

Joan R. Challinor
Robert L. Beisner

PART I

War, Peace, and American Culture and Society in the Revolutionary Era

In chapter 1, Linda K. Kerber describes the impact of the Revolutionary War on women and explores the ambiguous prospects of the peace that followed. In an unusual analysis of the connections between the amorphous eighteenth-century definitions of citizenship and the obligations to perform military service, she demonstrates that patriot women could claim their own revolutionary memories and a distinctive inheritance from the peace of 1783. In some respects they "redefined their political boundaries. . . ." They did not, however, create the instruments for collective action that might have produced significant political gains in postrevolutionary America.

In chapter 2, David F. Musto speculates on the psychological adjustments Americans made in their views of Britain and Britons, especially in the years after the New World nation had made its successful break from its mother country. Incorporating an assessment of recent psychohistorical approaches to early American history, Musto also offers insight into the contemporary strains between the United States and the third world. This essay should help Americans "empathize with the special relationship a young or small nation experiences when confronted with a world cultural power that threatens to engulf its formal independence."

1 LINDA K. KERBER

"May all our Citizens be Soldiers, and all our Soldiers Citizens": The Ambiguities of Female Citizenship in the New Nation

On 3 September 1783, Benjamin Franklin, John Adams, and John Jay made their way down the rue Jacob to the lodgings of David Hartley, the British Commissioner charged with the negotiation of the Definitive Treaty of Peace. The Peace of Paris they signed that day was a public triumph for the Americans and a personal triumph for Adams and Jay. They had not only negotiated firmly and effectively with their British enemy, they had outwitted their French allies, their compatriots in Congress, and their own colleague Franklin to resolve the War of the Revolution in a way which resulted in wider boundaries for the United States than the French had bargained for. Preparing for a celebratory ball, John Jay's wife, Sarah Livingston Jay, drafted a list of toasts, beginning with, "The United States of America, may they be perpetual."

Standing at the threshold of peace, Sarah Jay thanked those who had made it possible:

The Congress
The King and Nation of France
The United Netherlands and all other Free States
The Memory of the Patriots who have fallen

and welcomed a new era:

Gratitude to our Friends and Moderation to our Enemies
Concord, Wisdom, and Firmness to all American Councils
Liberty and Happiness to all Mankind

One toast, however, struck an ambiguous note: "May all our Citizens be Soldiers, and all our Soldiers Citizens." The words testify to the acceptance of a new relationship between the military and the republican state. Read carefully, the toast also reminds us that generalizations often do not apply to men and to women in precisely the same degree. American men, listening to the toast, knew they were citizens and might be soldiers; for men the two clauses were evenly balanced. American women, listening to it, knew they were citizens, but not soldiers. They heard a rhetorical imbalance in which the gender of the listener made a difference. What did Sarah Jay mean by it? What did her audience hear in her words?[1]

On the face of it, the toast is about *soldiers*. It refers to the military obligations of citizens. It also refers to the principle of no standing armies, inherited from the English Civil War and the Glorious Revolution. The upheavals of the seventeenth century had established for liberals the rule, as Lois G. Schwoerer has recently put it, that "a standing army in peacetime was a threat to freedom and a menace to the English Constitution." It followed that a republic must rely on militias. The Declaration of Independence had complained of standing armies in peacetime and the quartering of soldiers in private homes. A few years after Sarah Jay's celebration, the Constitution would give Congress the power "to provide for organizing, arming, and disciplining the militia." To begin with, then, Sarah Jay had in mind a future in which soldiers would be temporarily recruited in rotation from the general population of male citizens.[2]

The toast was also, and obviously, about *citizens*, a word that had particular resonance in the late eighteenth century. All but the youngest of Sarah Jay's American contemporaries had been born British subjects. But the concept of the *rebel subject* was an oxymoron, a contradiction in terms. The rebel had to find something else to become. Borrowing from the Roman Republic, the rebel subject was metamorphosed into an American *citizen*. Now that their political identity had been transformed, were women and men both the same sort of citizen?

What it took to become a citizen was not fully clear when John

Jay raised his glass. There was never a single precise moment when the United States placed itself in "a state of nature," as the traditional political metaphor would have it, and asked its inhabitants explicitly whether they wanted to be part of the new polity. Even before the Declaration of Independence, a congressional resolution of 24 June 1776 transformed subjects into *members* of the polity:"all persons residing within any of the United Colonies, and deriving protection from the laws of the same, owe allegiance to the said laws, and are *members* of such colony" (italics added). This was done, James Kettner explains in his study of citizenship in the United States, in order to legitimize countermeasures against Tory espionage and counterfeiting. Since British law defined treason as opposition to the king, revolutionary leaders found it difficult to take stern measures against dissidents so long as the colonies technically remained in allegiance to George III. Therefore, the resolution had a second part, which provided that "all persons, members of, or owing allegiance to any of the United Colonies . . . who shall levy war against any of the said colonies . . . or be adherents to the king of Great Britain . . . giving to him . . . aid and comfort, are guilty of treason against such colony." By this law, both women and men who had been subjects of the king were transformed into members of the colonies; once independence was declared, by a short further step, the colonies became states and the "members," presumably, became citizens, whether they liked it or not.[3]

To refuse citizenship required explicit and physical removal of oneself—by emigrating, by enlisting with Loyalist forces, or by going behind the British lines. In fact, Sarah Jay's aunt Margaret Livingston thought Loyalists had a point when they complained about a fait accompli.

I am not so unfeeling a patriot as not to Suffer exceedingly for the many families, who are now Leaving us, on their refusal to take the Oath to the State the tendering of which they Say, Should have been delay'd till we are, what we stile ourselves & which we have never yet been, our Independence to which they are to swear, being Still contested by a Large army in our Country.[4]

All were citizens, then, unless they had explicitly opted out. Were women also citizens? The usage of the word was fuzzy. It might be used in a general way to mean all permanent residents. But its roots in civic republicanism meant that the word carried with it the implication of political rights and privileges.

J. G. A. Pocock has characterized the classical republican tradition in this way:

Civic action, carried out by *virtus*—the quality of being a man (vir)—seized upon the unshaped circumstances thrown up by fortune [given emblematic form in the figure of a woman], and shaped it, shaped Fortune herself, into the completed form of what human life should be: citizenship and the city it lived in.[5]

Ancient Greece provided the model of the male citizen who made the city possible by taking up arms on its behalf; by the time of the Renaissance, Pocock observes, military commitment was integral to civil identification. Pocock cites, for example, the Florentine humanist Leonardo Bruni, who thought of "arms as the *ultima ratio* whereby the citizen exposes his life in defense of the state and at the same time ensures that the decision to expose it cannot be taken without him; it is the possession of arms which makes a man a full citizen."[6] This mode of thinking, this way of relating men to the state, had no room in it for women except as something to be avoided. As Hanna Fenichel Pitkin recently put it,

Machiavelli's sexual and familial imagery, meant to challenge men out of their concern with private, household matters of wealth and family into the more "manly" realm of political life, also has the opposite effect, arousing images of domination and submission and undermining that capacity for mutuality which citizenship requires. . . . Men are not inherently more fit for citizenship than women and will appear so only in a society where women are . . . denied access to public life.[7]

The assumptions of the classical republican tradition, summarized by Lawrence Cress as the "association of propertied independence, political personality and military obligation with political stability," persisted into the American republic. If Liberty were to survive, male Americans would have to take up arms in her defense. "In the eyes of revolutionaries," Charles Royster argues, "war put to the trial the military ardor and skill as well as the moral assumptions on which they based their hopes for American independence and liberty. To fail as defenders of ideals was to fail as Americans." In a formulation like this one, the connection to the Republic of male patriots (who could enlist) was immediate; the connection of women, however patriotic they might feel themselves to be, was remote. Royster summarizes popular attitudes at the beginning of the Revolution: "The first anniversary of the Declaration of Independence was celebrated with the toast, 'May only those Americans enjoy freedom who are ready to die for its defence.' " To be free required a man to risk death.[8]

The definition of citizen took a long time to stabilize in America. Although the obligation to bear arms on behalf of the king had once been central to the feudal understanding of the political order, it was not always explicitly articulated in Britain or in America; the theme of *allegiance* was increasingly stressed in the revolutionary era. State constitutions usually spoke of free native-born inhabitants as citizens; the Articles of Confederation recognized "free inhabitants." By 1828 Noah Webster's Dictionary was offering definitions that did not include military obligation and which stressed civic rights: for Webster, a citizen was simply

an inhabitant who enjoys the freedom and privileges of the city in which he resides. . . . In the U.S. a person, native or naturalized, who has the privilege of exercising the elective franchise, or the qualifications which entitle him to vote for rulers and to purchase and hold real estate.[9]

Military obligation was not central to the definition.

If a citizen had to possess civic rights, then women were not citizens, for they did not vote except briefly in New Jersey. But unmarried women could certainly hold property; women, whether married or unmarried, could be naturalized. Citizenship awaited precise definition. Yet we need that definition to determine what Sarah Jay had in mind. Did she mean to refer, simply, to the tradition of no professional armies? Or did she envision an extension of the classical tradition which linked citizenship to military commitment, or even anticipate something like the French concept of the population at arms, as displayed in the great *journées* of the French Revolution?

For Sarah Jay, even the framing of the toast was unusual; women were normally not expected to deliver themselves of political expressions. It had been the common sense of eighteenth-century political theory that women had "less patriotism than men." The idea that women ought to have no politics is older than classical Athens. Gender and political behavior were understood to be linked. Because women were excluded from honors and offices, the usual methods of attaching subjects' self-interest to the outcome of national policy, women's relationship to their nation seemed to be second-hand. They were thought to experience politics through husbands, fathers, and sons.[10]

But the prewar crises and the war of the revolution brought what Margaret Livingston called the "dreadful fruits of Liberty"—violence, uncertainty, disruption—to every dinner table. Even as they continued to write self-conscious variations on the theme that "politics is not my province" it was impossible for many women, like many male civilians, to ignore the highly charged political atmosphere in which they moved.[11] In many areas the Revolution was a guerrilla war, and soldiers moved through civilian property; one would have to be blind or foolish to continue to say that "politics is not my province" when soldiers were marching through one's corn, or quartering themselves in one's home, or raping one's neighbors. So it is not at all surprising to find political expression by women— not so much as radical challenge to the mores of the times as the commonsensical response to the reality that surrounded all civilians.

For example, Helen Kortright Brasher of New York at first resented her husband Abraham's political commitment. "All our domestick happiness appeared at an end," she wrote in a private memoir years later. "He would often say, my country first and then my family. In this we differed. I thought a man's family should and ought to be his first object. . . . My politics were the same as his." She felt hurt because he was "forever out or had his house surrounded with gentlemen conversing on politicks; every evening out at some meeting or other haranguing his fellow citizens, writing for the public prints." Although Brasher spoke first of her family and resented what she took to be excessive political involvement by her husband, she also took care to locate herself politically: her "politics were the same as his."[12]

Sarah Jay herself came from a highly political family. Her father, William Livingston, was wartime governor of New Jersey. John Jay called Sarah's sister Catharine his "best correspondent"; and Ca-

tharine, acknowledging her interests, once observed to her pro-
spective husband, "I . . . fancy I hear'd you exclaiming what a rage
this girl has for politics." Sarah Livingston Jay, born into a political
family and married into another, may have been better informed
and more sophisticated in her political interests than most of her
contemporaries; but she shared with many of her generation a "rage
for politics" engendered by the intensity of the prewar crises and
the war itself. Playing unaccustomed roles during the war would
inevitably affect how women approached the peace that followed.[13]
"[The] various emotions that must have been excited in the different
Parties by the Articles of Peace presents indeed a true picture of
human happiness which rarely exists without its shades as well as
its brighter colors," Sarah Jay observed shortly after the Peace of
Paris was signed.[14]

As the twentieth-century experiences of China, Algeria, Cuba,
and Israel have suggested, wars of national liberation may well be
distinctive in their ability to attract the support of women. Certainly
the war of the American Revolution drew many women from the
role of political observer into that of actor. Patriot women redefined
their political boundaries in at least four ways. Some of these
changed perceptions would persist into the postwar years in an
explicit way; others would remain subliminal. When peace came,
women had their own distinctive revolutionary memories, their own
form of a revolutionary inheritance.[15]

First, the consumer boycotts of the prewar years had been pred-
icated on the support of women, both as consumers—who would
make distinctions on what they purchased as between British imports and goods of domestic origin—and as manufacturers, who
would voluntarily increase their level of household production.
Women who had thought themselves excused from making political
choices now found that they had to make these choices, even behind
the walls of their own homes. After the war, control of their consumption patterns would remain the most effective political weapon
in women's small political arsenal. In 1787, for example, the "Patriotic and Economic Association of Ladies of Hartford" announced
that they would eschew conspicuous consumption as a patriotic gesture against the national debt. An anonymous columnist (it is impossible to tell whether male or female) offered their reasoning:

The sheep's wool that grows in this state is, I believe, not sufficient for
stockings for its inhabitants; what then must be the wretched situation,
particularly of the poor of this town, the approaching winter, when the
wool, which might cover the legs of hundreds, is diverted from that use

to form fashionable dresses and petticoats and "bustlers" which de-
form the shape.[16] Consumption boycotts were used during the
Quasi-War in the 1790s and persisted into the nineteenth century;
when women's abolitionist societies searched in the 1830s and 1840s
for a strategy to bring pressure on the slave economy, a boycott of
slave-made goods came naturally.

Second, the most radical of the revolutionaries included women
in the mobilized "Body of the People." When the Boston Sons of
Liberty called meetings of The Body of the People in 1770, they
were explicitly inviting everyone, "male or female, franchised or
not, free or bound." And when, in 1772, the Boston Committee of
Correspondence circulated the Solemn League and Covenant, establishing a boycott of British goods, they demanded that both men
and women sign it. Thus, for the first time in the revolutionary
crisis, an organized secular group attempted consciously to mobilize
women for political purpose.[17]

Third, the war itself created many occasions for direct displays of
political choices. Women were encouraged to display their patriotism by sending husbands and sons off cheerfully; that is, women's
behavior was expected to ease the problems of general mobilization.
Some women displayed their commitment directly, taking advantage of old expectations (that women did not make political choices)
by serving the side of their choice in secret ways. Thus Washington
suspected that women who got permission to cross from American
lines into British-held territory were often smugglers; Henry Livingston complained that women communicated to the British
"everything that passed among us." There were women who helped
prisoners escape; the British placed a bounty on the head of Elizabeth Burgin for helping two hundred American prisoners escape
in New York in 1779.[18]

Finally, there was the informal quartermaster corps popularly
known as the "Women of the Army." As Barton Hacker has recently
pointed out, the American Revolution was one of the last of what
might be called the early modern wars in the West. Thousands of

women and children traveled with the armies, functioning as nurses, laundresses, and cooks. Amazingly little attention has been paid to these women. They were not prostitutes, who were dealt with severely, nor traditional camp followers like Brecht's Mother Courage, who sold goods to soldiers. Often they were married to wagoners or sutlers and worked alongside their husbands. These women drew rations in the American army, and—an imitation of British practice—a limited number of them could be attached to each company. They often brought children with them, who drew half-rations; American regulations took care to insist that "suckling babes" could draw no rations at all, since obviously they could not eat. "The very rules that denied a place in the army to all women sanctioned a place for some," Hacker remarks. Washington was constantly issuing contradictory orders—whether the women of the army were to ride in the wagons so as not to slow down the troops, or walk so as not to fill important space. But he knew he needed them.[19]

It is true that cooking, laundering, and nursing were female skills, that the Women of the Army were doing in a military context what they had once done in a domestic one. But we ought not discount these services for that reason, or visualize them as taking place in a context of softness and luxury.

One observer of American troops . . . attributed their ragged and unkempt bearing to the lack of enough women to do their washing and mending; the Americans, not being used to doing things of this sort, choose rather to let their linen, etc., rot upon their backs than to be at the trouble of cleaning 'em themselves.

Washington was particularly shocked at the demeanor of the troops at Bunker Hill, some of whom apparently were so sure that washing clothes was women's work that "they wore what they had until it crusted over and fell apart."[20] A friend of Mercy Otis Warren's wrote a description of the women who followed the Hessians after the surrender of Burgoyne:

great numbers of Women, who seemd to be the beasts of burthen, having a bushel basket on their back, by which they were bent double, the contents seemed to be Pots and Kettles, various sorts of Furniture, children peeping throu' gridirons and other utensils, some very young Infants who were born on the road, the women bare feet, cloathd in dirty raggs, such effluvia filld the air while they were passing, had they not been smoaking all the time, I should have been apprehensive of being contaminated by them.[21]

Susannah Rowson's fictional Charlotte Temple, at the end of her rope, is bitterly advised to "go to the barracks and wash for a morsel of bread; wash and mend the soldiers' cloaths, and cook their victuals . . . work hard and eat little."[22]

Women who served such troops were performing tasks of the utmost necessity if the army was to continue functioning. They did not live in gentle surroundings in either army, and the conditions of their lives were not pleasant. Although they were impoverished, they were not inarticulate. The most touching account of Yorktown I know is furnished by Sarah Osborn, who cooked for Washington's troops and delivered food to them under fire because, as she told Washington himself, "it was not fair that the poor fellows should fight and go hungry too." At the end she watched the British soldiers stack their arms and "go off to await their destiny."[23]

Historians face a real problem in finding what these women thought they were doing. We have some testimony, like Sarah Osborn's at Yorktown. We know of the women of Philadelphia, who raised three hundred thousand paper dollars, but refused to merge it into the general fund, insisting on using it to buy fabric to make shirts, so that each soldier would know that he had received something special from the ladies of Philadelphia. We have Elizabeth Burgin's petition, in which she asks for a pension for wartime services. We have large numbers of widows' petitions asking for financial support from state legislatures and the Continental Congress, which rarely responded. We have the stunning petition of Rachel Wells of Bordentown, New Jersey, asking—in horrible spelling, but with intellectual clarity—for full payment on her war bonds: "I have Don as much to Carrey on the war as maney that Sett Now at the healm of government . . . say of me if She did not fight She threw in all her mite which bought the Sogers food & Clothing & Let them have Blankets."[24]

By the war's end, then, many women's self-perception had changed, but the mechanisms for collective action by women had not been developed. Rachel Wells's petition was tabled; Burgin did not get the pension to which she felt she was entitled. (She did get a charitable handout from George Washington, which she had not wanted.) Political theory was not modified to take into account what it might mean to perceive women's will as part of the general will. Without a strategy of collective behavior, without political theorists of their own, women did not immediately develop a mode of forcing the political community to take account of their distinctive interests. Nor had they begun to grapple with the implications of variants of citizenship which bore—for free blacks and Indians as well as white women—only limited responsibilities and obligations. As Edward Countryman recently put it, the radicalism of the Revolution

> was in some ways parochial and in some ways shortsighted. It was in many ways intensely selfish. . . . It was to . . . artisans, white laborers, small farmers, and expectant small capitalists that the policies of the 1780s appealed. It was these groups that tax, Tory, economic and land policies brought to the Revolution's support, and it was their support that was vital if the new order was to stand. Groups that had established their political identity in the Revolution, and no others, were in a position to struggle for their concerns in the liberal "new order of the ages."[25]

It would be for the succeeding generations of American women to institutionalize their political identity. The Revolutionary generation began by articulating their sense of resentment, like Charles Brockden Brown's fictional Mrs. Carter, who fumes, "I am tired of explaining this charming system of equality and independence." Sarah Jay's Aunt Margaret Livingston observed that women could not have "such romantic notions" of the Goddess of Liberty as men have. "Our sex are doomed to be obedient in every stage of life so that *we* shan't be great gainers by this contest."[26]

In the traditional governments of Europe, all men and women had been subjects of their rulers, but only some men had civic responsibilities and obligations. In the new American republic, an ideologically radical revolution had transformed all free adults—men and women—into "citizens" but had not yet clearly defined their rights and responsibilities. Some male citizens—those who could meet state age and property requirements—exercised the franchise; others did not. Rarely did anyone attempt to evaluate the precise boundaries of female citizenship.

One of the few occasions on which the relationship of women and the political order was carefully analyzed occurred in the context of a lawsuit which involved the question of whether married women were citizens. The case of *Martin v. Commonwealth of Massachusetts* is not as widely known as it deserves to be.

The lawsuit involved the interpretation of a confiscation law passed by the General Court of Massachusetts in 1779. That statute, which may well have been one of the most radical departures of the revolutionary period, explicitly encouraged the wife of the Tory absentee to break from her husband, to declare her own loyalty to the revolutionary state, to set herself at risk for the republic, and in so doing to protect her property. It provided that when the wife or widow of a Loyalist absentee "shall have remained within the jurisdiction of the United States, she shall be entitled to the improvement and income of one third part of her husband's real and personal estate, after payment of debts, during her life, and her dower shall be set off to her by the Judges of probate wills, in like manner as it might have been, if her husband had died intestate."

That is, the wife of the absentee would not be treated as were wives of traitors, who traditionally had their dower reserved to them. The wife of the absentee could only hold her dower *if she made her own political commitment*. The Commonwealth of Massachusetts promised to protect her property only if she remained in America, dissociated herself from her husband, and in effect declared her own political allegiance. The 1779 statute was eventually tested by a son of absentee loyalists who claimed an inheritance on the grounds that his mother's dower share had been improperly seized. The argument that ensued when the case of *Martin v. Commonwealth* finally worked its way up to the state's Supreme Judicial Court became in part an argument over the distinction between *inhabitants* of a state and *members* or citizens of a state.

William and Anna Martin were Loyalists who had fled with the British to Halifax and then to New York under British occupation before removing to England. Their abandoned property was confiscated and rented out by the state of Massachusetts in 1781. Barely twenty years later, just when a twenty-year statute of limitations was about to run out, the Martins' son William returned to claim his deceased parents' property. He petitioned the Inferior Court of Common Pleas in Suffolk County to the effect that a series of errors had been made, among them that the Martins had not been effectively notified of the threatened confiscation, that William Martin, senior, had only a life interest in the family lands, and that "the fee simple thereof belonged to . . . Anna Martin." William Martin, junior, claimed the properties as her son and heir and argued that his mother had been a *feme covert*, who had never been "liable to have her estates confiscated."

Thus the Martin case raised as a central issue the political and economic relationship of Anna Martin to the Commonwealth of Massachusetts. In arguing it, attorneys for both the plaintiff (Martin) and the defense (Massachusetts) made explicit their conceptions of the place of women in the civic community. In deciding it, the three justices of the Massachusetts Superior Court also articulated their own understanding of the relationship of married women to the political community and, indeed, their place in the political economy. This exchange is unusual for its forthright consideration of an issue which was usually left to implication: "Who are members of the body politic?"

The Solicitor-General for the state of Massachusetts was Daniel Davis, a Republican who argued that all inhabitants of the state were members of the body politic. If a married woman, "covered" in contemporary usage by her husband's legal identity, could levy war and commit treason, Davis was confident that she could be expected to declare her own political allegiance. Wives could choose to stay with the rebels. When Mrs. Martin had fled to England with her husband, she had made a political choice, and the rebel state owed her and her heirs nothing. To argue this way was to undercut coverture; it was to insist that the married woman could have a political will of her own for which she was responsible and for which she could be punished.

Martin's case was presented by Theophilus Parsons, a well-known Federalist who the following year would be raised to chief justice of the court in which the case appeared, and George Blake, an experienced attorney. They took the position that the court eventually upheld: Martin deserved the return of his property because it had been unfairly seized from his mother. Blake argued that as a married woman, Anna Martin had "no political relation to the state any more than an alien." (Years later, the abolitionist Sarah Grimke would ask plaintively, "Are we aliens because we are women?") Blake distinguished between inhabitants and members of the state.

He pointed out that married women were not required to take an oath of allegiance. He asked a string of rhetorical questions: "How much physical force is retained by retaining married women? What are the personal services they are to render in opposing by force an actual invasion? What aid can they give to an an enemy?" Women were not of service in defense of a country; in fact they were an impediment to that defense. Parsons, in his turn, added that the "statute extends to persons who have *freely* renounced their relation to the state. Infants, insane, *femes covert*, all of whom the law considers as having no will, cannot act *freely*. Can they freely renounce?"

The court upheld Martin. In his decision, Judge Theodore Sedgwick made the point that the married woman traditionally was not held to be guilty of actions performed jointly with her husband except of the "most . . . aggravated nature," because "she is viewed in such a state of subjection and so under the control of her husband, that she acts merely as his instrument." This subjection was implicit in the vow of obedience a women took at marriage. "Was she to be considered as criminal because she permitted her husband to elect his own place of residence? Because she did not, in violation of her marriage vows, rebel against the will of her husband?"[27]

The court's decision offered an androcentric interpretation of the relationship of women and the state. The Revolution had challenged white men to rebel against familial rule. The son of a Loyalist father was explicitly encouraged to rebel against his father's will. Adult white men, like Abraham Brasher, were encouraged to put their country's interests ahead of those of their families. But even for republican ideologues, it remained unnatural for daughters to reject familial direction, unnatural for women to reject their husbands' political decisions. The judges were horrified at the thought that the revolutionaries might be thought to have asked a women to rebel against the will of her husband, and concluded that the revolutionary legislatures had never really intended that women should be forced to choose between disobeying their husbands and losing their property. Faced with a choice between encouraging a woman's support for the Revolution and loyalty to her husband, and given a chance for sober second thought, American Federalists insisted that she choose loyalty to her husband, even if he had been a Tory. Thus retrospectively, American Federalists chose to establish as policy the more restrictive interpretative option open to them.

When lawmakers chose coverture over independence and dependence over autonomy, they set down clear limits on the transformation of the political culture. Watching the law as it affected women is one way of measuring the radicalism of the American Revolution—as contrasted, for example, to the French.

In his evocative opening chapter of *A Tale of Two Cities*, Charles Dickens paints a portrait of France a decade before the revolution, observing that the trees were growing which would become the guillotine and its tumbrels. As Sarah Jay planned her list of toasts for the Paris celebrations of 1783, there were women walking in the streets of that city who six years later would be marching in organized processions by trade, district, and parish to support the bourgeois National Guard commanded by Lafayette; there were Dames de la Halle in the stalls of the central markets who six years later would be marching ahead of Lafayette to Versailles to petition and ultimately to intimidate the king. Many of the women who went to Versailles were armed. In 1791, understanding that citizenship for men was linked to the duty of service in the National Guard, Pauline Leon would present to the Legislative Assembly a petition signed by three hundred women urging the creation of a women's battalion. They were citizens; they wished to be literally soldiers. There were women living in 1783 who would in 1793 organize the Society of Revolutionary Republican Women, which demanded radical reform in the penal code, a system of divorce, and full political roles for women.[28]

Meanwhile, in America, the family circle remained a woman's state and the meaning of citizenship for women remained ambiguous. It seems highly unlikely that Sarah Jay had in mind something approaching a *levee en masse*—a mobilization of all men and women in defense of the polity. Women themselves rarely raised the question; their male contemporaries were content to leave it alone.

Yet, the story is not complete. The Jacobins ruthlessly suppressed women's popular political societies; by 1794 they had been stamped out. By the time Theophilus Parsons considered *Martin*, the Jacobin phase of the French Revolution had passed; Thermidor had been succeeded by Napoleon's empire, accompanied by Napoleon's Code. And that Code negated all that was radical in the changes which revolutionary law had made for women—their authentic membership in the body politic, their active citizenship, their right to divorce. The major radical feminist experiment of the French was over as surely as was Massachusett's own small one.

It is the common sense of the matter that no group can expect specific benefits from a revolution unless it has, as a collective body, been a force in making that revolution happen. Women had indeed served in, and supported, the Revolution—but as individuals, not as collectivities—and in 1783 were not in a strong position to make demands as a group. Political republicanism in America rested heavily on citizens who had their own "stake in society" and were financially independent. If there were implications in the republican synthesis which women would find useful, they would have to seize these possibilities and transform them into reality. We should not be surprised to find that male politicians did not demand for women what women did not demand for themselves or to discover that the Founders did not integrate into political theory an extensive analysis of the proper relationship between women and the body politic. That relationship awaited definition. "I have Don as much to Carrey on the war as maney that Sett Now at the healm of government," Rachel Wells had asserted; but, as an individual, she had only the most marginal hope of influencing the government to grant her petition.

Before a distinctively female republicanism could be devised, certain preconditions needed to be established. Either married women would need to be able to manipulate property of their own, or property requirements for voting had to be eliminated. Both trends would develop in the half-century that followed the Peace of Paris. The first of these trends was accompanied by an ideological formulation which I have elsewhere called "Republican Motherhood": a set of ideas which enabled women to understand their domestic roles in a political context.[29] Economic, political, and ideological change would eventually facilitate the direct integration of women into the citizenry of the republic; but it would be left to Elizabeth Cady Stanton's generation to articulate emphatically the need for this integration. Historians see the pace of these developments most clearly in the long perspective of two centuries' remove.

Perhaps it is enough to understand that the Revolutionary generation had embarked on a great debate over the implications of the republican experiment that would persist into our own time. In preparing her toast to a republican understanding of the relationship between military power and civic responsibility, Sarah Livingston Jay epitomized the politicization—however hesitant at first—of her female compatriots. For conclusions, and for a fuller expression of what one of Sarah Jay's contemporaries had learned from the revolutionary experience, we can turn to Mercy Otis Warren, a woman older than Sarah Jay, but—like her—the daughter of one politician and the wife of another.

In 1784, the year after the Peace of Paris, Mercy Otis Warren wrote a verse play called *The Ladies of Castille*.[30] She apparently wrote it at the urging of her son Winslow, who had challenged her to write a play *not* on an American theme. Although she set it in the Spain of Charles V, her introduction made it clear that the civil war in Spain was to be taken as a metaphor for the revolutionary civil war in America. *The Ladies of Castille* is about two women of contrasting temperaments caught up in a revolutionary civil war: the soft and delicate Louisa, who introduces herself with the words, "I wander wilder'd and alone / Like some poor banish'd fugitive . . . I yield to grief"; and the determined Maria, who announces in her opening scene: "Maria has a bolder part to act—/ I scorn to live upon ignoble terms." The message of *The Ladies of Castille* is simple and obvious: even in the exigencies of war, women must keep control of themselves and of their options. The Louisas of the world do not survive revolutions; the Marias—who take political positions, make their own judgment of the contending sides, risk their own lives— emerge stronger and in control. Women who, like Louisa, ignore politics, do so only at great risk. It was the Marias—whose souls grew strong by resistance, who took gritty political positions—that survive and flourish. "A soul, inspir'd by freedom's genial warmth," says Maria, "Expands—grows firm, and by resistance, strong."

NOTES

1. Sarah Livingston Jay, Paris [after 3 September 1783], in *John Jay: The Winning of the Peace—Unpublished Papers 1780–1784*, ed. Richard

B. Morris (New York: Harper and Row, 1980), p. 581. See also, Sarah
Livingston Jay to Catharine W. Livingston, 14 December 1782: "I was
telling young Franklin the other day that he must aid me in contriving a
Ball when Peace is concluded" (p. 590).

2. Lois G. Schwoerer, *No Standing Armies: The Antiarmy Ideology in
Seventeenth Century England* (Baltimore: Johns Hopkins University Press,
1974), p. 188. For the debate over standing armies in America, see Lawrence Delbert Cress, *Citizens in Arms: The Army and the Militia in American Society in the War of 1812* (Chapel Hill: University of North Carolina
Press, 1982); and Lawrence Delbert Cress, "An Armed Community: The
Origins and Meaning of the Right to Bear Arms," *Journal of American
History* 71 (June 1984): 22–42. A decade after Sarah Jay's toast, Mary Wollstonecraft made quite a different attack on standing armies as "incompatible
with freedom; because subordination and rigour are the very sinews of
military discipline . . . the main body must be moved by command, like the
waves of the sea; for the strong wind of authority pushes the crowd . . .
forward, they scarsely know or care why." Women who were not brought
up to think for themselves, she suggested, were like soldiers in standing
armies. She also suggested that both women and soldiers were educated
to admire pomp and fancy dress and to obey their superiors without ques-
tioning. Miriam Brody Kramnick, ed., *Vindication of the Rights of Women*
(1792; reprint ed., Harmondsworth, England: Penguin Books, 1975), p. 97.

3. *Journals of the Continental Congress* 5 (June 1776):475–76, quoted
in James H. Kettner, *The Development of American Citizenship, 1608–
1870* (Chapel Hill: University of North Carolina Press, 1978), pp. 179.
Writing as Phocion the year after the Peace of Paris, Alexander Hamilton
put it this way:

> By the declaration of Independence on the 4th of July, in the year
> 1776, acceded to by our Convention on the ninth, the late colony
> of New-York became an independent state. All the inhabitants, who
> were subjects under the former government, and who did not with-
> draw themselves upon the change which took place, were to be
> considered as citizens, owing allegiance to the new government. This,
> at least, is the legal presumption; and this was the principle, in fact,
> upon which all the measures of our public councils have been granted.

Hamilton was writing in defense of the claim of Loyalists that they were
also citizens; "*Second Letter from Phocion*," New York, April 1784, in *The
Papers of Alexander Hamilton*, ed. Harold C. Syrett (New York: Columbia
University Press, 1962), 3:533.

4. Margaret Livingston to Susan Livingston [July 1778], Ridley Papers,

Massachusetts Historical Society, Boston. For disputed status of Loyalists, see Kettner, *American Citizenship*, pp. 183–84.

5. J. G. A. Pocock, *The Machiavellian Moment: Florentine Political Thought and the Atlantic Republican Tradition* (Princeton: Princeton University Press, 1975), p. 41. For insightful comments on the contrast between *Fortuna* and *virtus*, see Hanna Fenichel Pitkin, *Fortune Is a Woman: Gender and Politics in the Thought of Niccolo Machiavelli* (Berkeley: University of California Press, 1984), pp. 138–39.

6. Pocock, *The Machiavellian Moment*, p. 90.

7. Pitkin, *Fortune Is a Woman*, p. 306.

8. Cress, *Citizens in Arms*, p. 17; Charles Royster, *A Revolutionary People at War: The Continental Army and American Character, 1776–1783* (Chapel Hill: University of North Carolina Press, 1979), pp. 3–4, 32. See also, pp. 39–40.

9. For comment on the concepts of inhabitant and citizen as they appear in early state constitutions, see Mary-Jo Kline and Joanne Wood Ryan, eds., *Political Correspondence and Public Papers of Aaron Burr* (Princeton: Princeton University Press, 1983), 1:170–72, nn.1–16. The *Oxford English Dictionary* (1933), also links citizenship with privilege, but not necessarily with military obligation:

> 1. An inhabitant of a city or (often) of a town; esp[ecially] one possessing civic rights and privileges, a burger or freeman of a city. 2. A member of a state, an enfranchised inhabitant of a country, as opposed to an alien; in U.S. a person, native or naturalized, who has the privilege of voting for public offices, and is entitled to full protection in the exercise of private rights.

The sources on which definition 1 is based range from 1314 to 1848; definition 2 from 1538 to 1884.

10. Abigail Adams observed that women had every reason to be *indifferent* to public welfare, that when they displayed "patriotick virtue," the fact ought to be noted as especially heroic. Abigail Adams to John Adams, 17 June 1782, in *Adams Family Correspondence*, ed. L. H. Butterfield et al. (Cambridge, Mass.: Harvard University Press, 1963), 4:328. I have discussed this point at length in *Women of the Republic: Intellect and Ideology in Revolutionary America* (Chapel Hill: University of North Carolina Press, 1980; New York: W. W. Norton, 1986), chap. 2.

11. Margaret Livingston to [Catherine W. Livingston], 20 October 1776, Ridley Papers, Massachusetts Historical Society, Boston.

12. When the British occupied New York City, Abraham Brasher joined the Assembly in Esopus, after first making sure Helen and the children were settled in Paramus, well back, he hoped, from the fighting. At this

point, in 1776, Helen Brasher made her peace with the situation, telling Abraham, "Go my dear and serve your country. I will find the means to provide for the family." "Narrative of Mrs. Abraham Brasher," manuscript, New-York Historical Society.

13. John Jay to Catharine Livingston, 6 April 1783, Box 2, Ridley Papers; Catharine Livingston to Matthew Ridley, May 1783, Box 3, Ridley Papers, Massachusetts Historical Society, Boston.

14. Sarah Jay to Susannah Livingston, 22 November 1783, Jay Papers, Columbia University.

15. I have discussed the following themes in *Women of the Republic*, chaps. 2 and 3. See also, Mary Beth Norton, *Liberty's Daughters: The Revolutionary Experience of American Women* (Boston: Little, Brown, 1980).

16. *American Museum & Repository*, Vol. 2 August, November 1787.

17. Gary B. Nash, *The Urban Crucible: Social Change, Political Consciousness and the Origins of the American Revolution* (Cambridge, Mass.: Harvard University Press, 1979), p. 356. See also, "The Resolves of the Inhabitants of the Town of Gorham [Mass.] on the Port Bill," June 1774, signed by 220 men and six women (five of whom identified themselves as widows), in *Province in Rebellion: A Documentary History of the Founding of the Commonwealth of Massachusetts*, ed. L. Kivin L. Wroth et al. (Cambridge, Mass.: Harvard University Press, 1975), microfiche document #224.

18. Kerber, *Women of the Republic*, pp. 48–55.

19. Barton C. Hacker, "Women and Military Institutions in Early Modern Europe: A Reconnaissance," *Signs* 6 (Summer 1981):643–71.

20. Royster, *A Revolutionary People at War*, pp. 59–60; Hacker, "Women and Military Institutions," pp. 660–61.

21. Hannah Winthrop to Mercy Otis Warren, 11 November 1977, in *Warren-Adams Letters*, vol. 2: *Collections of the Massachusetts Historical Society* 73 (1923):451.

22. Susanna Rowson, *Charlotte Temple* [1794], ed. Clara M. Kirk and Rudolph Kirk (New York: Twayne Publishers, 1964), chap. 29.

23. Sarah Osborn in *The Revolution Remembered: Eyewitness Accounts of the War for Independence*, ed. John C. Dann (Chicago: University of Chicago Press, 1980), pp. 240–50.

24. Petition of Rachel Wells, 18 May 1786, *Papers of the Continental Congress*, National Archives Microfilm no. 247, roll 56, item 42, VIII, 354–55.

25. Edward Countryman, *A People in Revolution: The American Revolution and Political Society in New York 1760–1790* (Baltimore: Johns Hopkins University Press, 1981), pp. 288–89.

26. Charles Brockden Brown, *Alcuin: A Dialogue*, ed. Lee Edwards (New York: Grossman Publishers, 1971), p. 33; Margaret Livingston to [Catharine Livingston], 20 October 1776, Ridley Papers, Massachusetts Historical Society, Boston.

27. *Martin v. Commonwealth of Massachusetts* (1805), 1 *Massachusetts Reports*, 347–97. I have discussed this issue at length in *Women of the Republic*, chap. 4. A few years later, in *Kempe's Lessee v. Kennedy et al.*, February 1809, *U.S. Supreme Court Reports*, 5 (Cranch), 173–86, Richard Stockton, arguing on behalf of a Loyalist widow, tossed off the opinion that a *feme covert*

cannot properly be called an inhabitant of a state: the husband is the inhabitant. By the constitution of New Jersey, all inhabitants are entitled to vote; but it has never been supposed that a *feme covert* was a legal voter. Single women have been allowed to vote, because the law supposes them to have wills of their own (p. 177).

28. R. B. Rose, "Women and the French Revolution," *University of Tasmania Occasional Paper No. 5* (1976):10–134. See also, Darline Gay Levy and Harriet Branson Applewhite,"Women of the Popular Classes in Revolutionary Paris, 1789–1795," in *Women, War, and Revolution*, ed. Carol R. Berkin and Clara M. Lovett (New York: Holmes and Meier, 1980), pp. 9–36.

29. Linda K. Kerber, "The Republican Mother—Women and the Enlightenment: The American Perspective," *American Quarterly* 28 (Summer 1976):187–205; and Linda K. Kerber, "Daughters of Columbia: Educating Women for the Republic," in *The Hofstadter Aegis: A Memorial*, ed. Stanley Elkins and Eric McKitrick (New York: Alfred A. Knopf, 1974), pp. 36–59.

30. Mercy Otis Warren, "The Ladies of Castile," in *Poems: Dramatic and Miscellaneous* (Boston: I. Thomas, 1790).

2 DAVID F. MUSTO

The Problem of Dependency after America Became Independent

Americans did not easily or comfortably break the ties of dependency with the British Empire. Few petitioners for better treatment from Parliament in the years before the War for Independence wished or anticipated a full break with Britain. The adjustment of most Americans to this possibility took years of increasing estrangement from the parent nation, denigration of that previously succoring object, and proud expansion of colonial self-confidence.

Once independence was acknowledged by the mother country, the United States faced the difficult task of maintaining, at least to itself, the equality now won formally, but far from established in terms of military power, wealth, scientific or literary accomplishment, or strong institutions of culture. This apparently unequal status, compared to Britain and other European nations, was a humiliation to some Americans, but stoutly denied by others, denied so enthusiastically that patriots even claimed superiority to what they declared was an effete and decaying Europe.

The psychological adjustment of a young, weak, and culturally dependent nation, formed to achieve balance with the great states of Europe, is the subject of this essay. But there is a reason beyond a natural interest in the earliest history of our nation: by understanding ourselves two centuries ago, we may be able to empathize with the special relationship a young or small nation experiences when confronted with a world cultural power that threatens to engulf its formal independence. Our early intense fear of being "Britainized" can help us understand the fear and anger of other nations who now confront the dangers (and fascination) of "Americanization." Extreme denigration of American culture among third world nations while at the same time they thirst for American carbonated beverages, overpay for denim jeans, and yearn for our popular music is not simply a form of group hypocrisy. It is, rather, an understandable reaction to a powerful, attractive culture by nations striving to establish unique identities. Our pained response to cultural "anti-Americanism" should be greatly ameliorated by a knowledge of our own experience as a member of an eighteenth century "third world." A frank acknowledgment of the psychological defenses we employed early in our history would help us understand international reactions to a reversed role in the twentieth century.

This is hardly the first attempt to consider psychological themes and responses at the time of the War for Independence. John Adams noted the great shift in attitude among Americans that evolved in the period after the Stamp Act of 1764 until independence appeared no longer a fearful alternative to lawful protest, but an urgent necessity. This sea change was noted at the time although for many generations after independence the change was ascribed to factors and motives that were more patriotic than objective. Twentieth-century historians have viewed American nationalism as a more neutral phenomenon than did George Bancroft in his nineteenth-century *History of the United States*. Recently, the movement toward independence has been examined by historians using psychological models such as those of parent-child relationships. Before reviewing these modern analyses, let us consider an eyewitness account. After a lifetime of reflection, John Adams wrote a correspondent in 1818:

The revolution was effected before the war commenced. The revolution was in the hearts and minds of the people . . . The people of America had been educated in an habitual affection for England as their mother country . . . but when they found her a cruel Bedlam . . . it is no wonder that their filial affections ceased and were changed into indignation and horror. This radical change in the principles, opinions, sentiments and affections of the American people, was the real American Revolution.[1]

During the gradual unfolding of confrontation between those who would ultitmately seek independence and those who wanted their North American homes and lives to remain dependent on Great Britain, the dissatisfied eventually reached a fateful judgment of the intention of the British: rebellious colonists believed that British actions were evidence of a great conspiracy to enslave the inhabitants of the thirteen colonies. This conspiratorial concept undergirded the patriots' determination to continue the battle for, as they saw it, their inalienable rights as inheritors of the Anglo-Saxon political tradition.[2] Eventually, no action by the British, no word, could penetrate the conviction, the psychological matrix, through which outside information was interpreted. One painfully sad result of the colonists' suspiciousness is narrated in Bernard Bailyn's moving biography of the last Massachusetts royal governor, Thomas Hutchinson. Governor Hutchinson was vilified, hounded, and threatened by mobs, his home wrecked, his papers vandalized. Yet Bailyn describes him as:

honorable to a fault, sincere, industrious, and profoundly loyal to the community of his birth . . . more tolerant and more reasonable than those who attacked him and drove him into exile.[3]

When a calm appraisal of Hutchinson's life is juxtaposed with the accusations he endured during and after the War for Independence, it becomes obvious how important was psychological distortion—exaggerated denigration—to the achievement of separation from the symbols of colonial dependence. The neutrality with which the War for Independence is increasingly viewed is a sign of national maturity; we can examine the revolutionary era not only as the venerated period of our nation's origin, but also as a time when deep emotions twisted perceptions on both sides without either being fully conscious of the process.

I would like to review some of the psychological explanations applied to our early history by historians in the last decade or so as a way of explicating the psychological dynamics that colored the great controversy and the period after the Treaty of Peace (now known as the Treaty of Paris). First let us explore the metaphor suggested by John Adams, that is, the model of a family and the relationship between parents and children.

Noting a parallel between the American struggle for independence and adolescent protest and emancipation has been tempting for historians employing psychological themes, just as it was a favored metaphor for polemicists in the eighteenth century. Invocation of this developmental model acknowledges, as Adams recognized, that the establishment of national independence was as gradual, as emotionally difficult, and, in some instances, as misperceived as a child's transition to independence. One of the most interesting examples of this approach by a historian appeared shortly before the 1976 bicentennial when Philip Greven combined demographic studies with the psychology of the family to argue that structural changes in the family prior to the Revolution facilitated the break from Great Britain. Greven argued, from a demographic analysis of the first four generations of settlers in Andover, Massachusetts, that:

By the middle decades of the 18th century . . . the maturing fourth generation would not have found the idea of independence from parental authority at a relatively early age foreign to their own experience. Men were marrying significantly earlier than in previous generations; they were able to establish earlier, and with far less apparent hesitation and difficulty, their economic independence from their fathers; their autonomy was often accepted and even fostered by their parents: these facts suggest that their attitude toward parent-son relations had changed significantly from those of their fathers' and their grandfathers' generations . . . Surprising as it may seem, political independence in 1776 might have been rooted in the very character of many (but not all) American families . . . The nature of the family probably was one of the determinative factors shaping the responses of the people to the most important issues of the times.[4]

Winthrop Jordan also directed his attention to the familial analogy, especially the destruction of the father, King George III, in the affections of the colonists.[5] Jordan was intrigued by the rapidity with which monarchic imagery lost its hold on Americans in 1775 and 1776. He attributed the catalysis for rapid transition to republicanism to Thomas Paine's *Common Sense* and its virulent attack on monarchy. Jordan argues that Paine's tract, possibly the "most immediately influential political or social tract ever published in this country," crystallized the colonists' growing conviction that they had outgrown the parental relationship to Britain and the King and were now independent adults.[6] Jordan speculates about Paine's own life experiences that might have shaped this attack on strong parents (and monarchs)—a super-saturated solution—but here I want only to note that *Common Sense* was well timed to assist the maturation of the rebelling patriots from the role of child to that of adult.

At about the same time Jordan published his essay on "Familial Politics," E. G. Burrows and Michael Wallace published a substantial monograph entitled "The American Revolution: The Ideology and Psychology of National Liberation." In brief, Burrows and Wallace carefully analyzed the concepts of paternal and royal authority and image, and the notion that Britain and America stood in the relation of parent and child. They concluded that:

A sudden hardening of imperial policy in the early 1760s broke the spell of familial comity . . . and the imperial order began to come apart. The colonists in America, bitterly disappointed with the mother country, discovered that the idea they were children of England could also be used to legitimate, still in natural law, their opposition to her policies; in a remarkably short time they were prepared, except for the loyalist minority, to reject British rule altogether on the grounds that they had at last come of age.[7]

These are not peaceful descriptions of maturation. They suggest that the emotional strength required for a break from customary relations is drawn not just from growth in size and experience; instead, such momentous changes are often accompanied by a new, negative view of the previously nurturing source. For a time as the break comes about, nurturance, which had been a comfort, may be seen as a stifling, overcontrolling, and enveloping closeness threatening to any autonomy. What once nurtured must be put at a distance and rejected. Considering this description of adolescent development, it is understandable that historians of the American Revolution might find irresistible the model of youthful maturation as a kind of psychological map with which to trace the Revolution's rise, combat, and eventual achievement of independence. Perhaps we should not be surprised at the popularity of this model in the late 1960s and early 1970s, when youthful rebellion and the "generation gap" became so common as to be thought normative by many observers.

Following the achievement of independence, in the decades after 1783, Americans experienced the psychologically awkward state of being profoundly dependent on the trade and manufactures of Great Britain. Adoption of Hamilton's financial scheme to pay the war debt with tariff revenues made the United States even more reliant on Britain, with whom it conducted seven-eighths of its trade.[8] This seemed hard to a people so close to the peak of righteous indignation that had fueled the war; to a people still celebrating triumph over an evil and corrupt nation that had tried, Americans continued to believe, to "enslave" them. At best, American feelings about Great Britain were complex.

Positive attitudes toward Britain had been absorbed with a common cultural heritage. Just as American patriots and British polemicists could use identical literary sources in their toe-to-toe arguments over natural rights and the legal status of Parliament, so did many Americans, especially the more formally educated, share a common standard for cultural achievement with their peers across the Atlantic. As a result, literate Americans were stung by such criticisms as Abbe Reynal's assertion that "One must be astonished that America has not yet produced one good poet, one able mathematician, one man of genius in a single art or a single science."[9] Culturally ambitious Americans sought desperately to compete with Europe and refute the harsh claims of foreign critics.

Dr. Benjamin Rush announced that American diseases were more hearty and serious than those suffered in Europe: treatment had to be "heroic" to cure the bodies of patriots. Unfortunately Rush's ministrations and theories may have ended more lives than had British cannon. Even George Washington's death, after enormous volumes of blood had been drawn from the great hero's body, was attributed to some of Rush's theories, for Rush had seized upon bloodletting as a sort of American cure-all.[10] We are familiar with Thomas Jefferson's extensive refutation of European minimization of America's natural and cultural attributes in his *Notes on the State of Virginia*. Jefferson was particularly delighted to cite the discovery of mammoth bones in rebutting Buffon's accusation that animals in the New World were insignificant. Other Americans pointed to the accomplishments in the arts of West and Copley, in science of Franklin and Rittenhouse, and in literature of the "Hartford wits," although in the latter instance the evidence was persuasive chiefly to

American patriots. From a vantage two centuries later, we can understand how these carefully listed achievements assuaged an American sense of inferiority and were aimed to puncture an unquestioning British assumption of superiority. The British, on the other hand, appeared to spend little time compiling evidence of their superiority. Suffering no anxiety on this point, they found the insistent American claims more curious than persuasive.

In addition to competing by comparing numbers of like achievements as though they were stacks of poker chips, other Americans competed with Europeans by proclaiming their dissimiliarities. Thus, they portrayed America as a mirror-image of the other society: no titles, no nobility, no hereditary offices of government, no powerful centralized government, no ostentation in dress, manners, or ceremony. The United States, this purified image suggested, was superior in the only categories that really counted, morals and politics—and only corruption's twisted vision could perceive major deficits. The scenes that disgusted fastidious aristocrats in America were the boast of rural democrats. Rejection of British traits was a reaction as intense for many Americans as imitation or acceptance of British cultural standards was for others.

In the midst of ambivalence over British cultural styles, the new government of the United States encountered difficulty in harmonizing what its own citizens expected of it with what would impress major European powers. The United States was torn between creating an administration of stark republican simplicity and one that would meet minimal criteria meriting the respect of the courts of Europe. This conflict over style appeared clearly in the now amusing quest for an appropriate title for George Washington. Vice-president John Adams could not conceive the head of state possessing so meager a title as the descriptive term "president."[11] He had come from seven years in European capitals in which an ambassador from the most humble state would be accorded many more and much grander titles than "president."

It would be easy to ridicule Adams's attitude for we know both the outcome of this search for a title of grandeur and our own satisfaction with the title given the head of state, but ridicule would miss the point of Adams's objection. He knew titles had no real meaning—as he said, "This is all nonsense to the philosopher; but so is all government whatsoever."[12] But he believed that one of government's responsibilities was to order titles, honors, and ranks so that the natural competition of all persons would be channeled toward the greater good. Fearing the new government would lose status in the eyes of Europe if the head of state were not granted a title of familiar significance, Adams favored something at least as grand as "His Highness the President of the United States and Protector of the Rights of the Same."[13] Rejected by the House of Representatives, as well as by Washington, the title became something of an embarrassment to Adams.

This controversy, however, revealed the split between the mirror-imagists and the more egalitarian Americans. Out of the country during most of the War for Independence, Adams had not sufficiently realized how rejection of European ornamentation had become a sustaining force behind resistance to Britain. Washington tried to steer a course between monarchical styles and no style at all, but he was not able to please either side fully, especially after the French Revolution appeared to show that the future belonged to republican simplicity.

The outbreak of the French Revolution exacerbated controversy over British traits. France, a decadent and monarchical nation— even if it had supplied the essential aid to bring the United States into being—had decided to follow the lead of the New World and cast off the gold lace of artistocracy; all titles reverted to the universal "citizen." Americans remained divided. Republicans wanted more simplicity for themselves and aid for France; Federalists wanted a strengthening of the new Constitution, to consider a hereditary Senate and hereditary President, and to maintain the new nation's neutrality between Britain and France. More conservative Americans were proud of having, they believed, purified British legal traditions and wanted to hold onto a code of law based on a written constitution with the same fervor with which Protestants during the Reformation adhered to a true faith rescued from unnecessary ornamentation. French enthusiasts, on the other hand, thought a thorough purification had only begun. The popular divisions over symbolic and practical association with Britain were thus intensified by the French Revolution, during which each side found evidence justifying their suspicion of the other. Destruction of the French aristocracy was a blow for freedom to one group but an example of ungoverned intolerance to the other.

Complicating this postwar division over British culture was the psychological residue of an earlier argument against British domination of the colonies. Patriots attributed much of American backwardness to the mother country's repression during the war and in the struggles leading to the war. The deficits which did clearly exist—and about which Americans were keenly sensitive—could happily be ascribed to the enemy's political repression. This was a well-protected psychological position; its power is evident in the corollary proclaimed by patriots that the Revolution would be followed by a burst of literary, scientific, medical, and other accomplishments. Free citizens would flourish in a multitude of arenas, while the Old World would slip further into the shadows of decadence.

This faith in the future release of pent-up energies was not necessarily opposed to British cultural tradition or limited to a uniquely American culture. It was a convenient, self-serving explanation for fewer works of genius in North America than the patriots might wish to claim for their native land. After Independence, there was an initial burst of enthusiasm as Americans anticipated an era of rapid progress in all walks of life. In addition, Americans—especially the mirror-imagists—also expected the political life of the new nation to be purer, fairer, and much less tainted by what we might call politics as usual. The letdown was painful. Reaction took at least two forms: recrimination against those who had failed the Revolution's promise; and a cheerful denial of any disappointment whatsoever, accompanied by claims that America was wonderful in her accomplishments, just as had been hoped and expected. This idealization of a unique American culture was especially appealing, for it shifted competition with Europe both to less concrete forms, such as national morality, and also to homespun creations, that given the level of education and state of transatlantic communication, were not likely to be compared unfavorably by many Americans with foreign artifacts.

Yet those who had been educated in the British tradition and maintained contact with Europe found it more difficult to overlook the paucity of scientific and literary activity. The most realistic reaction to the cultural gap was probably that taken by John Adams in his famous—but then private—statement to Abigail Adams that he must study politics and war so that his children could study naval architecture, navigation and commerce, so that his grandchildren could study painting and music.[14] The view that a young, developing nation could not be expected to exceed or equal Britain or France simply because of independence, regardless of the power of free people to flourish in all fields, appears to have been expressed more often in private than publicly. The people craved exaggerated claims. Comforting distortions were understandable responses, and our sympathetic consideration of them should help us emphathize with young nations of our own time.

In recent years, a number of studies have been conducted on the complex relationship between powerful and weaker nations. Some interesting analyses have been made by Steven Pieczenik, a psychiatrist and political scientist. These studies reveal a wide range of possible interactions in an internationally dependent relationship, some of which are relevant to the present discussion.[15]

In a dependent relationship, the weaker partner may experience anger, jealousy, and envy. The stronger partner may attempt both to define the other in the relationship and to induce the partner to accept a definition of inferiority. For example, those aspects of the relationship considered to be "inferior in value and prestige" may be incorporated into the image of the weaker nation.[16] This is exemplified by the image of eighteenth-century America as a supplier of raw materials for Europe or a land of natural beauty, but not as a candidate to become a world power. A further instance was the assertion by Abbé Corneille DePauw that the weather in America was disordered and caused puny animals.

A further element noted in these relationships is repression by the weaker member of overt expressions of resentment in order to avoid a future confrontation. Pieczenik's work suggests the example of the relationship between the United States and the Latin American countries, but we also may see a similar reaction in the United States' refusal to be provoked into war with Great Britain in the late 1790s over the destruction of merchant shipping and impressment of seamen. Combative rhetoric and even blatantly hostile actions of the British navy, including the *Chesapeake* incident of 1807, brought only carefully measured reactions culminating in the embargo of foreign trade by the Jefferson administration. The war that finally came, in 1812, resulted in a return to conditions before the war; the nagging, humiliating issue of impressment remained unsettled. The decision of the British to agree to *status quo ante bellum* could even be described as generous.[17]

Today nations around the world fear the loss of their cultural identities to the force of "Americanization," whether in the form of music, soft drinks, or television programs. This suggests an advantage Americans obtained from the starkly democratic culture imbedded in the early national "mirror image." Such a powerful image served to offset the massive impact of British culture in books, manufactured articles, plays, hymns, clothes, social styles, and even the language itself. To avoid "Britainization," Americans developed an exaggerated counterimage as a defense against being engulfed psychologically by a dominant and powerful country.

At home, Americans railed at British disregard of neutrals' rights, impressment, failure to remove troops from western forts, and so on, while the American government quietly suffered indignities awaiting the day when American power would be sufficient to assert American rights. The government was in a most difficult position, and it is unsurprising that the Washington and Adams administrations were accused of being pro-British or that Jefferson's embargo was castigated for its passivity and self-denial in the face of British and French depredations on American trade. The dependent position of the United States created an unsatisfying interface between British power and American weakness. American claims for morality and assertions that a uniquely just state had been created in reaction to aristocratic and effete British culture were partly abstractions employed as a substitute for equality to Britain in more tangible areas. For decades, rhetoric was the chief weapon against the fear of "Britainization."

An example of "identification with the aggressor" may be evident in the proposals of some Americans to join the British in attacking Spanish possessions in South America at the turn of the century. In this scheme, discussed at one time or another by Alexander Hamilton, Rufus King, General Francisco de Miranda, and others, the United States would supply troops and the British a fleet to separate the Spanish Empire from its colonies in the Western Hemisphere.[18] In the view of Americans enamored of this plan, a war of liberation would result in a government "agreeable to both the Cooperators."[19] Such an invasion—or war of liberation—would have put the United States on a rough equality with Great Britain in the campaign and in the anticipated result. Of course, "identification with the aggressor" is not a conscious imitation, but a psychological process more noticeable to an observer. To the participant, the behavior serves to diminish a feeling of threat from the aggressor and to establish, at least in the dependent side, a sense of camaraderie between unlikely partners. The invasion of South America in partnership with Great Britain would have come close to fulfilling that definition, but certainly was not the whole motivation. At any rate, the scheme did not take place because Presidents Adams and Jefferson refused to sanction the plan.

The suggestions and examples here support the contention that psychological ties between the new United States and the old mother (or father) country were not fully appreciated by the actors in the drama of independence. I do not argue that these psychological themes and motives were more than a part of the many elements entangling America with Britain after the Peace of 1783, including geography, trade, and European rivalries. But I think it is important to take into account the psychological evolution that transpired from the beginnings of the movement for independence, through a long and frequently discouraging war, and then remained a force as a new nation emerged.

I have briefly sketched some of the motives for seeking, however ambivalently, to incorporate or to reject British traits. A feeling of security about American cultural values took many generations to establish. Even now Americans may not be totally confident about their culture, but they have secured enough familiarity and success with it to be able to look upon the early national protestations of achievement with amusement and only a little embarrassment. Comfortable now, we Americans can see the gap between promise and performance that the patriots could not, or preferred not, to see.

It is unfortunate that the widespread lack of familiarity with history prevents so many Americans from knowing about their predecessors' sensitivity to cultural dominance by others in the late eighteenth and early nineteenth centuries. Our surprise and confusion at the touchy reaction of less developed nations to "Americanization" might be lessened if we could recognize the similarity to our own experience. And we might, by understanding the psychology of our early dependency, also realize that the avid adoption of American ways across the world prompts a simultaneous resentment as an inevitable reaction against a powerful foreign culture. A lesson for international cooperation today lies within our own history and is a compelling reason for its study.

NOTES

1. John Adams to Hezekiah Niles, 13 February 1818, in *Works of John Adams*, ed. C. F. Adams (Boston: Little, Brown, 1850–1856), X:282–83.

2. Bernard Bailyn, ed. *Pamphlets of the American Revolution, 1750–1776* (Cambridge, Mass.: Harvard University Press, 1965), I:60ff.

3. Bernard Bailyn, *The Ordeal of Thomas Hutchinson* (Cambridge, Mass.: Harvard University Press, 1974), p. 376.

4. Philip Greven, Jr., *Four Generations: Population, Land and Family in Colonial Andover, Massachusetts* (Ithaca, N.Y.: Cornell University Press, 1970), pp. 281–82.

5. Winthrop Jordan,"Familial Politics: Thomas Paine and the Killing of the King, 1776," *Journal of American History* 60 (September 1973): 305.

6. Ibid., p. 295.

7. E. G. Burrows and Michael Wallace, "The American Revolution: The Ideology and Psychology of National Liberation," *Perspectives in American History* (1972): 303.

8. Thomas A. Bailey, *A Diplomatic History of the American People*, 8th ed. (New York: Appleton-Century-Crofts, 1969), p. 74.

9. Cited by Thomas Jefferson, *Notes on the State of Virginia*, ed. William Peden (New York: W. W. Norton, 1972), p. 64.

10. John Duffy, *The Healers: The Rise of the Medical Establishment* (New York: McGraw-Hill, 1976), pp. 93ff.

11. John Adams to Jabez Bowen, 26 June 1789, Adams Papers Microfilm Edition, Reel 115.

12. William Maclay, *Sketches of Debate in the First Senate of the United States, in 1789–90–91*, ed. George W. Harris (Harrisburg, Pa.: L. S. Hart, 1880), p. 41.

13. John Adams to Benjamin Rush, 24 July 1789, in *Old Family Letters, Series A*, ed. Alexander Biddle (Philadelphia, Pa.: J. B. Lippincott, 1890), I:46. See also: John R. Howe, Jr., *Changing Political Thought of John Adams* (Princeton, N.J.: Princeton University Press, 1966), pp. 176ff.

14. John Adams to Abigail Adams, after 12 May 1780, in *Adams Family Correspondence*, eds. L. Butterfield and M. Friedlaender (Cambridge, Mass., Harvard University Press, 1973), III:342.

15. Steve R. Pieczenik, "Some Psychological Consequences of Inter-

national Dependency," *American Journal of Psychiatry* 132 (April 1975): 428–43.

   16. Ibid., p. 429.

   17. Bailey, *Diplomatic History*, pp. 154ff.

   18. William Spence Robertson, *The Life of Miranda* (Chapel Hill, N.C.: University of North Carolina Press, 1929), I:163–87.

   19. Alexander Hamilton to Francisco de Miranda, 22 August 1798, in *Papers of Alexander Hamilton*, ed. H. C. Syrett (New York: Columbia University Press, 1975), XXII:156.

PART II

Peace and Expansion through Commerce, Cooperation, and Singular Initiative

In chapter 3, Harold D. Langley shows that while the peace of 1783 shattered economic relations with Great Britain, American merchants quickly seized new opportunities elsewhere. "Private ventures succeeded where conventional diplomacy failed," he writes, especially in South and East Asia. Confirming Adam Smith's apothegm that private traders form an international republic of their own, he explains how the "attractions of mutual profit overcame obstacles set by the diplomats" in the decades following the Revolution.

Ranging over several generations, James A. Field, Jr., in chapter 4 emphasizes the American faith that international peace could be secured through the product of the spread of republicanism and through free trade not only in commodities but in talents and ideas. Much that we think of as world politics could be left to the people. American reliance in the twentieth century on organized state and military power has wrenched a society that remains, even today, "in large degree . . . reformist, missionary, and 'republican'. . . ."

3 HAROLD D. LANGLEY

Trade as a Precursor of Diplomacy: The Beginnings of American Commercial Relations with the Pacific and Indian Ocean Areas, 1782–1815

"We have the World before us, and a navigation act on the principle of conducting our Commerce on the Footing of the most exact reciprocity with all Nations will tend more to increase than diminish our power."[1] So wrote John Jay in July 1783, two months before he joined with the two other American commissioners in signing the Definitive Treaty of Peace with Great Britain ending the War of the American Revolution. Jay's optimism was shared by a great many of his fellow countrymen engaged in maritime activity. Those who hoped for a speedy resumption of close trade relations with Great Britain, such as they enjoyed as colonists, were doomed to disappointment. But shattered hopes in one trading sphere led to new opportunities in others. Private ventures succeeded where conventional diplomacy failed.

The views of men of commerce were strongly influenced by the ideas set forth in Adam Smith's book *The Wealth of Nations*, first published in 1776. Men who never read the book itself heard its arguments discussed in newspapers and by like-minded men in all sorts of gatherings. It was the most influential economic treatise ever written, the foundation of the classical school of political economy. Smith argued that the world was made up of demanders and suppliers of movable goods. The producers and traders of movable goods were citizens of the world, not of just one country. They belonged to "the great mercantile republic." In the process of satisfying his own needs, a man of commerce was helping to create a network of complex and constantly changing links of interdependence in this republic.[2] This was a point of view that Americans found very attractive, especially when they were beginning to establish themselves as an independent nation.

In their studies of Anglo-American commercial relations between the end of the Revolution and the War of 1812, historians have focused on several issues: the economic dependence of the United States on trade with Great Britain; the failure of American efforts to retaliate against British restrictions; the inability of John Adams, the first American minister in London, to bring about reconciliation; and the treaty secured by John Jay's mission in 1794.[3] Attention has also been given to the questions of neutral rights, impressment, and the political and economic preliminaries of the War of 1812.[4] Those interested in the postwar relations with France have been concerned with the impact of the French Revolution and the wars of Napoleon on American commerce.[5]

Less well known is the story of American merchant ships in the Indian and Pacific Oceans and of their relations with the British, Dutch, and French in those regions. Americans engaged in trade with India and the French island of Mauritius played a significant role in the economic life of those areas. They also brought wealth to their own country and stimulated an interest in products of the Far East. In the process of developing trade with India, they carried cargoes to and from other areas of the Far East, as well as to Europe and their own country. Much of this trade in the Indian and Pacific Oceans was carried on without the benefit of formal trade treaties or consular representation. In their search for profitable cargoes, American captains made the first contacts with the regions in the Indian and Pacific Oceans at least a generation before they attracted the official, diplomatic attention of the U.S. government.

At the end of the American Revolution, the commerce of the thirteen states was in shambles. Long years of war and a blockade of the Atlantic coast had driven American merchant ships from the seas. Shipyards were destroyed or had virtually ceased business. With money scarce, one way to raise capital was to engage in privateering. With a little luck one might capture a British merchant vessel and sell it as a prize. On the other hand, if luck ran out, one might end up in a British prison. The desire of American merchants to resume peacetime trading was particularly strong during the long interval between the surrender of the British at Yorktown in October 1781 and the ratification of the Treaty of Peace two and a half years later. A number of American merchants could not wait until the diplomats and the politicians had finished their work.[6] They eagerly sought cargoes in such familiar areas as the West Indies. Others, more adventurous, looked to India and to the Far East.

Before the Revolution both American colonists and British subjects were forbidden to trade east of the Cape of Good Hope, beyond which the British East India Company held a trading monopoly. Now that the war was ending, a few American merchants wanted to send ships to India and the Far East. Such men soon found out that there were British merchants who were eager to undermine the monopoly of the East India Company, making it possible to work out arrangements mutually beneficial to British and American merchants.[7]

The first known attempt by Americans to tap the trade to India took place in 1782. An American ship flying Danish colors took on a cargo at Serampore, a Danish settlement on the Hooghly River near Calcutta. The details of the cargo and its eventual disposition are unknown, but a report of the incident was sent to the directors of the British East India Company warning that the Americans were preparing to send ships to India.[8] The company was thus alerted to a possible threat to its monopoly.

Nearly two years later, in December 1783, the fifty-five ton sloop *Harriet* sailed from Boston with a cargo of ginseng destined for China. At the Cape of Good Hope the captain of the *Harriet* met with a group of British East-Indiamen who were disturbed by the prospect of American competition in China. To keep the ship from going to China, the East India traders bought the *Harriet*'s cargo for double its weight in Hyson tea. The American captain returned to Boston with a handsome profit in less time than anticipated. This was hardly a lesson in how to discourage further market exploration.[9]

One of the most imaginative and enterprising Americans was Robert Morris of Philadelphia, the Superintendent of Finance of the United States. In this capacity as well as in his earlier role as the financier of the American Revolution, Morris had a number of connections with the business and maritime community. Sometime early in 1783 he met John Ledyard, who proposed a fantastic business scheme. The Connecticut-born Ledyard had served as a ship's corporal on the *Resolution* under Captain James Cook during that British officer's exploration of the Pacific northwest and Hawaii. Ledyard was impressed by the abundance of fur pelts that could be acquired from the Indians in the area of Vancouver Island. Subsequently he learned that such furs could be sold in China at an enormous profit. During the course of his voyage with Cook, the young corporal devised a plan for a trading pattern. Rum and hardware from New England would be carried to the Pacific Northwest and there traded for furs. The next stop would be Hawaii, where sandalwood and other stores would be loaded. Then on to Canton, where the furs and wood could be sold and the money used to buy tea. The tea would then be carried to New England and sold. Great profits seemed assured, but the Revolution prevented any attempt to gain them. Ledyard refused to serve against his countrymen and was imprisoned in the brig of the *Resolution*. While the ship was docked on Long Island in 1782, he escaped and returned to Connecticut. He then published an account of his voyage and visited various port cities in an effort to find backers for his trading plan. To most merchants of the time, Ledyard's scheme seemed wild and risky, especially since money was tight. But Morris was interested.[10]

A plan was devised for sending three vessels to China. One would go directly to Canton; the other two would first go to the Pacific Northwest to collect a cargo of sea otter pelts.[11] "I am sending some Ships to China in order to encourage others in the adventurous pursuits of Commerce," Morris wrote to John Jay.[12]

Unfortunately, plans went awry. The only salable cargo that the ship going directly to Canton could take was ginseng, a root coveted by the Chinese for its reputed medicinal properties. Ginseng grew wild in the eastern United States. It took time to collect, cure, and pack the cargo, estimated at nearly two million specimens. Moreover, the financial support needed from a group in New England was not forthcoming, so the plan to send the other two ships to collect furs was dropped. Disgusted and discouraged by this turn of events, Ledyard went to Paris where he talked to Thomas Jefferson and John Paul Jones about his plans.[13]

Gradually the backers of the venture were put together, the cargo collected, a new ship acquired, and a captain appointed—John

Green, on leave from the Continental Navy. Major Samuel Shaw, of a Boston mercantile family, was appointed as supercargo, or agent to dispose of the goods. The *Empress of China* sailed from New York on 22 February 1784. Six months later, on 23 August, Captain Green dropped his anchor at Macao, a Portuguese leasehold from which all foreign vessels had to approach Canton. Supercargo Shaw proceeded to sell the ginseng in Canton.[14] Though the ship carried $20,000 in silver coins, no port east of the Cape of Good Hope would accept anything but bullion or the Spanish milled silver dollar. Nor would the Chinese buy any manufactured goods. But Shaw succeeded in disposing of his cargo in exchange for teas and silks.

The profits of the first American trading voyage to China were modest. Indeed, there was hardly enough to go around. But the venture did generate some excitement. Shaw's published report on the voyage encouraged others to enter the China trade. The *Empress of China* had clearly demonstrated that Americans need not depend on the Dutch or the British for goods from the East. The United States government took notice in 1786 by appointing Samuel Shaw the United States Consul at Canton.[15]

Other Americans were now beginning to respond to opportunities in the East. Four weeks after the *Empress of China* left New York, the four hundred-ton ship *United States* sailed from Philadelphia. En route to China via Mauritius with a cargo of tobacco, ginseng, copper, naval stores, and hardware, it made a stop at Madeira. Here her master, Thomas Bell, took on some very good Madeira wine. Stopping at the old French leasehold at Pondicherry on the Coromandel coast, Bell was to find the British still in possession, but was greeted cordially and sold his wine. Bell then traveled overland to Madras, where, the British learned, he made inquiries about establishing an American presence, or factory, near Pondicherry. Without any official support from Congress, Bell had in mind a private venture.[16] On the basis of these and other reports, Lord Macartney, the British governor of Madras, decided that Bell and his associates were involved in experimental and speculative, but not very important, ventures. William Moore, the Irish supercargo on the *United States*, was allowed to remain in Pondicherry, where he presumably entered into trade for his employer.[17]

The next American vessel to reach India did not meet with such a cordial response. It was the *Hydra*, a former British frigate converted into a merchant vessel, which experienced far more difficulty. William Green, the supercargo, owned the ship in partnership with a Mr. Champlain of Rhode Island and some English merchants. Were the ship and cargo British or American? British officials in India were concerned that denying entry to the *Hydra*'s cargo might provide a pretext for keeping Indian goods out of the American market. What to do? When it was discovered that the supercargo Green had both French and American commissions, the Governor General and the Council requested that the *Hydra* replace its American colors with the French flag. This done, the cargo was unloaded without incident.[18]

Why was this trade with India tolerated by British officials? Why did the East India Company not have a policy in regard to American trade? The answers to these questions lie in the situation in India itself.

In 1787 much dissatisfaction was expressed over the administration of Warren Hastings, the Governor General of Bengal, and William Hornby, the President of the Council of Bombay. In August 1784 Parliament had approved the India Act, sponsored by William Pitt the Younger. This act had several purposes: it attempted to stop the territorial expansion of the East India Company and its interference in native affairs; it prohibited the company from declaring war except in cases of aggression; and the company itself was put under the control of the Crown. Further, a dual system of government was imposed, the company continuing to function under the supervision of a board of control sitting in London and of a governor-general in India.[19]

For the post of governor-general the British government wanted Charles Lord Cornwallis, the man who had surrendered to Washington at Yorktown in 1781. Cornwallis turned down the job in 1782 and again in 1785, but by 1786 the pressure on him was so great that he accepted the appointment as governor-general and as commander-in-chief of the East India Company's possessions in India. He landed in Calcutta on September 12, 1786, and took up his duties.[20]

During the interval between the passage of the India Act and the arrival of Cornwallis, the company had to cope with a native revolt (the Second Mysore War, 1780–84) that resulted in a shortage of silver, especially in Bengal. This led the British to encourage American trade with India, since ships carried the Spanish milled dollars needed in the China trade. The silver situation had improved greatly by the time Cornwallis arrived.[21]

Much of the dishonesty and corruption associated with the East India Company originated in the low salaries of its employees, who supplemented their income by taking advantage of opportunities for graft. Cornwallis raised their salaries to remove this temptation. In 1793 he promulgated other reforms in The Permanent Settlement, which stabilized the system of collecting revenue from the natives and made Bengal one of the richest areas in the country.[22]

Cornwallis faced other problems. One concerned the relatives and dependents of members of the company, who were in a position to acquire wealth illegally. It was possible to make a fortune in a few years, return to Great Britain, buy property, and join the landed gentry. Under the Cornwallis administration the opportunities to make quick fortunes diminished. Company officials and relatives who had already accumulated ill-gotten gains now faced the problem of getting their money out of the country. Sending anything to Great Britain in the company's ships was risky. American ships provided an ideal opportunity. They did not have to contend with a consular bureaucracy. American captains and supercargoes spoke the same language; many possessed an adventurous entrepreneurial spirit. They enjoyed lower insurance rates, especially in times when Europe was at war. Money could be sent to the United States and then transferred to Great Britain. A safer alternative was to convert the money into goods that could be sold on the American market. The proceeds of the sales could be invested in other goods or deposited in the United States or Great Britain. Thus the East India Company officers, former officials, and their relatives had their own reasons for welcoming ships from the United States. So it was that Americans participated in the trade of India—a trade closed to Englishmen who were not employees of the East India Company.[23]

By 1787 British consuls in New York and Philadelphia were reporting to their government that British subjects were shipping fortunes out of India in American vessels. They also advised that Indian goods were being carried illegally to British possessions in American ships. As an example of the trend, it was noted that the ship *Commerce*, which left Madras in 1788, carried goods worth £50,000. Of this total, £30,000 belonged to the owners, the other

£20,000 representing consignments from Europeans in Madras. Articles not sold in the United States were disposed of in Ireland, England, or elsewhere in Europe.[24]

American ships also began to participate in the carrying trade between other ports in India and with other regions of Southeast Asia. In 1787 the Providence firm of Brown, Benson, and Ives sent the ship *General Washington* with a mixed cargo of sailcloth, anchors, munitions, hams, porter, claret, chocolates, and cheese to a diverse market. After stops at Madeira and the Cape of Good Hope, the ship sailed for India and participated in coastal trading between Pondicherry and Madras. From Madras it went to Canton, then to the West Indies before returning to Rhode Island. The voyage was considered a success. On its next voyage it went directly to Bombay. In 1791 the ship was sold in Calcutta at a great profit.[25]

To replace it, Brown, Benson, and Ives sent a mixed cargo to India on the *John Jay*. Little is known about this voyage, but the ship returned to Providence with a cargo of Indian goods on which over $75,000 was paid in customs duties. The profits from the sale must have seemed worthwhile, for the *John Jay* made three additional voyages to India before being captured by a British privateer.[26]

Other American firms began to trade with India. Elias Hasket Derby, Jr., the son of a prominent Salem merchant, purchased two small vessels, the *Peggy* and the *Sultana*, on the French island of Mauritius in the Indian Ocean and used them in trade between Bombay and Mauritius and along the Indian coast as far as Madras. It was the *Peggy* that brought the first cargo of Indian cotton to the United States to the chagrin of Derby's father, aware of cotton harvests in the southern part of the United States. Nevertheless, the senior Derby in 1788 sent nine of his largest ships to tap the Indian trade. Return cargoes from Calcutta, Bombay, and Rangoon in 1789 earned him a profit of $100,000.[27]

Despite warnings from British consuls in the United States and Egypt, the East India Company continued to tolerate American trade with India. The policy was questioned in connection with the arrival of the ship *Chesapeake* off Calcutta in 1787. Its captain and owner was Irish-born John O'Donnell, formerly a military officer in Bombay and a merchant in Calcutta. To company officials in Calcutta he presented United States naturalization papers and a legal clearance for the ship, which sailed from Bordeaux to the Cape of Good

Hope. The ship, based in Baltimore, had originally sailed from Perth Amboy, New Jersey, but most of its crew were British subjects. O'Donnell may have been engaged in illegal commerce under the protection of the American flag. The advocate-general in Bengal, however, ruled that the ship could not be seized unless it could be proved that the cargo was the legal property of British subjects. This would be difficult to do. That fact plus political considerations involving Americans and other foreign traders dictated a policy of no action. Although his ship had been detained until the case was resolved, O'Donnell had nothing but praise for the treatment he received from the officials in India. The *Chesapeake* returned to Perth Amboy in June 1789 and disposed of her cargo of goods from Madras, Bengal, and Bombay.[28]

Other Americans were beginning to appreciate the opportunities that awaited resourceful Americans in India and the Far East. In March 1788 Thomas Jefferson, U.S. Minister to France, received a letter that William Coxe, Jr., a Philadelephia merchant, had sent to another merchant on the matter of American commerce. Coxe wanted the intermediary to tell the American ministers at London and Paris that:

The British nation possess an immoderate share of the trade of India and China. The Dutch also have a great deal of the former and some of the latter. It appears to me that it wou'd be sound policy in those nations who have very little of that trade to permit the Americans to enjoy the privilege of their ports. France for instance by permitting us to use Pondicherry wou'd give us an opportunity of acting with them in gaining ground upon the British.[29]

Coxe asserted that the Americans were favored in China because they resembled the British. The French acting in concert with the Americans would make gains in that part of the world. "The commerce with the East shou'd if it were possible be made common to all the powers of inconsiderable [*sic*] influence in that country."[30]

From his perspective in Philadelphia, Coxe then added the following revealing bit of news:

To our ministers you may also mention confidentially that the principal american sales of fine teas are made for smuggling to Ireland and the british Islands—of Nankeens to the same—and likewise to the french and spanish colonies but more largely to the latter. Foreigners have bought in this port double the quantity brought [*sic*] in the Canton.[31]

In 1788 George Washington wrote to Jefferson on the pending adoption of the Constitution and on matters of economic interest. On the subject of foreign commerce, he said:

Notwithstanding the shackles under which our trade in general labours; commerce to the East Indies is prosecuted with considerable success; salted provisions and other produce (particularly from Massachusetts) have found an advantageous market there. The Voyages are so much shorter and the vessels are navigated at so much less expense, that we hope to rival and supply (at least through the West Indies) some part of Europe, with commodities from thence.—This year the exports from Massachusetts have amounted to a great deal more than their imports. I wish this was the case every where.[32]

The traders needed hard currencies to commence their operations. At first, firms like the Crowninshields of Salem had to scrounge to get Spanish milled dollars through coastal trading and borrowing. Within a few years Americans hit upon a more profitable arrangement. Each autumn at Gibraltar they bought Spanish dollars at the rate of five shillings to a dollar. The East India Company always bought its Spanish dollars in the spring when the ratio of exchange was five shillings sixpence to the dollar. Thus Americans started annual operations in the East a sixpence ahead on every Spanish dollar.[33]

In addition, Americans found that the Indians, as well as most of the inhabitants of Southeast Asia, liked to chew the betel nut. Americans went to Ceylon to acquire quantities of the nuts, which they then took to India. There the nuts were sold for specie or used directly along with bullion or Spanish dollars in trade.[34]

Already suspicious of French activities during the Third Mysore War (1790–92), the British became apprehensive of French alliances with other native rulers. When the news reached India that the National Assembly of Revolutionary France had declared war on Great Britain, Holland, and Spain in February 1793, Cornwallis promptly seized Pondicherry and the small French outposts in Bengal, marking the end of French power in India.[35]

France's disappearance from India created problems for British merchants who were members or former members of the East India Company. Prior to the outbreak of the war, Englishmen in India bought bills payable in Paris from the French East India Company, thereby getting their money to the Continent. The seizure of French possessions in India put an end to these practices. To provide a new way to transfer funds, the British East India Company established a new arrangement in 1793 that allowed employees to buy bills on the London office. Because company officials still considered this unsatisfactory, they sought other channels for transferring money and goods. This worked to the advantage of the Americans.[36]

To the Americans, the elimination of French authority from places like Pondicherry, which had offered a way to evade British restrictions, seemed inconvenient. Yet they made the most of the great advantages of being the major neutral carrier in the region.

The focal point for dealing with the French now shifted to the island of Mauritius then known as the Isle of France, in the Indian Ocean.

Robert Morris was the first American to grasp the potential value of the island. Writing to the Marquis de Lafayette on 19 May 1784, Morris urged the Frenchman to use his influence to have a free port established at Port Louis, the main harbor of the Isle of France. "I consider it as almost certain," wrote Morris, "that America will find it more advantageous to trade with that port than to go to India." France could thereby attract more American commerce. The French did not announce that Port Louis was open to foreign trade until 1787, but American merchants did not wait for a formal opening. Between 1773 and 1785 nearly two hundred American ships visited the island. In December 1785 Elias Hasket Derby of Salem sent the *Grand Turk* to Mauritius. It arrived there in April 1786 and promptly sold its cargo. The ship was then chartered by a French merchant to carry freight to Canton. In China the ship took on a cargo of tea, china, and cinnamon which was sold in Salem. Derby made twice his capital investment on this venture. Delighted, he sent two other ships to Mauritius, one in 1786 and one in 1787, both of which yielded large profits. Ships owned by Derby or his sons carried one-tenth of the American trade with Mauritius between 1786 and 1800. American merchants in Boston, Philadelphia, and Baltimore also traded with Mauritius during these years.[37]

War between Great Britain and France in 1793 threatened Amer-

ican trade with Mauritius. The colonial assembly of the island em-
bargoed both American and British ships. Early in 1794 the embargo
against the Americans was lifted; but news of the repeal traveled
slowly, and only five American ships called at the island in 1795.[38]
American merchants were convinced they needed an official rep-
resentative in Mauritius. Thus, William Macarty, who had been
functioning as a commercial agent on the island since 1790, was
commissioned as a U.S. consul on 29 May 1794, and entered on his
duties in April 1795.[39]

When the news of this development reached American shippers,
trade with the island picked up. Between 1796 and 1798 an average
of forty American ships stopped at Mauritius each year. Those who
visited the island during that time found it a veritable hotbed of
privateering activity. French privateers captured English merchant
ships and brought their cargoes to Mauritius to sell. The Americans
found that the local market was often overstocked with British goods
brought from India, China, or elsewhere. The French had no means
to take these goods home or to other European markets. Thus,
American merchants found with delight that they could get what
they wanted at Mauritius without having to sail to Canton or the
ports of India.

Indeed, American captains found that they could buy captured
cargoes at anywhere from one-third to two-thirds of their original
cost. The French captains were happy to sell their loot quickly and
close at hand. Without the Americans, privateering would hardly
have been worth the effort to the French. The British in turn regarded the Americans as receivers of stolen goods. And lower costs
meant high profits for the Americans.[40]

If trade was beneficial to the Americans, it was vital to the French
authorities on Mauritius. Cut off from contact with the rest of the
world, they had to rely on Americans and other neutrals for news.
The island also needed food and supplies, which the Americans
brought. Thus the trade was advantageous to the French authorities,
the French captains, and to the Americans.

British authorities were well aware of the American activities on
Mauritius, hearing about them from passing Danish vessels. The
Danes were also the principal competitors of the Americans in the
transfer of English fortunes from India to Europe in the form of
salable goods.[41] For the most part the British chose to do nothing

about the American activities in Mauritius; British warships did not seize American merchant vessels engaged in trade with their enemy. On both official and unofficial levels a policy of conciliation was being followed in the hope that the Americans would be less inclined to trade with the French and the Dutch.

The extent of the American involvement in trade in the Indian Ocean and in the Far East now began to worry officials of the East India Company. Having earlier welcomed American trade with India, they now saw American merchants as serious rivals. An opportunity to combat American competition seemed to present itself when John Jay went to London to discuss outstanding issues between the United States and Great Britain. Out of these talks came the Jay Treaty of 1794.

This treaty redefined the terms of commercial relations between the two nations. Trade with the British Isles was placed on a most-favored-nation basis. The United States gained a small concession in regard to the West India trade. Concerning American contacts with India, Article 13 allowed vessels belonging to U.S. citizens to be admitted and "hospitably received in all the sea-ports and harbors of the British territories in the East Indies." It stipulated that while Americans could carry on trade between India and the United States, that they could not engage in the coastal trade of India. The British hoped to keep Americans out of areas important to the East India Company. In Congress, critics of Jay's work noted that American trade with India was less free after the treaty than before. Nevertheless, after much debate and a number of public demonstrations against it, the treaty was approved by the Senate. East India Company officials hoped that they had now resolved the American problem, but they were mistaken.[42]

The attractions of mutual profit overcame obstacles set by the diplomats. Regardless of the letter of the treaty, the Americans came under no restraints. Restrictions were not enforced; when they were applied, ways were found around them. What could not be shipped from British India went out through the Danish footholds at Serampore, near Calcutta, or at Tranquebar on the Coromandel Coast. Americans also frequented areas of India not controlled by the East India Company. They were soon cutting into the Portuguese markets at Surat on the Western coast.[43] Clearly American entrepreneurial spirit flourished.

So favorable was trade in the East Indies and in India itself, that more Americans were attracted to the markets there. Philadelphia merchants, who had been indifferent to the India trade after 1784, now came back into the market. Between 1795 and 1800 at least fourteen ships went from Philadelphia to India. In Massachusetts a merchant of Beverly sent the first ship from that port to Calcutta in 1798, selling the return cargo in New York City, where merchants invested in return cargoes. Salem began to emerge as the major American port for trade with the East Indies. The Indian goods that were being sold to American customers were sugar, silk, ginger, muslin, gunny sacks, gun copal, indigo, opium, and saltpeter. The Crowninshields of Salem in 1795 imported the first Indian elephant to the United States. This animal, landed in Philadelphia, became an enormously popular attraction.[44]

The great increase of American trade with India caused a group of New England merchants to petition the United States government to appoint a consul. The man suggested for the post was Benjamin Joy of Newburyport, Massachusetts, a private speculator who had been living in India for several years. President Washington and the Senate concurred in the choice, and in November 1792 Joy was appointed as consul at Calcutta "and other ports on the Coasts of India and Asia." Joy did not reach Calcutta until April 1794, where he found that the governor-general refused to recognize his official status. Officially received or not, Joy could remain as a private businessman, but, under the circumstances, he had little hope of accomplishing much. He stayed at his post only one year. The State Department then appointed another Calcutta businessman named W. J. Miller to the post. Also unacceptable to the governor-general, he nonetheless got along well with officials, possibly because he was a Scot. Miller stayed on in his unrecognized capacity and continued to participate in business. Other consuls followed Miller, but the British never officially recognized any until 1843.[45]

Meanwhile a famous Frenchman had become interested in the trade between India and Europe and the involvement of Americans in Indian commerce with Europe as well as their own country. The Frenchman was Charles Maurice de Talleyrand-Périgord, a former president of the French National Assembly temporarily exiled in the United States in the mid 1790s. Long interested in economic questions, and with both experience and training in financial and political operations, he turned his attention to the state of American business. He knew that Europeans were looking for a safe place for their capital in the midst of war. He was aware that America needed capital to develop. Could these two needs be brought together? Alexander Hamilton had charted the financial course of the nation, and a new stability was emerging. Talleyrand knew that American speculators were trying to sell land to European investors, but he doubted that much capital would be raised this way. Instead he devised a plan involving the United States and India.

Under Talleyrand's plan, American lands would be marketed in India as a means of transferring Anglo-Indian fortunes to the United States and of financing the American trade with India. Although American trade with India and Asia was expanding, many Americans were still reluctant to use their limited supply of capital for Asian ventures that would take at least two years to pay off, if at all. It seemed more prudent to make investments closer to home that required less time. Trade with the Orient also took specie out of the country, with a temporarily depressing effect on business. Talleyrand's answer to this was to form an Asiatic Bank in the United States that would relieve the drain of specie, attract European capital, and stimulate trade with Asia.[46]

Talleyrand had no luck in selling the Americans on his Asiatic Bank before returning to France in June 1796. Meanwhile his companion and fellow exile in America, Bon-Albert Briois de Beaumez, left for India in May 1796 to sell American land owned by the Holland Land Company. This plan also fell through, but Beaumez settled in India as a merchant.[47]

Though his schemes came to little, Talleyrand's statement about American trade with India remains interesting. After reviewing the need of the East India Company's employees and the native Indians to have access to foreign commerce, Talleyrand wrote:

All these circumstances combined strongly to invite Americans to turn their eyes toward Asia and to form there strong commercial ties before the French, after recovering from the wounds of their revolution, can rival them in that part of the world. The merchants of the United States have realized so well their favorable position that during 1795 they sent thirty-two expeditions to India instead of the five or six which ordinarily leave the continent. What will it not be when the return of peace permits them to bring to their shipments that economy which alone can assure durable profits and which characterizes wise and able merchants.[48]

To the west of India, Americans' lucrative trade with Mauritius was affected when news of the Quasi-War reached the island in April 1799. After much discussion, the local Assembly ordered the seizure of all American ships and alerted French privateers for action. Vice-Consul George Wilt argued against the seizures on the grounds that the quarrel between the two countries had been settled. A short time later word was received that the Directory in Paris had repealed the earlier instructions. Accordingly the authorities on Mauritius rescinded all but seizures of American merchant vessels operating under a letter of marque. The local privateers were displeased, and the cancellation of seizures had to be repeated again in September 1799. Nevertheless, on 4 January 1800, a privateer from Mauritius attacked the American ships *Louisa* and *Mercury* in the Indian Ocean.[49]

Meanwhile, Americans worried about trade with Mauritius convinced Congress to send out a special agent to seek a special agreement with the authorities. Samuel Cooper arrived on the island in December 1799; a month later a draft agreement favorable to the United States had been agreed upon. He then set out for the French island of Reunion in the hope of repeating his earlier success in Mauritius. By the time Cooper completed his labors and returned to the United States, the Quasi-War with France was over. A treaty of amity and commerce was signed in Paris on 30 September 1800.[50]

During the war years 1799–1800, only eight American ships came to Mauritius. With the return of peace the number rose to nineteen in 1801 and forty-six in 1802. Between 1804 and 1807 more than half of the trade by neutral ships was carried by Americans. After that, things began to go wrong. American trade declined and then stopped.[51]

The first reason for the decline was oversupply. Privateers had brought captured goods to Mauritius, where Americans purchased them. Between 1803 and 1810 a total of 167 ships were brought to the island as prizes, resulting in a glut of goods and a slump in the market.

A second reason was the deterioration of Franco-American relations as a result of Napoleonic wars. The United States tried to cope with the harassment of neutral commerce by passing the Embargo Act of 1807, barring all foreign trade; when that failed, it substituted the Non-Intercourse Act of 1809 aimed directly at France and Great Britain. For its part, France issued the Bayonne Proclamation of April 1808, which authorized the confiscation of American ships in French ports. The years 1809–10 found only ten American ships in Mauritius, and six of these were prizes brought in by privateers.

The third factor in the decline of American trade with Mauritius was the tightening of the British blockade of the island in 1808. Finally, the British seized the island later in 1810, landing troops from India in one of a number of operations in Eastern waters that deprived Napoleon of any close base for naval operations against India.[52]

In the meantime, Americans had been probing other regions in the Pacific Ocean. Remembering John Ledyard's view that the one item that the Chinese would buy in quantity was furs from the Pacific Northwest, a group of Boston merchants sent out two ships to test the market. John Kendrick of Massachusetts, the commander of the expedition and the captain of the *Columbia*, and Captain Robert Gray of Rhode Island in the *Lady Washington* left Boston in September 1787. Eleven months later they were in Nootka Sound, the center for fur trading on Vancouver Island. It was then too late in the year for trading, so the vessels anchored in a cove and the crew lived ashore in log huts. During the winter season they made chisels from scrap iron, which they subsequently traded for otter skins. By the summer of 1789, with provisions beginning to run low, a full cargo of skins had not yet been accumulated. The captains decided to trade ships and separate. Gray took the *Columbia* to Canton, where he traded his skins for tea and returned to Boston, having sailed around the world. But the voyage was not a financial success, in part because fourteen other American vessels had recently preceded the *Columbia* in Canton.[53]

Kendrick in the *Lady Washington* tried something different, going across the North Pacific from Vancouver to Japan. He reached the Yamato Peninsula on 6 May 1791. His reception was not cordial. The Japanese were not willing to trade with foreigners and especially not for furs. Kendrick did not know that the religious beliefs of the Japanese did not permit the wearing of the skin of anything that had once been a living thing. Even if he had known this information, he might have ignored it. On an earlier voyage to Canton, he had refused to pay the middleman's fee and had been banned from that port. Kendrick's contempt for national customs, traditions, and beliefs was now extended to Japan. It was a most unfortunate beginning of American contacts with that kingdom, and it ended in failure. Before leaving Japan, Kendrick left two notes for the officials in which he described American commercial activities in Asia. Kendrick was obliged to sell his cargo to the Portuguese at Macao, in the process making new enemies. Later in that same year (1791) Kendrick carried a second cargo of otter skins to Macao. Though the Portuguese governor refused him entrance to the port, Kendrick succeeded in selling his cargo.[54]

A little more than a month after Kendrick's original attempt, the American ship *Grace*, under Captain James Douglas of New York, tried to open trade with Japan. Douglas pretended that his ship had been damaged by a storm and that he needed to do a little trading for supplies. The Japanese were not moved and Douglas failed in his effort.[55]

The outbreak of war in Europe brought the Americans a new opportunity to penetrate Japan. After Napoleon conquered the Netherlands, the British Navy began to attack and capture Dutch ships. The Dutch East India Company had the right to send one cargo a year to the Japanese port of Nagasaki, and it was anxious to maintain this monopoly. It now began to look for an American ship to take the annual cargo to Japan.

The first American to be involved in this activity was William F. Stewart of New York. He had traded between British India and the Dutch East Indies, but he was not as successful as some of his countrymen and had lost two of his ships to creditors. Then came an opportunity to rent his ship to the Dutch. Under a Dutch East India Company charter, his ship, the *Eliza* of New York, carried a cargo to Nagasaki in the summer of 1797. The Japanese noticed that Stewart and his men spoke English, and they assumed that it was part of a British ruse to trade with them. Stewart assured the Japanese that the Americans were a different kind of English-speaking people. The captain's tact and diplomacy impressed both the Japanese and the Dutch. Stewart disposed of his shipment and was returning to Batavia with a cargo of copper and camphor wood when his ship struck a reef and sank. The captain and his men were saved.

Stewart appealed to the Japanese for help, and after many difficulties his ship was raised. While en route to the Philippines, the *Eliza* sank again, this time for good. Determined to return to Japan, Stewart turned his attention to raising money in the Philippines for another ship.[56]

While Stewart was struggling to achieve his ambition, another American ship, the *Franklin* of Boston under Captain James Devereux, reached Nagasaki in August 1799. Devereux succeeded in selling his cargo of sugar, cloves, tin, cotton yarn, black pepper, and sandalwood. In return he acquired a substantial number of Japanese items including cabinets, tea trays, knife boxes, fans, and baskets. The *Franklin* was the first American ship to bring Japanese goods to the United States.[57]

In 1800 the Dutch chartered the Boston ship *Massachusetts* for the annual trip to Nagasaki. Sailing in it was the newly appointed Dutch director of the warehouse on the island of Deshima. When they reached Nagasaki they found another American ship, *Emperor of Japan*, whose captain was the redoubtable William Stewart. The *Emperor of Japan* was flying the Dutch flag, Stewart having told the Japanese that his ship was the annual cargo vessel. When the real charter ship, complete with an official, arrived on the scene, Stewart was arrested by the Dutch and the cargo of the *Emperor of Japan* confiscated.[58]

There were other charters of American ships by the Dutch until 1809, when the *Rebecca* of Baltimore left Nagasaki to be captured by a British warship and taken to Calcutta. The Dutch then resumed sending their own ships to maintain the monopoly. Anglo-American relations gradually deteriorated until in 1812 the United States declared war on Great Britain. The war ended the activity of the United States in the North Pacific. Almost thirty years would pass before another American visited Japan.[59]

New trading patterns were emerging elsewhere in the Far East. The ships of Elias Hasket Derby were credited with being the first Americans to trade with Ceylon and Sumatra and among the first to go to Manila. They also made the first attempt to trade with Siam. Beginning in 1795 a number of American ships began appearing in Sumatra for the pepper trade, carrying tobacco, iron, dried fish, brandy, and gin to exchange in that Dutch outpost. Other captains, ostensibly engaged in whaling, smuggled American goods to the

Dutch-held Spice Islands. Direct trade was also carried on with
Batavia on the island of Java. Americans brought cargoes of cloth,
hats, wine, beer, seltzer water, stationery, and silver in the form
of trade dollars. In return they received spices, coffee, rice, and
Chinese goods.[60]

Rhode Island merchants who had purchased coffee in Haiti sought
a new source after a slave uprising in 1792 stopped production on
the island. They found it on Java in the Dutch East Indies, and
trade began in earnest in 1799. Between 1800 and 1807 Rhode Island
merchants sent fourteen ships to Batavia for coffee. The Dutch would
not allow foreign vessels to buy all the coffee they wanted and
insisted that designated amounts of sugar and pepper had to be
taken as well. Spanish silver dollars were in great demand in Java,
and the Americans discovered that the use of such specie greatly
facilitated their transactions. In 1802 the authorities in the Netherlands issued orders that coffee was not to be sold to neutrals, but
Americans could have it for silver.[61]

There were other difficulties to be overcome. American vessels
ran the risk of being seized by Malay pirates or by ships of the Royal
Navy. For example, the *John Jay*, captured by a British warship in
September 1804 while en route from Batavia to Providence, was
taken to Bermuda. The ship and cargo were condemned by a British
admiralty court because it was carrying bar iron, a contraband, in
addition to coffee, sugar, and pepper. But the ship was released on
bail.[62]

If there were risks, there were also benefits. When Denmark
entered the European war on the side of Napoleonic France in 1807,
the United States became the only neutral nation still involved in
the coffee trade. All this came to an end with the passage of the
Embargo Act by the United States Congress in 1807. Although this
act was replaced in 1809 by the less restrictive Non-Intercourse Act,
the Rhode Island merchants were not able to revive their coffee
trade before the outbreak of the War of 1812. After that war, the
trade again flourished for a time.[63]

Within a few years after the Jay Treaty went into effect, some
East India Company officials and a few British leaders became concerned that Article 13 of that treaty was being interpreted too
loosely. Efforts by the company to tighten the rules were resisted
by Henry Dundas, one of the king's principal secretaries of state,

who argued in 1797 in favor of more liberal commercial principles. The following year Lord Kenyon, a British judge, gave a broad interpretation to the article in the cases of *Wilson v. Marryat*.[64] In another case, when the governor-general of Bengal prevented an American ship from sailing for Manila in 1797 for fear of compromising British preparations to attack the Philippines, the British officials, uneasy about the detention, paid the captain to carry the cargo to the United States.[65]

But gradually opportunities for Americans declined in India. In 1805 the Jay Treaty expired, and the Anglo-Indian wealth in India ceased to be transported in American ships. The East India Company tried to do something about the range and diversity of the American activity by inserting in the Monroe-Pinckney Treaty of 1806 the requirement that only direct trade between the United States and British East India ports would be allowed. But that treaty was not ratified by the Senate, so trade continued much as before until it was undermined by the Embargo and finally by the War of 1812.[66]

At the end of the War of 1812, the East India Company lost its monopoly. The Commercial Convention of 1815 gave the United States most-favored-nation status in India, but confined its trade to four ports and imposed double duties.[67] In the 1820s American trade with India declined while that with China grew.

In light of the changed situation in India, both the American merchants and the State Department reassessed their needs and opportunities. Trade slowly shifted from India to China. No attempt was made to establish a consulate in Calcutta or elsewhere in India. The United States consulates at Port Louis on the island of Mauritius and at Manila in the Philippines, which were closed during the War of 1812, were reopened in 1816 and 1817, respectively. When the British returned the island of Java to the Dutch, the United States reopened its consulate there in 1818. The old order of things had passed, and new commercial arrangements were emerging.[68]

Ten years after the War of 1812, Americans were seeking new outlets for their commerce. Noting that Great Britain had made a treaty with Siam in 1826, the United States government decided to follow suit. Edmund Roberts, a former American trader in the Indian Ocean, was sent by President Andrew Jackson to negotiate treaties with Siam, Cochin China, Muscat, and Japan. In 1833 Roberts

signed a treaty with Siam modeled on that of the British. A similar
treaty was signed with the sultan of Zanzibar. Roberts was on his
way to Japan when he died in 1835. Nineteen years later Commodore Matthew C. Perry completed that work. For the remainder
of the nineteenth century, the diplomatic relations of the United
States were highlighted by its involvement with those areas of the
world with which American traders had made the first contacts long
before.[69] This was true of China, Japan, Hawaii, and the Philippines,
as well as of Italy and Eastern Europe. While in the pursuit of trade,
American merchants played an important role in making the citizens
of the United States more aware of the non-Western world. American diplomatic attention was eventually attracted to where interests
had grown, stimulated by merchants and shippers seeking profits.

NOTES

1. John Jay to William Bingham, 9 July 1783, in *John Jay: The Winning
of the Peace: Unpublished Papers, 1780–1784*, ed. Richard B. Morris (New
York: Harper and Row, 1980), pp. 536–38.

2. Ralph Lerner, "Commerce and Character: The Anglo-American as
the New-Model Man," *William and Mary Quarterly*, 3d series, 36 (January
1979):3, 6, 9–11, 17, 19.

3. For an overview of the trade problems of the Confederation period,
see Merrill Jensen, *The New Nation: A History of the United States during
the Confederation, 1781–1789* (New York: Alfred A. Knopf, 1950), pp. 194–
218; and Forrest McDonald, *E Pluribus Unum: The Formation of the American Republic, 1776–1790* (Boston: Houghton Mifflin Co., 1965), passim.
The philosophical underpinnings of American commercial policy are discussed in Felix Gilbert, *The Beginnings of American Foreign Policy: To
the Farewell Address* (New York: Harper and Row, 1961), pp. 51, 69–72,
84, 86; and in Paul A. Varg, *Foreign Policies of the Founding Fathers*
(Baltimore: Penguin Books, 1970), pp. 20–22, 27–38. For the attitudes of
Jefferson and Jay concerning commercial relations with France, see Julian
P. Boyd, "Two Diplomats between Revolutions, John Jay and Thomas
Jefferson," *Virginia Magazine of History and Biography* 66 (April 1958):131–
46. For the views of Thomas Jefferson, see Dumas Malone, *Jefferson and
the Ordeal of Liberty* (Boston: Little, Brown, 1962), pp. 154–60; and Merrill
D. Peterson, "Thomas Jefferson and Commercial Policy, 1783–1793," *Wil-
liam and Mary Quarterly* 3d series, 26 (October 1965):584–610. On Madison's views, see Drew R. McCoy, "Republicanism and American Foreign
Policy: James Madison and the Political Economy of Commercial Discrim-

ination, 1789 to 1794," *William and Mary Quarterly* 3d series, 31 (October 1974):633–46. On the background and negotiation of the commercial treaty with Great Britain, see Samuel Flagg Bemis, *Jay's Treaty: A Study in Commerce and Diplomacy* (New York: Macmillan, 1923); and Jerald A. Combs, *The Jay Treaty: Political Battleground of the Founding Fathers* (Berkeley: University of California Press, 1970). The role of Secretary of the Treasury Alexander Hamilton in regard to the treaty is discussed in Gilbert L. Lycan, *Alexander Hamilton and American Foreign Policy* (Norman: University of Oklahoma Press, 1969), chap. 12.

4. James Fulton Zimmerman, *Impressment of American Seamen* (New York: Columbia University Press, 1925); Irving Brant, *James Madison, Secretary of State, 1800–1809* (Indianapolis: Bobbs-Merrill, 1953); Bradford Perkins, *The First Rapprochment: England and the United States, 1795–1805* (Philadelphia: University of Pennsylvania Press, 1955); Bradford Perkins, *Prologue to War: England and the United States, 1805–1812* (Berkeley: University of California Press, 1961); Norman K. Risjord, "1812: Conservatives, War Hawks and the Nation's Honor," *William and Mary Quarterly* 3d series, 18 (April 1961):196–210; Reginald Horsman, *The Causes of the War of 1812* (Philadelphia: University of Pennsylvania Press, 1962); Roger Brown, *The Republic in Peril: 1812* (New York: Columbia University Press, 1964), pp. 161–76; J. Mackay Hitsman, *The Incredible War of 1812: A Military History* (Toronto: University of Toronto Press, 1965), chap. 1; Harry L. Coles, *The War of 1812* (Chicago: University of Chicago Press, 1965), chap. 1; Dumas Malone, *Jefferson the President: The Second Term, 1805–1809* (Boston: Little, Brown, 1974); and Drew R. McCoy, *The Elusive Republic: Political Economy in Jeffersonian America* (Chapel Hill: University of North Carolina Press, 1980), chaps. 9 and 10.

5. Alexander De Conde, *Entangling Alliance* (Durham: Duke University Press, 1958); Alexander De Conde, *The Quasi-War: The Politics and Diplomacy of the Undeclared War with France, 1798–1801* (New York: Scribners, 1966); Albert Hall Bowman, *The Struggle for Neutrality: Franco-American Diplomacy During the Federalist Era* (Knoxville: University of Tennessee Press, 1974); and Clifford L. Egan, *Neither Peace nor War: Franco-American Relations, 1803–1812* (Baton Rouge: Louisiana State University Press, 1983).

6. Robert G. Albion, William Baker, and Benjamin W. Labaree, *New England and the Sea* (Middletown, Conn.: Wesleyan University Press, 1972), pp. 55–73; Samuel Eliot Morison, *The Maritime History of Massachusetts, 1783–1860* (Boston: Houghton Mifflin Co., 1941), pp. 30–40.

7. Albion, Baker, and Labaree, *New England and the Sea*, pp. 54–58; G. Bhagat, *Americans in India, 1784–1860* (New York: New York University Press, 1970), pp. xxiii–xxvi.

8. Bhagat, *Americans in India, 1784–1860*, p. 3; Ole Feldbaek, *India Trade under the Danish Flag, 1772–1808* (Copenhagen: Scandinavian Institute of Asian Studies, 1969), pp. 64–74.

9. Morison, *Maritime History*, p. 44; Morison's account of this transaction is disputed by Philip Chadwick Foster Smith, who argues that the owner of the *Harriet* never intended to send his ship to China. Instead, he made a last-minute decision to sell his cargo of ginseng at Cape Town when it was too late in the season to ship it to Sweden. See Smith's *The Empress of China* (Philadelphia: Philadelphia Maritime Museum, 1984), pp. 24–25.

10. Smith, *The Empress of China*, pp. 14–20; Jared Sparks, *The Life of John Ledyard, The American Traveller* (Cambridge, Mass.: Hilliard & Browne, 1828), pp. 126–31.

11. Smith, *The Empress of China*, p. 29.

12. Robert Morris to John Jay, 27 November 1783, in *John Jay*, ed. Richard B. Morris, p. 651.

13. Smith, *The Empress of China*, pp. 31–44. John Paul Jones was interested in Ledyard's plan and thought that he could get King Louis XVI to finance it. But the King of Spain considered the Pacific coast to be Spanish territory, and he was not interested in encouraging any American poachers. As an ally of the King of Spain, Louis XVI would not allow French ships to break Spanish laws, so the project fell through. See Samuel Eliot Morison, *John Paul Jones: A Sailor's Biography* (Boston: Little, Brown, 1959), pp. 341–43. Ledyard then went on to Egypt, where he died in 1789.

14. Smith, *The Empress of China*, pp. 44–188.

15. Ibid., pp. 153–240. Smith states that at the beginning of the 1784 season in Canton the price of ginseng was about $15 a pound; but by the time various English, French, Dutch, and Danish ships had sold their shipments of it, the price was down to about $1.50 to $2.25 a pound. The profit from the voyage was between 25 to 30 percent. Representatives of the British East India Company kept a record of the prices paid for the cargo of *The Empress of China*, and a report on it was sent to the company's directors.

16. Holden Furber, "The Beginnings of American Trade with India, 1784–1812," *New England Quarterly* 11 (June 1938):235–36; Samuel W. Woodhouse, Jr., "Log and Journal of the Ship *United States* on a Voyage to China in 1784," *Pennsylvania Magazine of History and Biography* 55 (January 1931):230–53. The East India Company officials learned that the *United States* carried Captain Patrick Lawson and his wife from Madeira to Sumatra and that the two then took a ship from Sumatra to Bengal. The company officials knew that Lawson had sent a cargo from Calcutta under the Danish flag and that he was involved in illicit trade. See Bhagat, *Americans in India*, p. 5.

17. Furber, "The Beginnings of American Trade with India, 1784–1812," pp. 236–37.

18. Ibid., pp. 237–38. According to the articles of agreement, the ship was owned by William Green of London, the supercargo. The ship was to go to Bengal "under cover of an American house, whose name must be used for the Proforma, through the whole Transaction, and the Ship of course to be navigated under American Colors." Accordingly, the ship was sold to Christopher Champlin of Newport on 25 April 1784. See Worthington Chauncey Ford, ed., *Commerce of Rhode Island, 1726–1800* (Boston: Massachusetts Historical Society, 1895), 2:202–4. For a report on the *Hydra*'s visit, see C. H. Philips and B. B. Misra, eds. *Fort William-India House Correspondence and Other Contemporary Papers Relating Thereto: Foreign and Secret, 1782–1786* (Delhi: Controller of Publications, Government of India, 1963), 15:510–11.

19. Lucy S. Sutherland, *The East India Company in Eighteenth-Century Politics* (Oxford: Oxford University Press, 1952), chap. 13.

20. Marguerite Eyer Wilbur, *The East India Company and the British Empire in the Far East* (New York: Richard Smith, 1945), pp. 347–48.

21. Holden Furber, *Rival Empires of Trade in the Orient, 1600–1800* (Minneapolis: University of Minnesota Press, 1976), pp. 178–79; Bhagat, *Americans in India, 1784–1860*, p. xxii.

22. Wilbur, *The East India Company*, pp. 348–52.

23. Furber, *Rival Empires of Trade in the Orient*, pp. 180–81; Furber, "The Beginnings of American Trade with India, 1784–1812," p. 242; C. Northcote Parkinson, *War in the Eastern Seas, 1793–1815*, (London: George Allen & Unwin, 1954), p. 44.

24. Furber, "The Beginnings of American Trade with India, 1784–1812," p. 242; J. Franklin Jameson, ed., "Letters of Phineas Bond," *Annual Report of the American Historical Association for the Year 1896* (Washington, D.C.: U.S. Government Printing Office, 1897), 1:540–41.

25. Bhagat, *Americans in India, 1784–1860*, p. 25.

26. Ibid., pp. 25–26.

27. Richard Haskayne McKey, Jr., "Elias Hasket Derby, Merchant of Salem, Massachusetts, 1739–1799" (Ph.D. diss., Clark University, 1961), chap. 8; Bhagat, *Americans in India, 1784–1860*, pp. 14–15.

28. "The Beginnings of American Trade with India, 1784–1812," pp. 241–42; Syed Hasan Askari, ed., *Fort William-India House Correspondence and Other Contemporary Papers Relating Thereto: Foreign, Secret and Political* (Delhi: Controller of Publications, Government of India, 1976), 16:169.

29. William Coxe, Jr. to John Brown Cutting, March 1788, in *The Papers of Thomas Jefferson*, ed. Julian P. Boyd (Princeton: Princeton University Press, 1956), 13:3–4.

30. Ibid.

31. Ibid., p. 4.

32. George Washington to Thomas Jefferson, 13 August 1788, in *The Writings of George Washington*, ed. John C. Fitzpatrick (Washington, D.C.: U.S. Government Printing Office, 1939), 30:84.

33. Furber, "The Beginnings of American Trade with India, 1784–1812," pp. 255–56; Bhagat, *Americans in India, 1784–1860*, pp. 57–58, 74, 103.

34. Bhagat, *Americans in India, 1784–1860*, pp. 57–58.

35. Wilbur, *The East India Company*, p. 354.

36. Indian goods had to be paid for in specie, which always created a drain. In the case of Great Britain, Parliament limited the total amount of bills that could be drawn on the Company to £300,000 sterling a year. This amount was always exceeded, but it still did not meet the demand in India for bills to transfer their fortunes. See Hans Huth and Wilma J. Pugh, trans. and eds., "Talleyrand in America as a Financial Promoter, 1794–96: Unpublished Letters and Memoirs," *Annual Report of the American Historical Association for the Year 1941* (Washington, D.C.: U.S. Government Printing Office, 1942), 2:15–16.

37. A. Toussaint, "Early American Trade with Mauritius," *Essex Institute Historical Collection* 87 (October 1951): 374–78.

38. Ibid., p. 378.

39. Ibid.

40. Ibid., pp. 378–80; Parkinson, *War in the Eastern Seas, 1793–1815*, p. 47.

41. Parkinson, *War in the Eastern Seas, 1793–1815*, p. 44.

42. Furber, "The Beginnings of American Trade with India, 1784–1812," pp. 240, 243; Bemis, *Jay's Treaty*, chaps. 12–13. The text of the treaty is published as an appendix.

43. Furber, "The Beginnings of American Trade with India, 1784–1812," pp. 246–49. Furber points out that when a British judge cast doubt on the legality of American trade with India under the operation of the Navigations Acts, a clause was inserted in an act of Parliament to make easier the implementation of the Jay treaty. Another scholar points out: "Between 1795 and 1800, more than 107 American ships visited India and generally were engaged in coastal trading in Asia for months." He also states that between 1793 and 1812, United States ships were the main carriers of Indian manufactured goods. See Bhagat, *Americans in India, 1784–1860*, pp. 61, 71.

44. Bhagat, *Americans in India, 1784–1860*, pp. 36–37. Bhagat states that Philadelphia merchants adhered strictly to the provisions of Article 13 of the Jay Treaty and participated only in direct trade between India and the United States. For an overview of Philadelphia trade in the early nine-

teenth century, see Russell F. Weigley, ed., *Philadelphia, A 300-Year History* (New York: W. W. Norton, 1982), pp. 208–18. An earlier survey is Marion V. Brewington, "Maritime Philadelphia, 1609–1837," *Pennsylvania Magazine of History and Biography* 63 (April 1939): 93–117. On the activities of Salem and Beverly in the East Indies, see Morison, *Maritime History*, chap. 7, and pp. 141–42. The ships of Elias Hasket Derby of Salem carried the first native of India to the United States and the first zebra. See McKey, "Elias Hasket Derby, Merchant of Salem, Massachusetts, 1739–1799," p. 294.

45. Bhagat, *Americans in India, 1784–1860*, pp. 86–92. Between 1802 and 1843 the United States did not commission any consuls for Calcutta. In 1838 it made an unsuccessful effort to gain recognition for a newly appointed consul at Bombay. The British attitude toward Benjamin Joy is set forth in a letter of Sir John Shore, the Governor-General, to Henry Dundas, the President of the Board of Control, dated 7 March 1795. Shore described Joy as "a sensible, moderate, well informed man." The problem with recognizing him was stated as follows: "The only danger arising from the residence of privileged Consuls at this Presidency, is this, that they may cover the illegal trade of British Subjects, to a very great extent, & if Consuls are to be admitted here, they should be placed under such Restrictions as may prevent this Effect." See Holden Furber, ed., *The Private Record of an Indian Governor-Generalship* (Cambridge, Mass.: Harvard University Press, 1933), p. 67.

46. Huth and Pugh, *Talleyrand in America*, pp. 16–18.

47. Ibid. p. 22, n.13.

48. Ibid., p. 129.

49. Toussaint, "Early American Trade with Mauritius," p. 381.

50. Ibid., pp. 381–82. For the text of the treaty, see U.S. Navy Department, Office of Naval Records and Library, *Naval Documents Related to the Quasi-War Between the United States and France* (Washington, D.C.: U.S. Government Printing Office, 1938), 6:393–409.

51. Toussaint, "Early American Trade with Mauritius," p. 382.

52. Ibid., pp. 384, 386. When the British captured the Isle of France, they changed its name to Mauritius. The War of 1812 kept American ships away from the island. There was a brief revival of trade in 1818 and 1823 followed by a decline. Things picked up again in 1838, and in 1863 thirty-six ships called at the island, the largest number since 1810. There was a moderate amount of trade until 1870, when the opening of the Suez Canal late in the previous year began to be felt. The major portion of shipping now avoided the island. The United States finally closed its consulate there in 1911. See Toussaint, "Early American Trade with Mauritius," p. 387. For the British Admiralty's views about Mauritius and the capture of that

island, see Parkinson, *War in the Eastern Seas, 1793–1815*, pp. 364–411. The conquest of Java is described on pp. 412–17.

53. Tyler Dennett, *Americans in Eastern Asia* (New York: Macmillan, 1922), pp. 36–37, 242. Dennett points out that the first shipment of furs that Americans took to the East were seal skins collected in the Falkland Islands and taken to the coast of India before being finally sold in Canton in 1788. Morison, *Maritime History*, pp. 46–47. A recent work on the activities of American fur sealers in the South Pacific, the Indian Ocean, the Southeastern Pacific, Fiji, Australia, Polynesia, and Canton is James Kirker, *Adventures to China: Americans in the Southern Oceans, 1792–1812* (New York: Oxford University Press, 1970). A short, but well-illustrated, account of the China trade is Alfred Tamarin and Shirley Glubok, *Voyaging to Cathay: Americans in the China Trade* (New York: Viking Press, 1976).

54. Lee Houchins, "The Early American Experience in Japan, 1791–1809: A Reexamination," paper presented at the meeting of the Columbia University Seminars on Modern East Asia: Japan, 11 May 1973, pp. 7–8; William L. Neumann, *America Encounters Japan: From Perry to MacArthur* (New York: Harper and Row, 1963), pp. 6–7.

55. Dennett, *Americans in Eastern Asia*, pp. 243–44; Lee Houchins, "The Early American Experience in Japan, 1791–1809: A Reexamination," p. 4; Neumann, *America Encounters Japan*, p. 6.

56. Neumann, *America Encounters Japan*, pp. 7–9; Dennett, *Americans in Eastern Asia*, pp. 242–43.

57. Neumann, *America Encounters Japan*, pp. 9–10; Dennett, *Americans in Eastern Asia*, pp. 243–44.

58. Neumann, *America Encounters Japan*, pp. 8–9; Houchins, "The Early American Experience in Japan, 1791–1809," pp. 13–16. Houchins states that there are three versions of Stewart's escape from Batavia. One was that he stole an American ship while its master was ashore; another that he stole a Dutch ship loaded with rice; and a third one was that he sailed on an American ship bound for Mauritius. Stewart made another attempt to open trade with Japan in 1803. This time he brought letters addressed to Japanese officials and gifts, including a camel. He had also learned to speak Dutch. His efforts were not successful because the Japanese believed that he was responsible for some of the Dutch factory's debt and because they considered him an agent of the British.

59. Between 1797 and 1809 the Dutch hired eight different American vessels to make the trip between Batavia to Nagasaki. See Houchins, "The Early American Experience in Japan, 1791–1809," pp. 4–6; Charles Oscar Paullin, *American Voyages to the Orient, 1690–1865* (Annapolis, Md.: U.S. Naval Institute Press, 1971), p. 104. Paullin's information originally appeared as a series of articles in the *U.S. Naval Institute Proceedings* in

1910–1911. He points out that the first American whale ship entered Japanese waters in 1820, but by 1822 there were more than thirty in the area. Apart from the American ships under the Dutch flag, the last American commercial vessel to visit Japan before the War of 1812 was the *Eclipse*, presumably from Boston, under Captain Joseph O'Cain, which came to Nagasaki in 1807 under the pretext of needing provisions. The Japanese suspected that this was an excuse to trade, so the ship was furnished with provisions and forced to depart. See Paullin, *American Voyages to the Orient, 1690–1865*, pp. 104–5. Dennett says that the *Eclipse* was chartered by the Russian-American Company at Canton to carry a cargo to Kamchatka and the Northwest Coast and was flying the Russian flag. Since the Japanese had been angered by Russian conduct at Sakhalan the previous year, they had an additional reason not to be hospitable. See Dennett, *Americans in Eastern Asia*, pp. 242–43.

60. McKey, "Elias Hasket Derby, Merchant of Salem, Massachusetts;" pp. 255–94; Parkinson, *War in the Eastern Seas, 1793–1815*, p. 46.

61. Sharom Ahmat, "Some Problems of the Rhode Island Traders in Java, 1799–1836," *Journal of Southeast Asian History* 6 (March 1965):94–96.

62. Ibid., p. 98. According to Congressman Jacob Crowninshield, who as a former ship captain and a member of a prosperous mercantile family of Salem prepared a report on American trade in 1806 at the request of Secretary of State James Madison, there were fifty American ships trading with Batavia in 1805. He believed that more than forty of these carried away cargoes of sugar, coffee, and paper that were paid for by specie, iron, liquor, wines, and American-grown provisions. Similar cargoes were carried by American ships from Europe to Batavia. Likewise sugar and coffee, after being landed in the United States and duty paid on them, were shipped to Europe. Some of these latter ships were seized by the British in the Atlantic. Others, carrying cargo from India to the United States, were seized by the British at the Cape of Good Hope on the grounds that it was illegal for Americans to begin voyages to India from Europe. See John H. Reinoehl, ed., "Some Remarks on the American Trade: Jacob Crowninshield to James Madison, 1806," *William and Mary Quarterly*, 3d series, 16 (January 1959): 103–4.

63. Ahmat, "Some Problems of the Rhode Island Traders in Java, 1799–1836," pp. 92–100.

64. Furber, "The Beginnings of American Trade with India, 1784–1812," pp. 249–50.

65. Ibid., p. 251. According to Jacob Crowninshield, by 1805 there were from three to five American vessels in Manila every year and this had been the case for several years. They purchased sugar and indigo as well as

Chinese goods brought there by Chinese junks as well as by the Portuguese from Macao. He noted that in 1802 an American ship had been chartered to carry a cargo from Manila to Acapulco in Mexico. The Americans usually purchased their cargoes with dollars and with European goods. In 1805 a ship from Salem carried Virginia tobacco to Manila, where it sold well and returned home with a cargo of sugar and indigo. See Reinoehl, "Some Remarks on the American Trade: Jacob Crowninshield to James Madison, 1806," p. 104.

66. Bhagat, *Americans in India, 1784–1860*, pp. 41–48, 67–68; H. R. Ghosal, "Indo-American Trade during the French Revolutionary and Napoleonic Wars," *Journal of Indian History* 41 (December 1963):426–29. Crowninshield stated that he had made five voyages to India beginning in 1786 and 1787 and that by 1806 more than two hundred American ships were constantly involved in the Indian trade each year, with American capital of eight to ten million dollars. Prior to the Jay Treaty, he wrote, American ships carried thirty to fifty cargoes of Bombay cotton to China each year, each cargo averaging a half million pounds. By 1806 few American vessels went to Bombay because of the enforcement of restrictions in the Jay Treaty. In Calcutta and Bengal the situation was different. An average of thirty to fifty American ships went to Calcutta each year carrying Spanish dollars, iron, lead, brandy, Madeira and other wines, tar, small spars, and a variety of European articles. In some years as much as three million dollars' worth of goods from Calcutta were imported into the United States. Americans were in the habit of buying white cotton manufactured goods directly from the native merchants rather than from the English residents because they were cheaper. This led to jealousy on the part of the English merchants and to complaints against the American trade. Crowninshield claimed that with the British enforcing the carrying of Indian goods directly to the United States, Americans were still able to transship them to Europe and to undersell Indian goods shipped from London. Aware that the British were trying to squeeze the Americans out of the trade in the Indian Ocean area, Crowninshield urged the secretary of state to implement retaliatory measures against British trade with the United States. See Reinoehl, "Some Remarks on American Trade: Jacob Crowninshield to James Madison, 1806," pp. 102, 109–18.

67. Furber, "The Beginning of American Trade with India, 1784–1812," pp. 264–65.

68. Bhagat, *Americans in India, 1784–1860*, p. 90.

69. Dennett, *Americans in Eastern Asia*, chaps. 4–14.

APPENDIX

Statistical evidence on the extent of American trade to the East is difficult to come by. Adequate import and export statistics begin only in 1821. Inquiring Americans themselves had difficulty getting accurate figures. The notes on commerce that Gouverneur Morris shared with Thomas Jefferson in 1784 stated that the United States consumed East India goods valued at £500,000 sterling, but do not say what the total was based on.[1] A little more than two years later, when Secretary of State Thomas Jefferson sent to Lafayette an estimate of the imports and exports of the United States, he added:

Calculations of this kind cannot pretend to accuracy, where inattention and fraud combine to suppress their objects. Approximation is all that they can aim at. Neither care or condour [sic] have been wanting on my part to bring them as near the truth as my skill and materials would enable me to do.[2]

Jefferson in this report lumped "East India goods" with imports from Europe and Africa.[3]

When Assistant Secretary of the Treasury Tench Coxe published his compilation of statistical information in 1794, he gave figures on the import tonnages and duties paid in 1789–92 and on imports in 1790, but did not include places of origin.[4] He notes that exports were six times the amount of national taxes and duties. He also states that "all ships and vessels depart from the United States fully laden, excepting a part of the East India traders."[5] His table summarizing the value and destination of exports from the United States for the period 18 October 1792 to 30 September 1793 again lumps together the material destined for the European countries and their colonial possessions. Nevertheless, the table is of interest for its attempt to assess the relative volume of trade and because it includes a figure on the East Indies. Coxe shows export highlights as follows:[6]

	Dollars
to dominions of Russia	5,769
to dominions of the United Netherlands	3,169,536
to dominions of Great Britain	8,431,239
to dominions of Spain	2,237,950
to dominions of France	7,050,498
the East Indies generally	253,131

No one better appreciated how misleading economic data could be than Samuel Blodget, Jr., a pioneer American statistician. In a manual published in 1806, he noted that:

Hence, if a cargo of flour be entered at 8 dollars cost, to net 12 abroad, if the proceeds be invested in foreign articles, the *apparent* custom-house balance would be 50 per cent against the country, though in fact a *great gain, although* often a larger debit in the deceptive account in question; add to this, if a ship is either hired abroad, or sold, both the hire and sale often swell this *nominal* debit; so when our merchants ship specie to India, or bills, no *outward* entry is made of *either*, but often *a large return cargo*, and of course a debit appears in the *nominal* statements of the *custom-house balance of trade*.[7]

In 1835, when Timothy Pitkin published *A Statistical View of the Commerce of the United States of America*, he gave the following details on the American commerce with the British East Indies.[8]

Year	Imports	Exports
1795	$ 742,523	
1796	2,427,717	$66,316
1797	1,764,290	21,325
1798	2,977,324	39,075
1799	1,521,213	7,296
1800	3,391,027	130,416
1801	5,134,456	71,617
1802	(No data)	83,489

For the years of 1802, 1803, and 1804, Pitkin provided only average figures: $3,530,000 annually for imports, $130,000 for exports.[9] Although he included no figures for the years 1805–20, he did supply the following information:

Prior to the year 1816, much the greatest part of the imports from the British East Indies, consisted of low priced cotton goods. During the years 1802, 1803 and 1804, the value of white cottons, from this country, was estimated, on an average, at about $2,950,000. By the tariff of 1816, all cotton goods, the original cost of which, at the place from whence imported, (Except nankeens, directly from China,) was less than twenty five cents per square yard, and charged with duty accordingly. This minimum price was fixed, for the purpose of excluding entirely from the American market, the low priced India cottons, and thereby afford protection and encouragement, both to the American cotton manufacturer, and the American cotton planter. This duty had the intended effect, and since that period few India cottons, of this description, have been brought into the United States.[10]

Pitkin went on to say that the Treasury Department kept no record of the specie shipped to the British East Indies prior to 1821. As for domestic produce, very little was ever carried to India, mostly flour, whale oil, spermaceti and tallow candles, hewn timber and other lumber, manufactured tobacco, and some other unnamed articles. To Pitkin, this indicated that there must have been a great balance of trade against the United States.[11] There is no reference to the fortunes carried out of India in American ships in the form of goods. Nor did Pitkin refer to ships that stopped in European ports to take on goods before proceeding to Indian Ocean destinations.

As for American involvement in other parts of the East, Pitkin offered the following statistics.[12]

Bourbon and Mauritius

Year	Imports	Exports
1795	$ 805,928	$. . . . .
1796	1,464,174	42,609
1797	996,794	58,792
1798	1,116,284	147,718
1799	262,221	3,900
1800	234,894	. . . .
1801	. . . .	128,487
1802	(no data)	153,261

Manila and the Philippines

1795	61,150	. . . .
1796	. . . .	. . . .
1797	232,674	. . . .
1798	. . . .	. . . .
1799	24,329	. . . .
1800	142,969	14,112
1801	351,011	. . . .
1802	(No data)	. . . .

China and the East Indies (generally)

1795	1,114,103	1,023,242
1796	2,459,410	1,352,860
1797	2,319,964	387,310
1798	2,309,304	261,795
1799	3,219,262	595,249

1800	4,613,463	1,047,385
1801	4,558,356	1,374,506
1802	(No data)	877,267

North West Coast and South Seas

1795	. . . .	44,063
1796	. . . .	23,607
1797	. . . .	15,607
1798	. . . .	79,515
1799	. . . .	72,941
1800	23,441	827,748
1801	18,079	343,338
1802	(No data)	160,707

Whatever their merit otherwise, these statistics refer only to trade directly to and from the United States. They tell us nothing of the profits earned by Americans in carrying goods between Indian ports, or between India and Europe. But they do offer a fascinating glimpse of early American patterns of trade in the Pacific and Indian Oceans.[13]

NOTES TO APPENDIX

1. "Abstracts of Gouverneur Morris' Letters on Commerce," May 1784, in *The Papers of Thomas Jefferson*, ed. Julian P. Boyd (Princeton: Princeton University Press, 1853), 8:353.

2. Thomas Jefferson to the Marquis de Lafayette, Paris, 17 July 1786, in *The Papers of Thomas Jefferson*, 10:145.

3. Ibid., 10:147.

4. Tench Coxe, *A View of the United States of America* (Philadelphia: William Hall, Wrigley & Berriman, 1794), pp. 421, 423.

5. Ibid., p. 432.

6. Ibid., p. 476.

7. Samuel Blodget, Jr., *Economica: A Statistical Manual for the United States of America* (Washington, D.C.: Samuel Blodget, Jr., 1806), p. 127. For those who argued that the specie sent to the East Indies caused a scarcity of money in the United States, Blodget pointed out that $100,000 sent to India purchased two hundred thousand pieces of nankeens or muslins. If 130,000 of these pieces of cloth were taken to the islands of the East Indies and sold for almost two dollars each, the money earned could be invested in coffee that could serve as cash for remittances to Europe.

8. Timothy Pitkin, *A Statistical View of the Commerce of the United States of America* (New Haven: Hezekiah Howe & Co., 1835), pp. 188, 261.

9. Ibid., p. 188.

10. Ibid.

11. Ibid., p. 189.

12. Ibid., pp. 258–62.

13. Similar statistics and with the same shortcomings were published by Dr. Adam Seybert in his *Statistical Annals Embracing Views of the Commerce . . . of the United States of America* (Philadelphia: Thomas Dobson & Son, 1818), which gave figures for the years 1789–1799. Using a British source, he computed that Americans sent about one-half million dollars in Spanish dollars to Bengal every year and about the same amount to China. See Seybert, p. 55n. Subsequently, the U.S. Congress published a great deal of data for the years 1790–1820 in *American State Papers, Class 4: Commerce and Navigation*, 2 vols. (Washington, D.C.: Gales & Seaton, 1832–1834). This compilation, built upon earlier works noted above, fails to give a true picture of the range and volume of American trade with the Indian and Pacific Ocean areas from 1783 to 1812.

4 JAMES A. FIELD, JR.

Winning the Peace: The New Diplomacy in a World of Change

As all know by now, winning a war does not accomplish much unless one wins the peace that follows and unless the hard necessities of conflict bring forth the hoped-for kind of settlement. As to the Peace of Paris of 1783, it may be said that the United States has come pretty close to winning it two or three times; that we are still working on the problem; and, interestingly, that we are still working with much the same aims and assumptions that were common coin two hundred years ago.

These aims and assumptions deserve some comment. Many societies, no doubt, find themselves torn between inclination and necessity, or idealism and realism, in their conduct of foreign relations. Yet, for the Americans, with their remarkably idiosyncratic attitudes toward the outer world, such conflicts are perhaps more painful than for most. Certainly their tendency to return to the inherited inclinations whenever the pressures of necessity diminish has been unparalled over the past two centuries.

These attitudes and inclinations were the legacy of the second half of the eighteenth century. It seems nowadays widely, if not universally, agreed that the Revolution was the product of a constellation of ideas derived in part from antiquity, in part from John Winthrop, in part from the *philosophes*, and in part from the radical English republican counterculture of the time—brought together

and charged with new energy—the whole passing under the name
of "republicanism." Included in this constellation were utopian
hopes for the transformation of America—a "new creation" on the
"western shore"—by political separation from the monarchical and
luxurious corruptions that marked Great Britain and the European
powers; the creation of a new polity distinguished by self-determination, minimum government, and a strong localism (later transmuted into federalism); an energetic people sustained in its virtue
by church, school, and college; and a society based on widespread
ownership of property and a general equality of station in which
status would derive only from merit. For the realization of this
earthly millenium, the nature of the social and political environment
was crucial; as the poet and diplomat Joel Barlow put it, "nations
are educated like individual infants. They are what they are taught
to be." For the perfection of the environment, the central question
then, as it has been ever since, was the limitation of power.[1]

So far so good; but in current formulations the concept of republicanism seems curiously limited and circumscribed within national
bounds, politically, economically, and culturally. Such a delimitation
is hard to square with the nature of the republican vision, or with
the way domestic and foreign issues blended in political discourse,
or with the fact that it was (and is) easier to be persistently idealistic
about distant and imperfectly understood situations than about ward
politics at home.

Eighteenth-century assumptions, whether religious or philosophical in origin, of an identifiable something called the human race
suggested that the republican revolution need not remain a revolution for one country only. If reason could triumph "o'er the pride
of power" in America to produce a consenting government, it might
also do so elsewhere. The central concern for economics in advanced
contemporary thought had no national limits: when joined to the
need for trade in an undeveloped staple-exporting country, it
pointed outward to lands beyond the oceans and toward that dissolution, early foreseen by Turgot, of all mercantilist empires. From
this concern and this need came the formulation of the Model Treaty
of 1776 and enduring efforts on behalf of policies of reciprocity, all
of which, fortunately, could be justified on a higher level as tending
to "human happiness," the assimilation of the nations, and the coming of the reign of peace.[2]

Equally, the strong American faith in the power of applied science to improve the lot of man, embedded by the Reverend Samuel Hopkins in his portrayal of the imminent millennium and reinforced by current necessity, had no political bounds. Certainly the Americans needed such things as roads and canals, steamboats, and cotton gins. But so, surely, did others: carrying the "torch of science," an American "philanthropic band" would voyage outward "to find and bless a thousand peopled isles . . . with every useful art." And finally, to those touched by the Great Awakening, Christ's Great Commission—"Go ye into all the world, and preach the gospel to every creature"—carried a similarly universal message.[3]

Such attitudes, when combined with the Americans' taste for power and their commitment to limited government, had important implications for the nation's relations with the outer world. These would be characterized in purpose by continuing millenial hopes for the improvement of America and of humanity in general; in content by persistent efforts to diminish the role of power in the world by the removal of Europe from America, the liberalization of international trade, and the development of international law; and in style by the largest possible component of individual activity. Like much at home, much in international intercourse would be "reserved to the people."

But the implementation of republicanism, the regeneration of society at home (and, for the visionaries, of societies elsewhere) depended first of all upon separation from Britain, and here, with the Continental Congress's opening of the ports to the trade of all nations in April 1776, necessity crept in. Reluctant though they were to involve themselves in the political relations of states or to make other than commercial treaties, the revolutionaries found themselves forced to seek alliance with France. This move to league themselves with the monarchical, hierarchical, luxurious, papist, French-speaking power—"off-spring of the Scarlet Whore"—which within the memories of all had been inciting the Indians against the frontier, betokened a certain desperation. It may also, of course, have suggested a certain residual self-confidence.

Since the Americans from the beginning have been consistently picky about those with whom they associate themselves, this was certainly our first "strange alliance." With ingenuity, nevertheless, the French could be made ideologically palatable. Joel Barlow could praise the "Gallic sages" for urging "their king to lift an aiding hand" and "Great Louis" himself for supporting self-determination and "the liberal, universal cause." On the more practical level, although the suitoring around the courts of Europe by the representatives of the "virgin state" gained little, the advanced commercial principles of the Model Treaty were written into the Treaty of Amity and Commerce with France, which John Quincy Adams later described as the foundation of all American foreign policy. During the war, the formation of the Armed Neutrality at least nourished hopes for the spread of liberal commercial principles. And in the negotiations for the peace of Paris, Dr. Franklin and his colleagues did what they could for the liberation of commerce, as well as for the distancing of European power by the greatest possible extension of the boundaries of the new nation and by proposals for Canadian border disarmament.[4]

In time, the war was won and "The World Turned Upside Down." A shaky independence had been gained. Yet, despite success in the aim of political separation, necessities, both economic and political in nature, pressed heavily upon the new country. Internal confusion, especially with regard to commerce and its regulation, led to a Newtonian triumph of systems engineering in the form of a constitution which divides the power among the three branches and power itself among the general government, the states, and the people. This accomplishment, which permitted Dr. Franklin at the conclusion of the Constitutional Convention to pronounce the painting on the presiding officer's chair a rising, rather than a setting, sun, was followed by the adoption of a Bill of Rights, further restricting the power of the new government. Under the new dispensation, the hope that diplomacy would shortly wither away and the distaste for traditional modes of international discourse gave rise to a Department of "State" with numerous domestic duties, an expressed preference for consular—as opposed to ministerial—representation abroad, and a minimal military establishment.

For the moment, the new powers over taxation, commerce, and diplomacy augured well. Supported by the skills in naval architecture and navigation which produced the world's most efficient merchant marine, the Hamiltonian reforms proved coducive to prosperity. The upshot, rare in history, was a new country which shortly found itself established on a sound financial basis.

Still, necessities pressed. Since the mercantilist views of the anti-American Lord Sheffield worked to close the former colonials out of their accustomed trades, thought was given to possibilities of commercial retaliation and emphasis placed on seeking out new opportunities in the Mediterranean and Far East. But in the political field, there came at least brief encouragement. As General Washington was being inaugurated, troubles were developing in France. Shortly, the meeting of the Estates General and the fall of the Bastille suggested that the French were indulging in the sincerest form of flattery, that the "first chapter of the history of European liberty" was being written, and that the principles of republicanism indeed had general validity.[5] But excesses followed, and soon Europe descended into war from which, with but brief interludes, it would not emerge for more than twenty years.

War begets the king, and these wars not only brought unprecedented exercises of power by the belligerent governments, but also placed unwanted demands on that of the United States. Yet, if the old means still had to be employed, it seemed possible that they could be used in new ways and for the new purposes. Of this possibility, time would be the judge. For the moment, the needs of the warring powers led to an explosive and lucrative expansion of exports and reexports and of the merchant marine. But with the passing years this expanded commerce found itself between the millstones of the belligerents.

There followed a persistent diplomacy aimed at the vindication of neutral rights and the limitation of belligerent aggressions and at the further distancing of European power in America. These measures were in some degree served by the Jay and Pinckney treaties: the first secured the northern border and certain commercial benefits, in India if not in the West Indies; the second advanced the Florida boundary and opened the Mississippi outlet for the growing export trade of the Ohio Valley. These developments gave President Washington the opportunity to retire, leaving to his countrymen in his Farewell Address and his "Great Rule" a political testament which reemphasized the virtues of commerce and the hazards of political connections and which, despite the large role of Hamilton in its drafting, still contained a large measure of the republican idealism of the New Diplomacy.[6]

This idealism, or segments of it, together with the necessities of the time, continued to influence policy. The last decade of the old century and the first of the next brought limited wars for the protection of commerce: the first against the French in the West Indies and the second, undertaken by the peaceful "anti-commercial" Jefferson, a transoceanic effort against Tripoli. While this second war was in progress, the struggle against France continued; with assists from the Santo Domingan mosquito and the European situation, Jefferson gained a final opening of the Mississippi. Fortuitously, but quite acceptably, the desired acquisition of the left bank of the river and New Orleans was accompanied by a further removal of European power through the acquisition of the great emptiness to the westward by the novel and rational method of cash purchase.

But as war in Europe was resumed, pressures became too great. The growth of American shipping had attracted British seamen and so stimulated impressment. Belligerent actions expressed in captures, Orders, and Decrees restricted the freedoms "comformable to law and reason" claimed by the Americans; and further complications came from the threat of Indian hostilities on the western frontier. The resort to "peaceful coercion" in the form of economic warfare, an effort to move governments by putting pressure on their subjects and a remedy overestimated since the Stamp Act crisis, never quite succeeded.[7] In the second war for independence from overbearing European power, narrowly not a triangular or "prismatic" conflict with both England and France, the country managed to survive. And if one added to the Treaty of Ghent the later arrangements with Britain which expanded commerce, extended the northern border, and limited armaments on the Lakes; and the Florida Treaty with Spain, which produced a further distancing of Europe, it was possible to claim that the enterprise had been a considerable success.

In the years after Waterloo, the country emerged, a little hesitantly, into the sunny climate of the nineteenth century. Europe, the greatest repository of power, and so still the "Great Satan," now shrunken by the American wars for independence and exhausted by her own conflicts, was resting. In these happy circumstances, necessity could give way to inclination, the government could concentrate upon the facilitation of commerce, and individuals could direct their foreign relations—commercial, evangelical, philanthropic, or educational—as they saw fit.

In this new age the liberation of international trade proceeded steadily, if gradually, as the American reciprocity policy made headway among the European states. A new southward look—occasioned both by the Spanish-American wars for independence (which temporarily provided more evidence of flattering imitation and promise of the brighter republican future) and by the pursuit of seal, sea otter, and beaver for the China trade—brought commercial treaties with the new South American states and contacts with the American West Coast. There followed a wider outward look. The East Indies trade, earlier stimulated by favorable tariff provisions and by the Jay Treaty, so grew in the years after 1815 as to elicit British concern about possible American colonization of southern Africa.[8] Efforts to expand economic ties beyond the Atlantic led to commercial treaties with Turkey in 1830, Russia in 1832, Muscat and Zanzibar and Siam in 1833, and to a first abortive effort toward Japan.

With this progressive opening of the world economy came a renewed expansion of American shipping, whose earnings went far to offset the country's unfavorable balance of trade. Tonnage in foreign commerce, exponentially expanded in the period of neutrality during the great wars, had fallen radically after 1812 and revived only briefly with the peace. But the 1830s saw the start of a second period of growth which led steadily to the merchant marine's greatest moment in the decade of the fifties.[9]

This expansion was accompanied by that of the Navy, designed as a commerce-protecting instrument and so employed against France, Tripoli, Great Britain, Algiers, and most recently the West Indies pirates. As the new trade routes developed, there followed the establishment of permanent overseas squadrons: the Mediterranean Squadron in 1815 to watch over Barbary, the Pacific Squadron in 1818 to cover the west coast of South America, the West Indies Squadron in 1822 to deal with endemic Caribbean piracy, the Brazil Squadron in 1826, and the East Indies Squadron in 1835. Their task was to show the flag and protect shipping, and protect it they did; from Monroe to Buchanan, the government employed these forces with a certain vigor to teach the importance of rational commerce to the benighted inhabitants of the West Indies, the isles of Greece, the Falklands, Sumatra, and Paraguay.[10]

Commerce, no doubt, was central to the New Diplomacy; but for Americans it was hardly limited to the exchange of material goods. Jonathan Edwards had hoped that America would become the Old World's source of both material and spiritual treasure; John Adams had seen the settlement of America as the start of a providential scheme for "the illumination of the ignorant . . . all over the earth." And by now those dwelling in darkness were receiving the attention of other teachers. From the start, the republican ideology had contained a large religious component, a distillation of the Great Awakening, of Edwards's vision of a golden age within history, of Samuel Hopkins's idea of "disinterested benevolence," and of the millennial expectations of the time: in 1778 Joel Barlow had equated the Revolution with the Second Coming. Nor had success in war and the achievement of independence diminished the importance of religion. At home the concern for salvation and the devotion to disinterested benevolence would contribute to the necessary virtue of the citizenry; abroad, like commerce, it would work to unite the human race and prepare the way for the millennium. Thus, even so worldly an individual as David Humphreys, "friend of Washington," diplomat, poet, and entrepreneur, could write

To cure the pangs that nerve-torn nations feel, . . .
Come, emanation from the King of Kings,
Religion! come, with healing on thy wings![11]

Surprisingly, perhaps, the commencement of the American export trade in Protestant Christianity derived largely from the zeal of college students. The resolve of a few Williams undergraduates in 1807 to carry the gospel to the heathen led to the founding in 1810 of the American Board of Commissioners for Foreign Missions, shortly to become the country's first multinational corporation. Two years later the first missionaries to the heathen sailed to India; in 1819 workers were sent to Palestine and to the Sandwich Islands; in time other fields were occupied, including ultimately those in the Far East. It may be noted that in these various deployments the missionaries, like the traders and the frontiersmen, were generally out ahead of the government and the diplomats.

Except in Hawaii, where the whole society was shortly revolutionized, these devoted workers had small success in their aim of conversion. But in the export of Americanism, the unintended secondary consequences were remarkable. The presence of missionary

wives and female workers brought to traditional societies the shock-
ing realization that in some parts of the world women stood "upon
a par with men."[12] The concern for a Gospel religion called for the
translation of Bible and tract into local vernaculars and for the foundation of overseas missionary presses. To profit from Bible and tract
required literacy, and there followed the establishment of missionary schools including, startlingly, schools for females. In time the
perceived benefits of education, emphasized by increasing contact
with the West, led to demands from constituents for higher schools,
while the practical bent of the Americans encouraged a widened
curriculum. The emphasis on education and on the conversion experience suggested, to members of traditional cultures, the radical
idea of the possibility of change. As testimony from their hosts amply
confirms, the Americans taught not only Protestant Christianity, but
also—and more importantly—modernity (or republicanism). And,
in some cases, they taught revolution.[13]

In a text much favored by contemporary divines, the prophet
Daniel had foreseen that in the last times "many shall run to and
fro and knowledge shall be increased." In the first decades of independence, the prophecy appeared to be coming true, as from an
early date merchants and missionaries were joined in far places by
other Americans motivated by curiosity, adventure, the desire to
earn a reasonably honest dollar, and the rational assumption that
the needs of all branches of humanity were much the same. Taking
service in foreign parts, these synarchists (like the merchants and
missionaries) saw the world as their province and as a market for
their skills; over the years, their labors in joint rule of administration
produced a remarkable record in the extension of modern skills to
outer areas.

In the late eighteenth century, an American served as commander
of the Russian Black Sea Fleet; two stood for election to the French
National Convention (and one was elected); one served as secretary
to the Bey of Algiers; Robert Fulton busied himself in weapons
development in both France and England. In the first half of the
nineteenth century, the list includes a physician to the Bashaw of
Tripoli, a commander of the Egyptian artillery, a commodore in the
Argentine and the commander-in-chief of the Mexican navy, two
Ottoman chief naval constructors, an Afghan general, a consulting
engineer for the first Russian railroad, the builder of the port of

Valparaiso and of the first South American railway, and the director of the Hawaiian government press. When to the influence of these volunteers is added that of the missionaries, of American sea captains, and of American merchants established in European, South American, and Asiatic ports; of foreign reporters such as Tocqueville and Grund; and of the "America letters" sent home by immigrants, it may be presumed that the American gospel was getting a hearing from those who had ears to hear.[14]

In the late 1840s, territorial expansion—now some twenty-five years in abeyance, leapt forward once again. But this was expansion with a difference. In the early years the efforts to extend the national boundaries and distance the threat of Europe had involved a large component of purposeful governmental activity. But from the time of the Florida Treaty, the advance of individual Americans into "foreign" territory made the role of the federal government less that of initiator than of registrar of deeds. The Texans accomplished their own revolution. The movement of pioneers into Oregon led the Hudson's Bay Company to move its headquarters to Vancouver Island and so opened the way to a settlement. In 1847 the Mormons trekked to empty Utah. Although domestic political pressures, the confusion of Mexican politics, and some residual paranoia about British and French intrigues led to war with Mexico, the end result would hardly have been different had Polk been more patient. In 1846 the conquest of the vast province of California was accomplished by a few hundred men; two years later the discovery of gold at Sutter's Mill brought forth an invading horde of individuals totaling in number about twice that of the entire army in the War with Mexico.[15]

The year of the Treaty of Guadalupe Hidalgo, which brought the greatest extension of the area of freedom over the "empty land waiting for inhabitants" described by Tocqueville, was significant on the ideological, as well as the western, frontier. A spate of revolutions in Europe and the appearance of new constitutional regimes again raised hopes that the dangerous power of the Old World might be checked at its source by political reformation. The outburst of popular enthusiasm that followed brought contributions of assistance, some movement of volunteers to fight in the good cause, and speedy (and, in some cases, premature) recognition of new regimes by functionaries on the spot. But once again, as in the earlier French revolutions, reaction triumphed; and as hopes faded, the American response was limited to rhetorical animadversions upon the European tyrants and assistance to fleeing revolutionaries by American consuls and by ships of the Mediterranean Squadron. Over the long run, it would seem, the most important consequences for the United States of these revolutions were domestic: the arrival of the Germans of 1848; and the first introduction of the beard, quickly affected by liberty-loving young men, as a consequence of the visit of the "Hungarian Washington," Louis Kossuth.[16]

This check to the overseas extension of the republican institutions was certainly regrettable. But at home by mid-century (if one could overlook the growing sectional tensions) the most optimistic visions of the founders had been realized. Territorial expansion had brought the transcontinental two-ocean republic. The Author of Events had signified His approval of this development by arranging for the discovery of California gold. The government remained mild, unoppressive, and economical, with annual expenditures not totalling some two dollars per capita. Along with territorial expansion had come that of foreign trade, which in dollars per capita now exceeded any period since the wartime boom of the first years of the century. American ideas of commercial reciprocity were largely accepted throughout the world. The 1846 repeal of the Corn Laws and passage of the Walker Tariff had given new vitality to that "imperialism of free trade" by which the British and Americans had for some time been cheerfully and profitably imperializing each other through the exchange of capital and manufactured goods for cotton.

In this uniting of the world by commerce as in maintaining the balance of trade, the American merchant marine remained preeminent. Tonnage in foreign trade now almost tripled that of the previous high of 1810; the sails of American ships whitened the oceans; American clippers, the model for the world, had reduced shipping costs and shipping time. Around the world, American, and indeed all, commercial activity benefited from the activities of the Navy: in its protective role; in its exploring efforts, which had followed up Wilkes's great tour of the Pacific with exploration of the Dead Sea, the Amazon, the River Plate, and the West African coast, and the charting of the western North Pacific; and in the oceanographic research of Matthew Maury, which had reduced the times of ocean passages by up to 30 percent. And, of course, there was the ne-

gotiation of new commercial treaties, of which Perry's with Japan
remains preeminent, both in its consequences and in the symbolism
of the American package of artifacts by which the Commodore sought
to beguile the islanders into joining the march of progress: a miniature steam railway, a telegraph line, and small arms; such books
as Audobon's *Birds*, Bancroft's *History*, and works on farming, domestic architecture, and geology; and liberal quantities of whiskey
and champagne.[17]

The expansion of peaceful commerce and the improvements in
navigation went hand in hand with continued preaching to the outer
world. The overseas missionary effort continued to grow: by 1855
voluntary expenditure for this work totalled perhaps a third of a
million dollars a year and by 1865 over half a million. Hawaii had
long since been Christianized, and the work was now concentrated
first in India, Burma, and Ceylon; secondly in the Near East; and
with the rapidly growing Chinese effort in third place. The missionary emphasis on education had brought Yung Wing to this country, to graduate from Yale in 1854 and later return as leader of the
China Educational Mission. In the midst of the Civil War, American
philanthropy would create the capstones of the Near Eastern educational effort with the founding of Robert College at Constantinople
and the Syrian Protestant College (later American University) at
Beirut.[18]

The educational work was not limited to the missions and their
offshoots. In 1851 the Japanese castaway Manjiro, rescued ten years
before from an uninhabited island by an American whaler, returned
to his native land after schooling in New Bedford, service on another
American whaler, and gold mining in California to be treated both
with extreme suspicion and as a source of useful knowledge; although
closely watched, he rose in time to a position in the bureaucracy,
taught Western skills, and accompanied early Japanese missions to
the outer world. Having sat at the feet of Horace Mann, Domingo
Sarmiento went home to Argentina to create, with the aid of Yankee
schoolmarms, the finest educational system in Latin America. The
American movement for women's rights, first exported on the back
of the antislavery movement, occasioned Harriet Taylor Mill's famous essay on the "Enfranchisement of Women" and through her,
in time, converted her husband. The American peace movement,

with freedom of trade as one important component, gave rise to a series of mid-century European conferences.[19]

In the mechanic arts, American small arms, locks, clocks, reapers, and plows were by mid-century the standard of the world. In 1851 the Yankees carried off special prizes for reapers, India rubber, and meat biscuit at the great London Exhibition, while the yacht *America*, in her encounter with the Royal Yacht Squadron, proved herself so fast that the Queen's inquiry could receive only the mournful answer, "Your Majesty, there is no second." To these accomplishments one may add the increasing cultural impact of east coast literati, of P. T. Barnum, of such variegated southerners as the exotic and scandalous Ada Menken and Paul Morphy, chess champion of the world, and most importantly for the New Diplomacy, of Henry Wheaton's notable works on international law.[20]

Such a conglomeration of successes—territorial, ideological, philanthropic, mechanical, and cultural—was surely all the founders or contemporary patriots could have asked. Two events of the time may be taken to symbolize both the triumphs and the continuing aspirations. The first of these was the launching, in the fall of 1853, of Donald McKay's *Great Republic*, at 4,555 tons register both the largest extreme clipper ever built and the largest merchant ship up to that time. The second was the completion in 1858 of the first Atlantic cable. If the ship was a purely American artifact, the cable reflected the increasing Anglo-American symbiosis: the technology involved was largely British, but the moving spirit was that of Cyrus Field.[21]

Equally, the American celebration of the "Glorious Work" of the cable's completion was no narrowly nationalistic one. In New York the account of "THE CABLE CARNIVAL" filled the entire front page of the *Herald* and ran over far into the interior. Fourteen inches of headlines described the cosmic significance of "The Reunion of All the Nationalities," the participation of civic dignitaries and reverend clergy, of the jack-tars of both nations, and of the ladies who made "Broadway a Garden of Female Beauty." But beyond the sermons, dinners, toasts, and fireworks, and most significant of the spirit of the age, was President Buchanan's cabled message to Queen Victoria expressing the hope that "the Atlantic telegraph, under the blessing of heaven, prove to be a bond of perpetual peace and friendship between the kindred nations, and an instrument destined by Divine Providence to diffuse religion, liberty, and law throughout the world," and proposing, in accordance with American tradition, that the "nations of Christendom" declare it "forever neutral," and its traffic not subject to interruption even in wartime.[22]

Over time, no doubt, these hopes would be in some degree borne out. As the cable network grew, it certainly diffused a great many things. But for the immediate future it was not to be so. Twelve weeks after her launching, a fire spreading from shore burned the *Great Republic* at her dock. Ten days later the Nebraska Bill was introduced into Congress. Soon the Atlantic cable failed and so shortly did the Union. Before liberty and law could be diffused throughout the world, much blood and treasure had to be spent in diffusing them at home. But in the end the ordeal was survived and the Union restored, and to many (as after all our wars) it seemed that progress would continue much as before.[23]

As always, they were both wrong and right. The great unexploited possibilities of the West, now linked to the eastern metropolis by the new railroads, brought on a new age of furious internal development and of lessened concern with the oceans and the far shores. The merchant marine—victim of the depression of 1857, Confederate raiders, British technological superiority, and archaic navigation laws—entered a period of steady decline: by the century's end, tonnage in foreign trade would be less than during the Jefferson administration. Although the cruising squadrons were reestablished, "somewhat irreflectively," as Captain Mahan later observed, a similar decline in tonnage and personnel overtook the Navy. What remained was adequate enough for the perceived duties of showing the flag, protecting missionaries, and checking on Central American émeutes; but the lack of shipping to protect, the woes of Grantism, and congressional conservatism made for technological lag.[24]

The extraordinary internal development and the decline of the maritime interest were but two manifestations of great and irreversible changes that were taking place. These changes, long, but dimly comprehended, were the consequence of the trick of steam, played by the all-wise Creator on those whom he had endowed with coal underfoot and with the skills to use it. In America, steam brought an enormous leap in productivity, visible to all in the growth of

railroads, in the new industrial cities, and in the movement of the
vast new agricultural surpluses from the heartland to the seaboard.
But it also brought a threat to early ideals of a society (and, indeed,
a world) with no very rich or poor, in the appearance of growing
gaps between industrialist and worker, between city and farm, and
between those parts of the world that were industrializing and those
that were not. Among the early political results of these gaps were
the Granger and Populist revolts against the metropolis in America
and the sudden descent of the European powers upon Africa.

The decline of the Navy and merchant marine was no doubt
conducive to sentimental regret. But on another level it could be
argued that, once the French had gone home from Mexico and the
Alabama claims had been settled, the dreams of the founding generation were once again coming true in the diminution of the governmental role in foreign relations. Along with naval decline came
the almost total evaporation of the great Civil War army, as indeed
of diplomatic activity. Presented with a series of somewhat incon-
sequential executive initiatives, the Senate proceeded to reject treaties at twice the rate of antebellum days, while a variety of
embarrassing incidents with new personnel brought suggestions for
the abolition of the diplomatic corps. Once again, international relations became the province of the individual, and we may imagine
John Adams looking down approvingly upon this realization of his
hope that his study of "Politicks and War" would enable his sons to
study naval architecture, commerce, and agriculture and their sons
the fine arts.[25]

So if, to later historians, the period came to represent "the nadir
of diplomacy," that diminution of the role of government was just
what the revolutionaries would have wished. Foreign trade, even
if carried by others, continued to grow. A new prosperity came upon
the foreign missionary movement, where new expansion, most no-
tably in the Far East (despite the declining importance of Asiatic
commerce), brought new foundations of Christian colleges. At home
a renewed idealism among college undergraduates manifested itself
in the foundation in 1886 of the Student Volunteer Movement. But
while the watchword of the day, as early in the century, was "the
evangelization of the world in this generation," the old distinction
between the Gospel and the American gospel, originally insisted
on, but never easy to maintain, was wearing thin. The early concern

had been the extension of God's Kingdom, but by the end of the century a former missionary at Beirut could find it in himself to publish three fat volumes totalling 1,600 pages on *Christian Missions and Social Progress.*[26]

For those concerned less with gospel religion and more with modernization, the postwar years offered continued opportunity. Again the synarchists set forth: to China to provide her first ambassador to the West, to help staff the Imperial Customs Service, to direct naval training, and to advise governors and viceroys; to Japan to teach Western learning, advise the navy and the foreign office, organize agricultural development, and introduce baseball; to Korea to serve as military and foreign policy advisers; to Egypt to staff the army, map unsurveyed provinces, and assist in southward expansion; and throughout the world to seek out and open up mineral resources. The governing assumption in these activities of a common humanity with common goals, an inheritance from the eighteenth century, reached its apogee in early twentieth-century China, where a number of Americans moved back and forth, without exciting remark but with undoubted consequences, between missionary endeavor, the American diplomatic and consular corps, the service of the Chinese government, and duty on the new Far Eastern desk of the State Department in Washington.[27]

Further encouragement for believers in the traditional ideological package came from the new applications of science in communication and transportation. Whether the new cables worked to diffuse "religion, liberty, and law" may be debated; but they certainly worked to extend the healing ministrations of trade. As these cables tied together with preexisting telegraph networks, the length of the managerial arm was increased and the administration of such early multinationals as Singer Sewing Machine, Eastman Kodak, and Standard Oil, not to mention distant extractive industries, became feasible. But to say this is merely to point out a second trick of steam and a second consequence of the coming of the higher-energy society. Increasingly, over the future, the old individualistic synarchists would be replaced by servants of such collectivities as the new multinational corporations, the new philanthropic foundations, and the government.[28]

Still, for the moment, individuals mattered. Through their facilitation of transatlantic travel, the new ocean liners encouraged the mingling of international elites, the development of the transatlantic novel, and the phenomenon of international marriage—which produced, in the unions of American heiresses to British milords, a curious private dollar diplomacy prefiguring such later efforts as Lend-Lease and the Marshall Plan. Taken together, the old missionaries, the new managers, and the newly married could be seen as forming the nucleus of a New Tribe, functionally—rather than geographically—defined, whose influence increasingly transcended national boundaries.[29]

At the same time that these developments were knitting up the world, the new cables and the new steam navies had their consequences for the conduct of divisive national diplomacies. For the first time, dispatches could arrive without regard to shipping schedules; for the first time, foreign correspondents could excite their publics with daily reports of distant horrors; and with these developments, the lives of the foreign offices were changed. For the United States, the quick-response problem was first evident in the Cuban question and the *Virginius* affair of 1873; but once South America had been tied in by a British cable to Brazil and an American line down the Pacific coast to Chile, Monroeist diplomacy was put upon a day-to-day basis. Yet, while the tools were new, the purpose of this diplomacy remained the old imperative of distancing European power, as seen in statements of concern for the isthmus, in the anti-British actions of Patrick Egan in Chile and of the Navy in the Brazilian revolution, in Cleveland's response to the Venezuela crisis, and in the Hay-Pauncefote negotiations.[30]

The final, and perhaps the most serious, trick that steam played on the Americans was to provide a society that had always seen power as the enemy with great potential national power. As this realization began to dawn and to be transmuted—with some help from the activities of the European imperialists—into a new Navy for hemispheric defense, a reconciling memory could be drawn upon. The triumphs of the Grand Army of the Republic, memorialized in song and story (and on patriotic and pension-seeking occasions), made it clear that at least under certain circumstances republicans could use power to do good. This dawning view would fit well with the new strenuous morality of the Progressive Era.

The consequences of all these changes were wholly unanticipated. In 1821 John Quincy Adams had pointed out emphatically that

America, "well-wisher to the freedom and independence of all," was "vindicator only of her own." But freedom was still being "hunted round the globe," and in 1898 a long-continued island revolution led to the exercise of power for good by freeing the Cubans and then onward to an unplanned, open-ended involvement in Eastern Asia. In 1917 a long-continued war in Europe led Woodrow Wilson to reinvent the New Diplomacy of the eighteenth century; but by this time the conduct of a war to end war and "make the world itself at last free" required a two-million-man American Expeditionary Force, as well as a continuing involvement in transatlantic affairs. Although the inheritors of the old ideals continued to expand trade, advance technology, and practice philanthropy on an astounding scale, the environment was new. And this was all-important: as Barlow had known, nations "are what they are taught to be."[31]

So much had changed. For the Americans, still trying to win their peace, the central problem of the second century of independence turned out to be the uncomfortable one of employing great power in the service of an antipower ideology. Again, as before 1815, foreign policy became important; more than at any time since then, external necessities came to press upon the new nation. Yet, despite torrential change, the inclinations, one may say, have remained surprisingly the same: both proponents and resisters of policy still draw most of their arguments from the same old republican grab bag. Nowadays one can discern certain signs of fatigue. Now, as on earlier occasions, the question may be how long the advocates of the New Diplomay can maintain their motivation, which is rooted in necessity. But remarkably enough, two centuries after the Peace of Paris, America remains in large degree a reformist, missionary, and "republican" society.

NOTES

1. Bernard Bailyn, *The Ideological Origins of the American Revolution* (Cambridge, Mass.: Belknap Press of Harvard University Press, 1967), esp. pp. 55–77; Gordon S. Wood, *The Creation of the American Republic* (Chapel Hill: University of North Carolina Press, 1969); R. E. Shalhope, "Republicanism and Early American Historiography," *William and Mary Quarterly* 39 (April 1982): 334–56; Felix Gilbert, *To the Farewell Address: Ideas of Early American Foreign Policy* (Princeton: Princeton University

Press, 1961), pp. 33–43; Joel Barlow, *The Prospect of Peace: A Poetical Composition... July 23, 1778* (New Haven: Thomas & Samuel Green, 1778); Joel Barlow, *A Letter to the National Convention of France* (New York: J. Fellows, [1793]).

2. James A. Field, Jr., *America and the Mediterranean World, 1776–1882* (Princeton: Princeton University Press, 1969), pp. 6–17; Bernard Fay, *The Revolutionary Spirit in France and America* (New York: Harcourt, Brace, 1927), pp. 69–70; Gilbert, *Farewell Address*, pp. 48–87; Drew R. McCoy, *The Elusive Republic: Political Economy in Jeffersonian America* (New York: W. W. Norton, 1982), pp. 76–86.

3. Samuel Hopkins, "Treatise on the Millennium," *Works of Samuel Hopkins* (Philadelphia: Doctoral Tract and Book Society, 1852), 2:274–75, 285–87; Field, *Mediterranean World*, pp. 19, 22–24; Mark 16:15.

4. Joel Barlow, *The Columbiad, A Poem* (Philadelphia: C. & A. Conrad Co., 1807), VII, lines 13–14; Adams to R. C. Anderson, 27 May 1823, *Writings of John Quincy Adams*, ed. W. C. Ford (New York: Macmillan, 1913–1917), 7:460; Richard B. Morris, *The Peacemakers: The Great Powers and American Independence* (New York: Harper and Row, 1965).

5. Jefferson to Diodati, Paris, 3 August 1789, *The Papers of Thomas Jefferson*, ed. Julian Boyd et al. (Princeton: Princeton University Press, 1950–   ), 15:326.

6. Gilbert, *Farewell Address*, pp. 115–36.

7. John M. Murrin, "The Great Inversion, or Court versus Country," in *Three British Revolutions, 1641, 1688, 1776*, ed. J. G. A. Pocock (Princeton: Princeton University Press, 1980), pp. 389–92.

8. Vernon G. Setser, *The Commercial Reciprocity Policy of the United States, 1774–1829* (Philadelphia: University of Pennsylvania Press, 1937); Charles C. Griffin, *The United States and the Disruption of the Spanish Empire, 1810–22* (New York: Columbia University Press, 1937); Eric Rosenthal, *The Stars and Stripes in Africa* (London: Routledge, 1938), pp. 92–99.

9. J. G. B. Hutchins, *The American Maritime Industries and Public Policy* (Cambridge, Mass.: Harvard University Press, 1941), pp. 221–86; U.S. Bureau of the Census, *Historical Statistics of the United States: Colonial Times to 1957* (Washington, D.C.: U.S. Government Printing Office, 1960), p. 445.

10. C. O. Paullin, *Diplomatic Negotiations of American Naval Officers, 1778–1883* (Baltimore: Johns Hopkins Press, 1912); Dudley W. Knox, *A History of the United States Navy* (New York: Putnam's, 1948), pp. 140–55, 188–89; Andrew Jackson, "Third Annual Message," 6 December 1831, "Fifth Annual Message," 3 December 1833, in *A Compilation of the Messages and Papers of the Presidents*, ed. James D. Richardson (New York:

Bureau of National Literature and Art, 1908), 2:553, 3:27; Francis Rawle, "Edward Livingston," in *The American Secretaries of State and Their Diplomacy*, ed. S. F. Bemis (New York: Knopf, 1928), 4:249–54.

11. Field, *Mediterranean World*, pp. 13, 68, 78–79, 91; *Works of John Adams*, ed. C. F. Adams (Boston: Little, Brown, 1850–1856), 1:6; Sacvan Bercovitch, *The American Jeremiad* (Madison: University of Wisconsin Press, 1978), pp. 68–103, 128.

12. Jonathan Allen, "Farewell Sermon," 5 February 1812, quoted in R. Pierce Beaver, *Pioneers in Mission* (Grand Rapids, Mich.: W. B. Eerdmans, 1966), pp. 276–77.

13. Clifton J. Phillips, *Protestant America and the Pagan World: The First Half Century of the American Board of Commissioners for Foreign Missions, 1810–1860* (Cambridge, Mass.: Harvard University Press, 1969); Field, *Mediterranean World*; James A. Field, Jr., "Near East Notes and Far East Queries," in *The Missionary Enterprise in China and America*, ed. John K. Fairbank (Cambridge, Mass.: Harvard University Press, 1974), pp. 23–55; Bercovitch, *American Jeremiad*, pp. xii–xiii.

14. American synarchists can be discovered in quantity in such works as Tyler Dennett, *Americans in Eastern Asia* (New York: Macmillan, 1922); Merle Curti and Kendall Birr, *Prelude to Point Four: American Technical Missions Overseas, 1838–1938* (Madison: University of Wisconsin Press, 1954); Robert S. Schwantes, *Japanese and Americans: A Century of Cultural Relations* (New York: Harper & Bros., 1955), Fred H. Harrington, *God, Mammon, and the Japanese: Dr. Horace N. Allen and Korean-American Relations, 1884–1905* (Madison: University of Wisconsin Press, 1961); and Field, *Mediterranean World*.

15. David M. Pletcher, *The Diplomacy of Annexation: Texas, Oregon, and the Mexican War* (Columbia: University of Missouri Press, 1973); U.S. Bureau of the Census, *Historical Statistics*, pp. 13, 737.

16. Eugene N. Curtis, "American Opinion of the French Nineteenth Century Revolutions," *American Historical Review* 29 (March 1924): 249–70; A. J. May, *Contemporary American Opinion of the Mid-Century Revolutions in Central Europe* (Philadelphia: University of Pennsylvania Press, 1927); Field, *Mediterranean World*, pp. 216–37.

17. Douglass C. North, *Growth and Welfare in the American Past* (Englewood Cliffs, N.J.: Prentice Hall, 1966), pp. 109–10; Vincent Ponko, *Ships, Seas, and Scientists* (Annnapolis, Md.: Naval Institute Press, 1974); Frances L. Williams, *Matthew Fontaine Maury, Scientist of the Sea* (New Brunswick, N.J.: Rutgers University Press, 1963); Arthur C. Walworth, *Black Ships off Japan: The Story of Commodore Perry's Expedition* (New York: Knopf, 1946).

18. Field, "Near East Notes," pp. 32–38; Edmund H. Worthy, "Yung

Wing in America," *Pacific Historical Review* 34 (August 1965): 265–87; Field, *Mediterranean World*, pp. 297, 355–59.

19. Marc Pachter, ed., *Abroad in America: Visitors to the New Nation, 1776–1914* (Reading, Mass.: Addison-Wesley, 1976), pp. 92–113. Sarmiento wrote admiringly that "the North Americans live without a government . . . " and with hardly any army; Watta Stewart and William Marshall French, "The Influence of Horace Mann on the Educational Ideas of Domingo Faustino Sarmiento," *Hispanic American Historical Review* 20 (February 1940): 12–31; J. Fred Rippy, "Yankee Teachers and the Founding of Argentina's Elementary School System," *Hispanic American Historical Review* 24 (February 1944): 66–69; [Harriet Taylor Mill], "Enfranchisement of Women," *Westminster and Foreign Quarterly Review* 55 (July 1851): 289–311; John Stuart Mill, *The Subjection of Women* (London: Longmans, Green & Co., 1869, but written 1861); Merle Curti, *The American Peace Crusade* (Durham, N.C.: Duke University Press, 1929).

20. Horace Greeley, *Glances at Europe . . . Including Notices of the Great Exhibition, or World's Fair* (London: Dewitt & Davenport, 1851); Henry Wheaton, *Elements of International Law* (Philadelphia: Lea & Blanchard, 1836, and subsequently published in French, Mexican, Italian, Chinese, and Japanese editions); Henry Wheaton, *History of the Law of Nations in Europe and America* (New York: Gould, Banks, 1845); Elizabeth F. Baker, *Henry Wheaton, 1783–1848* (Philadelphia: University of Pennsylvania Press, 1937).

21. Arthur H. Clark, *The Clipper Ship Era, 1843–1869* (New York: Putnam, 1910), pp. 235–43; Bern Dibner, *The Atlantic Cable* (New York: Blaisdell Publishing Co., 1964). On the very large subject of Anglo-American symbiosis, it may suffice to instance here the Barings, with their American marriages, land purchases, assemblages of capital for American development, and American senior partner, Joshua Bates of Massachusetts; George Peabody, also of Massachusetts, London banker, transatlantic philanthropist, and the man who gave the Morgans their start in international finance; and the English scientist James Smithson, whose bequest to the United States, received in 1838, gave rise to the Smithsonian Institution, organized by act of Congress in 1846.

22. *New York Herald*, 2 September 1858; P. M. Kennedy, "Imperial Cable Communications and Strategy, 1870–1914," *English Historical Review* 86 (October 1971): 730.

23. For interesting examples of expectations of continuity and assessments of America's role in the world, Charles Sumner, "Prophetic Voices about America," *Atlantic Monthly* 20 (September 1867):275–306; Charles William Eliot, "Five American Contributions to Civilization," speech at Chautauqua, N.Y., 19 August 1896, in *American Contributions to Civili-*

zation, and Other Essays and Addresses (New York: Century Co., 1898), pp. 1–35.

24. A. T. Mahan, *From Sail to Steam* (New York: Harper, 1907), p. 196; Lance C. Buhl, "Maintaining 'An American Navy,' 1865–1889," in *In Peace and War*, ed. Kenneth J. Hagan (Westport, Conn.: Greenwood Press, 1978), pp. 145–73.

25. Sarmiento's earlier comment (supra, n. 19) still (or once again) held true: from 1875 to 1895 federal expenditures per capita were in the area of $5 to $6 per annum; marveling at the contrast between the situation of the United States and that of the juxtaposed and competitive European powers, a British military writer in the late 1870s noted the remarkable shrinkage of the great Civil War army to a force of a mere 30,000 at a time when the British were maintaining some 190,000 men under arms, the Germans 400,000, the French 450,000, and the Russians 750,000; *Encyclopaedia Britannica*, 9th ed., s.v. "Army"; Richard W. Leopold, *The Growth of American Foreign Policy* (New York: Knopf, 1962), pp. 91–92; John Adams to Abigail Adams, Paris, May 1780, in *Adams Family Correspondence*, ed. L. H. Butterfield and Marc Friedlaender (Cambridge, Mass.: Harvard University Press, 1973), 3:342.

26. R. Pierce Beaver, "Missionary Motivation through Three Centuries," in *Reinterpretation in American Church History*, ed. Jerald C. Brauer (Chicago: University of Chicago Press, 1968), pp. 113–51. The changing attitudes of those involved may be followed through Hollis Read, *The Hand of God in History* (Hartford: Robbins & Co., 1849); Thomas Laurie, *The Ely Volume; of The Contributions of Our Foreign Missions to Science and Human Well-Being* (Boston: Congregational House, 1881); and James S. Dennis, *Christian Missions and Social Programs* (New York: Fleming H. Revell Co., 1898–1906).

27. The worldwide deployment of American mining engineers began with J. Lawrence Smith's venture to Turkey in the late 1840s and Raphael Pumpelly's visit to Japan in 1861; Field, *Mediterranean World*, pp. 248–49; Curti and Birr, *Point Four*, pp. 22–24, 214. On the second generation, mostly trained in the American West, see Clark C. Spence, *Mining Engineers and the American West* (New Haven: Yale University Press, 1970), pp. 278–317; the best known of these, John Hays Hammond and Herbert Hoover, were rather latecomers in the enterprise. On interchangeable roles in China, one may cite such individuals as Charles Denby, Jr., William Pethick, William W. Rockhill, Willard Straight, and E. T. Williams.

28. Mira Wilkins, *The Emergence of Multinational Enterprise: American Business Abroad from the Colonial Era to 1914* (Cambridge, Mass.: Harvard University Press, 1970); *Encyclopedia of American Foreign Policy*, 1978 ed., s.v. "Philanthropy," by James A. Field, Jr.; Curti and Birr, *Point Four*.

29. Dixon Wecter, *The Saga of American Society* (New York: Scribner's, 1937), pp. 405–16; W. T. Stead, *The Americanization of the World; Or, the Trend of the Twentieth Century* (New York: H. Markley, 1902); James A. Field, Jr., "Transnationalism and the New Tribe," *International Organization* 25 (Summer 1971): 353–72.

30. James A. Field, Jr., "American Imperialism: The Worst Chapter in Almost Any Book," *American Historical Review* 83 (June 1978): 644–48; Robert L. Beisner, *From the Old Diplomacy to the New, 1865–1900* (New York: Crowell, 1975); Charles S. Campbell, Jr., *The Transformation of American Foreign Relations, 1865–1900* (New York: Harper and Row, 1976).

31. J. Q. Adams, "Fourth of July Oration, 1821," *Niles' Weekly Register*, 21 July 1821, p. 331; Thomas Paine, "Common Sense," in *Life and Writings of Thomas Paine*, ed. Daniel E. Wheeler (New York: V. Parke, 1908), 2:58; Field, "American Imperialism"; Felix Gilbert, "The 'New Diplomacy' of the Eighteenth Century," *World Politics* 4 (October 1951): 1–38; Woodrow Wilson, "Speech for Declaration of War," in *The Papers of Woodrow Wilson*, ed. Arthur S. Link (Princeton: Princeton University Press, 1967–   ), 41:527; Barlow, *Letter to the National Convention*.

PART III

The Varied Paths to Peace in the Nineteenth and Twentieth Centuries

For the Bicentennial symposium, Reginald C. Stuart in chapter 5 sought to understand why peace was maintained in the nineteenth century between an expansionist United States and the vulnerable Canadian provinces; how, in short, "the British North American provinces escaped becoming part of the United States between 1783 and 1871" despite recurrent Anglo-American-Canadian crises. Although he identifies several important constraints on U.S. annexationist impulses, the fact that a union with Canada never occurred, he believes, illustrates "that the work of peace is truly work, as well as partly an accident of history. Peace, even between two broadly similar and sympathetic, although distinct, peoples, is perpetual labor."

In chapter 6, Russell F. Weigley contends that peace along the lengthy U.S.-Canadian border was largely the result of an imbalance of military power. So long as Britain enjoyed military predominance, strife usually marred U.S.-British-Canadian relations. The more American military power grew—a power "usually wielded for benign purposes"—the more an undefended border became a reality. Thus Weigley demonstrates that "armed strength is not always a source of mischief and destruction. Peacekeeping is sometimes its consequence."

100

Michael A. Lutzker's chapter 7 is part of an ongoing study of crises that did not result in war. In analyzing the avoidance of war between the People's Republic of China and the United States over the offshore islands of Quemoy and Matsu in the 1950s, he provides an unusual examination, first, of what brought the hostile parties to the brink of war, and then, of what prevented their actually tipping over the brink. Understanding the dynamics of escalation from crisis to actual war is of obvious yet vital importance in the nuclear era. His essay also suggests that even when statesmen have succeeded in preventing disputes from escalating into war, they have often failed to summon the courage to eliminate the sources of the disputes themselves, thus paving the way for repeated crises over the same issues.

5 REGINALD C. STUART

United States Expansionism and the British North American Provinces, 1783–1871

As well as establishing American independence and sketching the outlines of the future Canadian nation, the Treaty of Paris eventually created the field of Canadian-American relations. Canadian historians have been more concerned than their American colleagues both with the unfolding interrelationship of the two countries and the issue of American designs on the provinces down to and after Canada's confederation in 1867. C. P. Stacey, for one, reminded us years ago that the border was neither undefended nor unfailingly peaceful between 1783 and 1871. On the one hand, however, provincials assumed an American aggressiveness, perhaps drawing more from their heritage as the world's original anti-Americans because of the French and Loyalist foundations of Canada than they did from historical reality. On the other hand, American suspicions of menace from the north faded after 1815, despite a popular Anglophobia that politicians in the United States frequently exploited.[1]

It is important to understand how the British North American provinces escaped becoming part of the United States between 1783

The author is grateful to the Social Sciences and Humanities Research Council of Canada and the Senate Research Committee of the University of Prince Edward Island for their generous financial support of the project from which this chapter is drawn.

and 1871. Why did a general territorial expansionism not sweep north? Why did clear, repeated, even frequently angry and strident ambitions for the provinces not translate into a concerted annexationist policy? The Canadians and British were aware of and trembled for provincial vulnerability, as Stacey demonstrated when he documented the efforts put into fortifying the boundary. But why did American policymakers not exploit periodic Canadian interest in joining the United States? Why did American ideological enthusiasm for the Upper and Lower Canadian rebellions of 1837 and 1838 fail to arouse United States policymakers to seek more than stronger neutrality laws? Anglo-American crises dotted the diplomatic landscape from 1783 to 1871. What led all but one to a peaceful resolution? Until historians explore how American views of the provinces developed over these years, we will have no satisfactory answers to such questions, nor much understanding of the historical roots of the celebrated American-Canadian harmony.

Until 1871 a voracious expansionism did seem to grip American foreign policy and the American people. Explorers, fortune hunters, entrepreneurs, filibusters, settlers, missionaries, even artists and photographers ventured into the nooks and crannies of North America with scant regard for political boundaries.[2] French Louisiana, Spanish Florida, Mexican Texas, an Oregon jointly occupied with Britain for a time, the northern Mexican provinces from Texas to California, and Russian America all were embraced by the American union. By 1871 Canadians still stood independently, and could feel secure. United States territorial expansionism had waned, at least for the moment. Commercial and missionary expansionism remained, but the leaders and workers of these movements had a global orientation, however much they projected American values. To the north, Confederation had absorbed British Columbia; Canada now stretched from the Atlantic to the Pacific coasts.

The Treaty of Washington of 1871, although ostensibly Anglo-American, was really a triangular arrangement. It dealt with American-Canadian, as well as American-British issues, and by concluding that treaty the United States recognized Canada in a number of ways. First, Canada's prime minister, John A. Macdonald, was a member of the British negotiating party. The British dominated their team, but the Americans dealt directly with a Canadian leader on Canadian matters. Furthermore, the treaty could not take effect without Canadian ratification, an American recognition of Canada's quasi-independent status. Finally, the penultimate American-Canadian boundary dispute over San Juan Island and possession of channels in the Strait of Juan de Fuca in the Pacific Northwest went quietly to arbitration.

Many forces had combined to produce America's whirlwind expansionism down to 1871. A drive for foreign markets, partly because of commercial ambitions and partly because Americans saw trade as a means of encouraging social and political, as well as material, progress, was the most consistent theme. Sectional politics, along with national ideology, produced spasmodic lurches in different directions toward specific targets. National fears, especially of Great Britain, similarly directed attention in specific directions. Finally, historical accidents and individual ambitions can be found behind this broad expansionism. And some Americans did not seem reticent about suggesting that the remaining British territory in North America should forthwith become part of the new republic. Benjamin Franklin had probed this possibility while the work of peace was still in its preliminary stages prior to 1783.[3] In the years before the War of 1812, national frustrations and resurgent Anglophobia generated talk about driving Britain from North America as retaliation for wrongs committed against the United States.[4]

Some statesmen, such as John Quincy Adams, mused that the entire continent should eventually form one nation. James Madison seemed to embark on a policy to achieve that ambition during the War of 1812, and Thomas Jefferson, Henry Clay, and James Monroe, among others, made several statements that support a thesis of aggression against Canada.[5] Actually, westerners and others who believed that Britain used Canada as a base to arrest American expansion into the old Northwest and monopolize the fur trade through controlling the Indian tribes proved the most eager for conquest, but only of the upper province.[6] Madison and his close advisors seem to have seen the provinces as hostages to force the British to settle on the issues of trade restriction, seizures, and impressment. American ambition for ownership of the provinces during the War of 1812 was limited, at best.[7]

American expansionism accelerated after 1815, assisted by economic growth and the end of the Napoleonic Wars, and evidence can be found for ambition toward the provinces. A. B. Woodward, an influential Michigan politician, wrote to John Quincy Adams that it was "the duty of the American administration to make a serious effort to obtain the whole of the British possessions on this continent by negociation." Joseph Sansom, a veteran on a visit north, believed that Upper Canada was fundamentally American anyway and would "sooner or later fall into our hands." In 1830, a correspondent of Daniel Webster, Henry Dearborn, urged that the United States should buy out the British. Dearborn was interested in the overseas timber trade and believed that annexation by purchase would eliminate a major competitor. There was no trace of the work of peace in his remarks, but he did reflect the entrepreneurial spirit of the Age of Jackson, if only because he did not see how the British could refuse to sell provided the price was attractive enough.[8] In 1839, Lewis Linn, a Missouri senator and Oregon lobbyist, noted that if they had to, Americans should drive Britain out of North America to gain international respect. John L. O'Sullivan, editor of the stridently partisan and expansionist *Democratic Review*, stated in 1845 that provincial progress was a prelude to early independence from Britain, "soon to be followed by annexation, and destined to swell the still accumulating momentum of our progress." Early in his career, Charles Sumner of Massachusetts thought that the annexation of Canada would balance the increased power that slavery had acquired through the acquisition of Texas. And the *New York Times* noted in response to the crisis over the provincial fisheries in the 1852 season:

Let our British friends at the North make us unpleasantly sensible of their existence; let them stand one moment in the way of the national prosperity and obvious destiny, and there is no telling how soon we shall swallow them, headland and inland, lake, river and town. We speak more in sorrow than in arrogance. We shall have to do it; that is all.[9]

In sorrow or eager ambition, editors, politicians, and private citizens applauded the annexation movements that sprang up in the provinces after 1846 when Britain's transition to a policy of free trade shattered the protected imperial markets that the provincials had always enjoyed for their forest, land, and sea products. And during the American Civil War, when British policies seemed anything but neutral to the beleaguered defenders of Union, many politicians and citizens felt betrayed and directed their anger on Canada. They applauded when Secretary of State William Henry Seward announced a passport system along the northern border to control the movement of Confederate agents from the provinces and notified the British that the United States intended to cancel the Reciprocity Treaty of 1854 that had freed up portions of American-provincial trade.[10]

After 1865, rumblings of annexation erupted occasionally into shrill calls that reflected partisan ambitions more than a genuine interest in an American-Canadian merger. As American consuls in Montreal pointed out in their dispatches, conciliatory policies and quiet encouragement of Canadian annexationists would do more than cheering on the Fenians. These Irish ultrapatriots organized into paramilitary units, threatening and attempting periodic "invasions" of Canada less to liberate the provincials from British control, as they professed, than to stir up Anglo-American difficulties to further home rule for Ireland.

Treasury officer E. H. Derby evaluated the results of reciprocity in 1865 and suggested that annexation would solve many problems. But, congressmen would see when the secretary of the treasury submitted Derby's report, England's hold over the provinces was precarious, and, "if a perfect union cannot be effected, the plan of a zollverein . . . is a near approach to it." In 1866 Nathaniel Banks, the "political general" of the Civil War who played a prominent role in Reconstruction policies in Congress, moved to annex the provinces. At the same time, James Gordon Bennett's *New York Herald* published aggressive editorials. George Bancroft, staunch Democrat, former diplomat, and historian, saw the purchase of Alaska as the first step in the absorption of the provinces. In 1869 Minnesota business interests worked to have the United States acquire the Red River colony. The year seemed rich with opportunity for Minnesotans with provincial contacts. Louis Riel led a rebellion of the discontented French-Indian *métis*, but Riel made an arrangement with the Canadian government, and prospects for annexation of the British northwest evaporated. During the same year, Charles Sumner, angry with Britain and bidding to shape American foreign policy from his chairmanship of the Senate Foreign Relations Committee, openly declared that a cession of Canada would wipe the Anglo-American slate clean.[11] Given all this, how did the provinces remain British?

British power was the most obvious reason for the provincial escape. Despite popular Anglophobia, despite periodic crises and spasms of anger directed against Britain, American policymakers respected British might. Negotiators from Franklin forward discovered that Britain would never willingly surrender the provinces to the United States. The defense of Canada in the War of 1812 proved the point, as did the commitment to fortifications after 1815.[12] Apart from that, New Englanders were strikingly aware of America's vulnerable coasts and maritime interests. American national pride generated periodic confrontations with Britain, ultimately resolved by the good sense of negotiators and administrations on both sides. The work of peace after 1815 was not smooth and easy, but it did have its effect.

A growing sense of Anglo-Saxon commonality reinforced the deterrent qualities of British power, as did internal partisan politics in the United States, the diversity of American continental interests, and thrusts for territory that drew Americans west and south rather than north. Southerners, in particular, were responsible for this geographic thrust. Expansion to them meant more territory for the slave system, especially by the 1830s. In 1833, Britain abolished slavery within the Empire, thus providing new refuges for runaways, and, if the provinces were to enter the union, they would come in as free states, something southerners adamantly opposed. Conflicting cultural values within the United States helped to shape not only domestic politics, but external relations and policies in the antebellum period.

The Loyalist heritage in all the provinces except the embryo settlements west of Lake Superior in the 1860s was a major factor in the equation. Loyalists had lost property, homes, families, health, and dignity, no matter what their social status, because of their beliefs during the American Revolution. Dispersed into exile throughout the British Empire after 1783, many Loyalist refugees from British enclaves and the frontier formed communities from Nova Scotia to as far west as near the Detroit River. They were the principal founders of New Brunswick in 1784 and transformed Nova Scotia from a few scattered settlements with a naval base into a populous maritime province by the War of 1812. Others, victims of the cruel civil strife in rural areas of the rebelling colonies, trickled through the forests or up the waterways connecting the new United States with the remaining British provinces in the interior. The first American settlers on the Niagara and Detroit frontiers found Loyalists there, with Indian allies and British protectors. A strong antirepublicanism and anti-Americanism was therefore part of the provincial heritage from 1783 forward, reinforced by the War of 1812 when provincials defended their homes against an invader from the south. Over time, anti-Americanism became a staple of an emerging British provincial patriotism and was a ready reflex for politicians to exploit during the Confederation era. Loyalism was as profound a force for the provincials as revolutionary republicanism was for Americans, and it discouraged local interest in annexation to the United States.

Although in the years immediately following the Revolution Americans referred to the "Tories" to the north and feared the British use of the provinces as a base to thwart American interests, the image of a British menace from the provinces waned after 1815. John C. Calhoun wanted enough American troops on hand to balance those maintained by the British in the provinces, but in practice, British soldiers always far outnumbered those of the United States. It is true that Americans placed great reliance on the potential of their militia in the northern border states, but the idea of an undefended northern frontier seems to have had a greater reality on the American than on the provincial side.[13] The Rush-Bagot Agreement of 1817 reduced naval forces on the Great Lakes, although not immediately upon ratification. And the American garrisons withered in the old Northwest as the Indian menace subsided.[14] In 1812, Lewis Cass of Michigan had been a brash young officer in General William Hull's invasion force crossing the Detroit River intoUpper Canada. In 1836 he was secretary of war and reported to Congress:

Our inland border rests, in the southwest and northeast, upon the possessions of civilized nations, and requires defensive preparations to meet those contingencies only which, in the present state of society, we may reasonably anticipate. In the existing intercourse of nations, hostilities can scarcely overtake us so suddenly as not to leave time to move the necessary force to any point on those frontiers threatened with attack.[15]

Standing forces remained small in the United States in the antebellum period, widely scattered in frontier posts to the west and in coastal garrisons. As a result, few federal troops were available to police the border when the provincial rebellions of 1837 encouraged idle and idealistic Americans to filibuster for the next year or so to "liberate" the provinces from the British yoke. General Winfield Scott, who had a reputation along the northern border to match his imposing appearance, relied largely upon his own personality and the official declarations of President Martin Van Buren's government to contain expatriate Canadian insurgents and their American sympathizers.[16]

Neither British nor American administrations wanted trouble over border incidents after 1815. The boundary dispute that led to the so-called Aroostook "War" of 1839 had simmered for some time, not urgent because the region was vacant. But Maine blocked any settlement that surrendered its territorial claims, and the federal government in Washington would not assert its constitutional authority for fear of political repercussions and for the fabric of the union. Rhetoric vastly exceeded violence when the Aroostook War erupted, but the incident aggravated nerve endings. Van Buren's administration worked to soothe both the Mainers and the British. Secretary of State Daniel Webster tried to muster local support in Maine by waging a propaganda campaign in the newspapers and with local Whig politicians favoring compromise, spending secret funds to do so. Winfield Scott once more donned the cloak of borderland peacemaker.[17] There was no popular support for a policy of force outside of Maine, and Webster summarized the common view when he wrote, "I have never contemplated it as a probable event, that two great nations would go to war . . . on such a question. I have never expected such a result and do not expect it now."[18] This was a spasm in Anglo-American relations, rendered dangerous by local passions and politics, but not an incident that reflected an expansionist thrust toward the provinces. Even Mainers wanted only the disputed territory and eventually accepted a compromise.

Anglo-American border disputes after 1815 never produced an American mobilization against a foreign assault, and the work of peace produced acceptable compromises in time. The nature of America's expansionist ideology reinforced this work-a-day tendency to seek peaceful solutions. Whether this ideology provided a rationalization for ambition or a spur to action is debatable. An eclectic blend of strident nationalism, republican idealism, commercialism, sectional ambitions and fears, racial belief, partisan perspectives, and views on proper foreign policy explained variously for expansionistic Americans where their country should move and why.

Prior to 1815, expansionism was primarily defensive and strategic, although it had contradictory elements. For example, expansionists leaned to republican ideas of acquiring territory for future generations of agrarians and believed that American ideals could be spread and assured through a growth of overseas trade; but they were also receptive to just-war and natural-rights doctrines that argued against territorial acquisition through conquest. At the same time, free-trade ideas led Thomas Jefferson, James Madison, and others to claim that the rivers and oceans should be open to all and to adopt policies of force to pursue such ends. When the Spanish closed the Mississippi River to American traders from the Ohio Valley in 1803, for example, references appeared to the United States' right to rule all of North America.[19] But such views reflected rhetorical outbursts rather than government policy or national ambitions that commanded genuine support.

American territorial development after 1783 built upon the Louisiana windfall of 1803. The sustaining national ideology of expansion nevertheless became increasingly complex. Westward and southward movement appeared linked with the idea of geographic predestination, but advocates rarely talked of moving north. Perhaps thoughts of the climate proved a deterrent along with British power and restrictions on settlement from the United States. American frontier migrants had drifted into the provinces before the War of 1812, but after 1815 tended to move west, discouraged by legal barriers and encouraged by both natural lines of travel and the demise of Indian power in the old Northwest. Editors and politicians in the United States talked about an American right to exploit natural resources, arguing that farmers made superior use of the land to hunters, gatherers, and traders. An article of faith among American agrarians, and apparently easily applicable against Mexicans or Indians, both perceived as lesser peoples, the superior use doctrine could not be applied with much consistency against fellow Anglo-

Saxons.[20] In Oregon, however, Americans argued that their settlers had precedence over British hunters and trappers. Commercial ambitions and power politics probably prompted O'Sullivan of the *Democratic Review* to write that the British should steer clear of America because it was an asylum for freedom, but such rhetoric was too bound up with opportunism and old fears of British encirclement to stand alone.[21]

If ideology had the power to direct American policy toward the provinces, it should have been in the 1830s. Jacksonian nationalism ran strong. American settlers in Mexican Texas rebelled against Mexican rule in 1836 in a "struggle for liberty" that sympathetic southerners claimed was a replay of rejecting British "tyranny" in 1776. These southerners were largely sincere in their rhetoric, although their awareness of fellow slaveholders working for an independent country that would surely maintain slavery was a major factor in their judgment. Combined, these themes justified assistance to the Texans that saw official toleration of violations of American neutrality laws. Even while the Texan War of Independence raged, apparently republican rebellions broke out in the Canadas in the fall and winter of 1837. Surely here, too, was a replay of 1776, and with the same "tyrant" as the oppressor.[22] O'Sullivan's *Democratic Review* stated:

If freedom is the best of national blessings, if self-government is the first of national rights, and if the "fostering protection" of "paternal government" is in reality the worst of national evils—in a word, if all our American ideas and feelings, so ardently cherished and proudly maintained, are not worse than a delusion and a mockery—then we are bound to sympathize with the cause of the Canadian rebellion.[23]

Americans along the northern borderland responded fervently at first. Some organized or attended rallies, donated or solicited funds, collected arms, received refugees when the rebellions fizzled, and even volunteered to fight for Canadian independence. The Washington, D.C., *National Intelligencer* claimed great interest, and border newspapers exhibited various levels of enthusiasm and excitement. On 5 December 1837 an *Intelligencer* correspondent in the provinces wrote "I have not the least doubt they [the rebels] will succeed in the end. Their cause is an inspiring one, and will enlist the sympathies of all the United States border counties of Lower Canada, even to the pitch of enthusiasm." Two days later, "Bunker Hill" wrote that his countrymen "cannot be insensible to the condition of fellow Americans re-enacting the drama of our own glorious Revolution."[24] Ideological empathy, human sympathy, a bumptious energy, individual recklessness, if not irresponsibility, flared among border Americans. A volunteer army of liberation collected under Rensselaer van Rensselaer, son of the War of 1812 general, on Navy Island, just above Niagara Falls. Citizens ignored the demands of neutrality here, as they had in Texas.

In this case, however, Martin Van Buren's administration breasted the popular stampede. For one thing, the enthusiasm was restricted to a narrow band along the border. For another, Congress was apathetic at best, far more concerned about the Seminole War in Florida, the slavery issue, Texan independence, the economic depression that followed the Panic of 1837, and the implications of all these issues for partisan politics. Perhaps the Canadian rebels were unfortunate in their timing, but Van Buren insisted upon neutrality, defining a legalistic diplomatic path. He relied upon federal marshalls, local state governors, and Winfield Scott to calm the frontier and enforce the neutrality laws. The *"Caroline* Affair," during which provincial troops rallied to Navy Island and burned an American vessel servicing the rebels and their supporters, raised the specter of an invasion of American soil and complicated the issue. But the resultant patriotic flush faded, and no aggressive movement collected around the cause of the Canadian rebellions.[25]

Ideological identification with the provincial rebels did not run deeply in American society in 1837 and 1838. Interest flagged when the rebellions collapsed, except among a cluster of the largely un-employed faithful who formed Hunters' Lodges and other secret societies along the border to carry the cause of Canadian inde-pendence. Most Americans who examined William Lyon Macken-zie's leadership in Upper Canada calmly were unimpressed. After an initial hero's welcome as a refugee, Mackenzie faded into relative obscurity. Beyond the border towns, the press condemned the hot-heads who sought to compromise the national interest. The New York *Albion* seemed biased when it talked about the *"stand-still"* French who refused to accept the progressive British lead, but many Americans entertained a low opinion of the French in Quebec because of their alleged ignorance and the supposed tyranny of Catholicism and the priests.[26] One New York paper believed that the English government was "more paternal, more liberal, more free, more tolerant to the Canadians than they were to the American colonies in 1776." The *National Intelligencer* at times seemed more sympathetic to the provincial government than the rebels. The editor noted that "the Canadians must fight their own battles," and many echoed his view. Senators and congressmen, alarmed by the troubles, defended Britain's right to quell rebellion and the American government's right to restrain misguided citizens, however natural their sympathies.[27]

President Van Buren's policies also sustained a thrust in American foreign relations evident since the 1790s. When the Wars of the French Revolution erupted, the United States was a young, weak nation, with links of interest and sentiment to both principal antagonists. A debate began in administration circles, spread to Congress, and then among the politically active public on whether the United States should honor the terms of its 1778 treaty with France. Ideological sympathies to brother republicans notwithstanding, George Washington's administration defined the national interest as avoiding entanglement in wars that did not relate directly to American honor and survival. This commitment to neutrality became a polestar for future policymakers. Even the War of 1812 was fought partially to enforce American neutrality. During the Latin American and Greek rebellions between 1808 and 1825, administrations would extend no more than moral sympathy to rebel entreaties for assistance. Where Americans did take direct action, it was in the form of filibustering, private enterprise guerrilla warfare, as to aid settlers in West Florida rebelling against Spain or Texans rebelling against Mexico. In both these cases, however, the rebels were clearly expatriate Americans and the United States government was not officially involved. Many Americans had moved into the provinces prior to 1812; but by the 1837 rebellions, those remaining, although identifiable and often active in provincial politics, had become largely assimilated into provincial society. They rebelled as provincials, not Americans. The New York and Vermont filibusters resembled in form those who had crossed the Texas border from southern states in 1836, but Van Buren took neutrality more seriously when dealing with the British. This was not only diplomatically prudent, but politically safe. Once away from the vicinity of the border, newspapers generally urged neutrality in the Canadian rebellions.[28] Ideology can be discounted, if not eliminated, as a force generating policy toward the provinces.

Commercial ambitions, on the other hand, demonstrably shaped American expansionism in the nineteenth century. A commercial outlook was as much a part of the American character as republicanism. And republicanism itself had a commercial streak. American farmers would require carriers and markets for their produce in order for agrarianism to flourish beyond a subsistence level. Even before the entrepreneurial and aggressive Jacksonian times, Americans looked abroad for commercial opportunities. New England mercantile interests lobbied for control of the Pacific Northwest during the early decades of the nineteenth century, supported by Oregon missionaries and settlers. Captain Charles Wilkes, who surveyed not only the western coast of North America as part of his oceanographic assignment from 1838 to 1842, but went on to map the Pacific Ocean, stimulated commercial attention by his reports of the spacious harbors of the Pacific slope. John Charles Fremont, son-in-law of Missouri expansionist Thomas Hart Benton and best known by his explorer's title of "The Pathfinder," provided even more publicity for the commercial opportunities of the far west, including possible trade in the Pacific basin. San Diego, San Francisco, and Puget Sound became indispensable ports. By the 1840s, ideology and commercial ambitions were mutually reinforcing and buttressed President James K. Polk's territorial expansionism.[29]

An aggressive American commercial culture sought opportunities in the provinces from 1783 forward. Shortly after the Treaty of Paris, New Englanders reestablished their colonial connections with what were from 1784 the Maritime provinces of Nova Scotia and New Brunswick. They required emergency assistance because a flood of Loyalist refugees swamped both local agriculture and the ability of British officials to supply food and shelter. By 1812 a flourishing coastal trade, not all of it legal, had developed. Farther west, in the Champlain Valley and along the land necks and river crossings of the Great Lakes basin and its drainage system, similar borderland economies developed progressively from the 1790s forward. John Jacob Astor's contacts with Montreal fur men suggest an early multinational corporation, albeit with provincials as the senior partners.

The promotors of the Erie Canal believed that their projected water-
way would tap provincial, as well as interior, American markets and
tie the northwest to the eastern seaboard. The provinces formed a
natural part of New York's commercial hinterland. Official interest
in American-provincial trade appeared in 1816. This exchange shot
up with the end of the War of 1812, the official statistics not including
the smuggling that continued in the Bay of Fundy and in the woods
near the border settlements of Vermont and western New York.[30]

After 1815 the British provinces became a partial extension of the
American economy even as they remained within the British Imperial system. By 1819 exports from the United States to the northern provinces exceeded those to the West Indies by a ratio of three
to two, although much of that provincial figure also found its way
to the West Indies. As stands of virgin timber dwindled in Maine,
Vermont, and northern New York, American lumbermen looked to
New Brunswick, the northern shores of the Great Lakes, and into
the Ottawa Valley. In the 1840s, Americans invested in sawmills at
Hull, Arnprior, and Pembroke, Upper Canada. And the builders of
the American railroad grids in the northeast and northwest in the
1850s poked branches into the provinces to tap raw materials and
markets.[31]

The remnants of England's protectionist system did not deter
American entrepreneurs who saw opportunities in the provinces.
The Erie Canal began to transform New York into an entrepôt for
the Canadas, as well as the American northwest and the Great Lakes,
as its promoters had forecast. From 1783 forward, Americans also
sought access to the St. Lawrence River in the belief that this would
benefit economic development in the Great Lakes region. By the
1820s, visitors commented on how freely American bank notes circulated in the provinces.[32] *Niles' Register*, the *American Almanac*,
and other United States periodicals began to publish information
about economic and political activity in the provinces by the 1830s.[33]
After 1833 the American government could appoint consuls in provincial ports. Their incomes derived solely from commissions, and
the increase in numbers of these consuls in the provinces testified
to the entrepreneurship of the Jacksonian period, as well as the
steady growth in American-provincial trade. These consuls also increased the flow of information on the provinces through their reports to the Department of State. Frequently, the consuls went

beyond a mere recording of the movement of goods or the rendering of services to Americans to discuss social activity, provincial politics, and imperial relations.[34]

By the 1840s interested Americans could learn much about the provinces from a variety of sources. Those with access to consular reports, especially those from Israel Andrews, read suggestions for eventual economic union with the United States. Andrews, born in New Brunswick, was a naturalized American. He grew up in the Maritime borderlands region and returned to New Brunswick as consul at St. John in 1843. He immediately initiated a flood of data and opinion on American-provincial relations and worked indefatigably for what became the Reciprocity Treaty of 1854.[35] By 1859 several congressional reports focused on American-provincial trade, and the House Committee on Commerce reported in 1848 that removing legislative restraints "would enable us to divert a considerable proportion of the import and export trade of the upper province of Canada from the St. Lawrence route to American channels."[36] Americans could view the provinces variously as both potential economic partners and as rivals.

The work of peace of 1783 had created two separate, but comparable, political, social, and economic entities in North America speaking a common language, except for the French Canadian settlements along the lower St. Lawrence River. As the economies of both regions developed, they became intertwined, especially along the borderland region. The provinces never became states of the union, but they did become extensions of the blossoming American economy. New York was an entrepot for the Canadas, especially after completion of the Erie canal system; Americans in the Great Lakes basin used the Welland canal and the St. Lawrence River as outlets; goods moved back and forth across the frontier for local consumption; and when railroads came in the northeast, they provided more efficient communications channels for this trade, just as the railroad across Upper Canada from Buffalo to Windsor proved a more efficient route than going south of Lake Erie for Americans shipping to Detroit.

These developing economic links produced the first formal diplomatic arrangement between the provinces and the United States (through Great Britain, of course) in the Reciprocity Treaty of 1854. The background to this treaty lay in provincial eagerness for closer links with the United States after the British jettisoned their Corn Laws in 1846 and thus threw the provincials onto a world market in which they were at a serious disadvantage. At first forecasting economic disaster, many provincial merchants believed that salvation lay only through establishing free trade with the United States. Some even argued for political annexation.[37]

Reciprocity with the provinces aroused some hostility in the United States, some enthusiasm, but mostly massive indifference. Southern representatives, increasingly sensitive to their minority status in both the House and Senate after the compromise of 1850 admitted California as a free state without the customary balance of a new slave state, feared that reciprocity was a masquerade to reduce their national influence even further as a prelude to the eradication of their "peculiar institution." Certain northern economic interests—Maryland coal producers, New England fishermen, Michigan lumbermen—feared that provincial competition would drive them out of business. Israel Andrews waged a lonely campaign to overcome these obstacles, evidently viewing reciprocity as a personal mission. After 1852, he had President Franklin Pierce and his secretary of state William L. Marcy, as well as certain influential congressmen and senators, Stephen A. Douglas among them, as allies. Pierce wanted to extend American commercial influence and settle a fisheries dispute with the British that some Americans suspected had been fabricated to pressure the United States into accepting reciprocity. Intense lobbying, administrative influence, and ample British lubricants supplied by the Canadian Government General, Lord Elgin, during a visit to Washington, D.C. in 1854, combined to create a favorable majority in Congress. The Reciprocity Treaty passed in 1854.[38] Although it seemed a break with the past, the treaty recognized the growing importance of American provincial trade. And the United States tacitly recognized as well the economic independence of the provinces by agreeing that each provincial legislature had to ratify the treaty before it would take effect.

Some Americans believed that the Reciprocity Treaty reflected a natural evolution in American-provincial relations since the two societies were on converging pathways. Such views were not aggressive. They rather built upon a sense of historical inevitability. James Monroe had thought about this as early as the 1780s and would do so again in the era of the War of 1812, as would John Quincy Adams.[39]

Commenting on the work of Nova Scotia writer Thomas Chandler Haliburton, a reviewer mused that "it needs no spirit of prophecy to foresee that the time must come when . . . the whole continent . . . [will] present the unbroken outline of one compact empire of friendly and confederated states."[40] William Duane spoke before the Historical Society of Pennsylvania on the Continental Congress and Canada during the Revolution, concluding:

The adoption of Canada into our family of confederated states is now a more probable event than it was at the most prosperous period of either of our wars with Great Britain. The people of that Province have long been watching with interest the progress of the United States, and, finding no sufficient explanation in climate, soil, and productions for the great difference between that progress and their own, they have been led to regard the different forms of government as the main cause.[41]

Duane assumed that provincials and Americans were really the same kind of people, who wanted the same things, viewed "progress" in the same way, and yearned for the same political freedoms that republicans apparently enjoyed. This was an underlying assumption for believers in the historical convergence of the provinces with the United States.

Influential proponents of reciprocity such as George Bancroft, a Jacksonian and patriotic historian, could therefore conclude that the British determination to grant provincials greater autonomy would not only smother political agitation in Canada, but link provincial and American self-interests. Israel Andrews was convinced that political union would inevitably follow reciprocity.[42] Andrews, like other American consuls in the provinces, exaggerated local interest in annexation and projected his own dreams onto the provincial reality. John M. Clayton, a consul in Montreal before becoming secretary of state in 1849, capsuled such misperceptions:

The establishment of reciprocity would instantly allay all agitation. It would defer the question of annexation to a more distant day while it would no less insure the ultimate accomplishment of this great measure, not by violent and dangerous disruption, but by breaking link by link the chains which bind the Countries to the Mother Country and by establishing that community of sympathies and interests between the two countries which would render annexation an inevitable political necessity.[43]

By the 1850s the convergence idea found widespread expression. "Why," asked the *Merchants' Magazine* of New York in 1852, "should we seek to keep asunder States which Time and Events, Nature, and Science thus unmistakably join together?" The *New York Times*, which regularly reported on provincial affairs, noted that Canadian eagerness for reciprocity reflected "a conviction on the part of their people that all their interests are in the main identical with those of this country." Transportation promoter John Poor of Maine agreed, subscribing to views of Anglo-Saxon solidarity and superiority common in the 1850s. And the *North American Review* asserted that the reciprocity treaty would "tend to make us one people, and absorb us, irresistibly, although insensibly, into each other."[44] President Franklin Pierce and William Marcy, reflecting a view of their times, supplied Israel Andrews with the funds he requested to lobby both American and provincial politicians in behalf of the Reciprocity Treaty.[45]

Provincial-American union did not follow reciprocity, but greater trade did. It is difficult to say how much of this resulted directly from the treaty. Historians do not agree on the matter; and it seems likely that expanding economies on both sides of the frontier, coupled with improving transportation systems, would have generated much of the growth even without a formal agreement.[46] Even so, supporters of reciprocity took satisfaction from rising figures, even as opponents charged that the treaty damaged American interests. A variety of opinions emerged on the impact and significance of reciprocity. E. H. Derby, for example, who conducted a detailed study of reciprocity's impact on the American economy, hinted that provincial American amalgamation lay in the future regardless of the Treaty's fate. John Potter, the American consul in Montreal at the end of the Civil War, believed that the treaty should be cancelled to pressure provincials into exchanging political independence for guaranteed prosperity by union with the United States. William Henry Seward, secretary of state at the time, was content to encourage a customs union and await the forces of historical change, which he believed favored convergence.[47]

American views on the provinces, in what emerged as their time of confederation at the close of the Civil War, covered a similar spectrum. At one end lay a belief that the provinces should never be part of the United States; at the other lay a concern for annexation as soon as possible. There were expressions of approval, indifference, and outrage over the creation of the Dominion of Canada in 1867.[48] Among the more extreme views were annexationist editorials by James Gordon Bennett in his *New York Herald* and a few speeches in Congress, for example, those by "radical" Republican Zachariah Chandler.[49] But Americans were distracted by the agonies of Reconstruction and ill-inclined for foreign adventures on an official level.

The most reasoned views seemed to come from those who subscribed to the convergence thesis. As Charles Francis Adams, the American minister in London, remarked to William Henry Seward, the British refused to believe that the United States did not covet Canada. "It is of no avail to represent to them that ever were it admitted to be our policy . . . the true way to bring it about would be patience, conciliation and the establishment of a harmony of interests that would bring on that end as a perfectly natural result." Horace Greeley, once a proponent of continental expansion and now a reforming Republican, stated: "And if territorial expansion is best for us and for mankind, it will be achieved without war by the simple force of political gravitation. We expect that the Canadas will be States of the Union at some not distant day." Faith in convergence counseled patience and trust in the historical inertia built up by geographic proximity, shared economic interests, a common language, and similar institutions.[50]

An expansionistic cadre did emerge in the post–Civil War era in the United States; however, its targets were in the south and west, not the north, apart from the acquisition of Alaska. Seward and supporters of the purchase viewed the region as one section of a commercial highway for Americans seeking opportunity in Asia. Only local interests in Minnesota agitated for annexation of Manitoba in 1869 during the Red River Rebellion.[51] They could arouse no enthusiasm outside their own circle.

By this time also, many Americans had come to realize that the provinces were not simply an extension of their own society.[52] Travelers from 1815 onward had noted this from time to time. When William Darby journeyed from New York to Detroit through Upper Canada in 1819, for example, he found that "though speaking the same language, enjoying a similar system of jurisprudence, and regulated in their private conduct by the same religion, yet in political opinion, a wide difference exists between the Canadians and

the people of the United States."[53] Others found the large French-
Catholic population in Lower Canada an important, and repugnant,
difference with the United States.[54] Observers of the Canadian rebellions of 1837 also concluded that the two Anglo-American societies were really quite distinct. Even Israel Andrews, for all his belief
in convergence, acknowledged in 1848 that a "national character"
was emerging in the provinces.[55] And as American consuls appeared
in more provincial ports, they developed habits of dealing with provincials as nearly separate nationals from both Britain and the United
States, whatever their private views about an eventual American-
provincial merger.[56] The *Merchants' Magazine* noted on the conclusion of the Reciprocity Treaty that the provinces now had a quasi-
independent status. And some would have agreed with Roscoe
Conkling's prognostication to the New York Chamber of Commerce
in 1859: "Another nation may be raised up on this continent."[57]

As the provinces confederated, editorial opinion in the United
States generally suggested that Americans had no right to interfere
in the emergence of the Dominion of Canada. The *National Intelligencer* saw Confederation as a step toward Anglo-American peace.
The *Merchant's Magazine* believed that the "provinces will now feel
themselves a nation, and the annexation to this country of Canada,
or any portion of it, must be considered from this time forth as
impossible."[58] Canada's external relations continued to flow through
the British foreign office, and its legislation remained to a degree
controlled by Great Britain's parliament; but Canadian leaders began operating as a quasi-independent state and hired George W.
Brega to lobby for their interests in Washington.[59]

The Treaty of Washington confirmed the official American tendency to view Canada as a quasi-independent nation. John A. Macdonald, Canada's first prime minister, was one of the British
delegates who negotiated the agreement. Hamilton Fish, secretary
of state, and Charles Sumner, chairman of the Senate Foreign Relations Committee, suggested that the British might want to trade
Canada for the claims arising out of the depredations on American
shipping committed by the Confederate raider *Alabama* during the
Civil War and from America's sense of grievance over what it considered as Great Britain's unneutral stance during the conflict. But both
believed that annexation could occur only with the free consent of all
parties, and Fish dropped the idea when the British were unrespon-

sive. In common with most Americans who gave a thought to the future of Canada, both men seemed unaware that anti-Americanism was part of the cement of Confederation.[60] The American government accepted that Canada must ratify the Treaty of Washington before it could take effect, since it dealt with provincial-American, as well as Anglo-American matters. That, too, was a tacit recognition of Canada's quasi-independence. Finally, British Columbia and Manitoba entered the Confederation in 1871, and this indicated clearly that even the sparsest settlements in the British North American provinces had escaped incorporation in the United States.[61]

The reasons why the British North American provinces escaped American expansionism between 1783 and 1871 seem clear enough, although their relative strengths are difficult to gauge. One is tempted to say that the architects of the peace of 1783 wrought better than they knew, but such hyperbole would only rival the cliche of the undefended border as a distortion of the facts. The forces at work were many, shifting, and complex, extending over a considerable period of time given the youth of the countries involved. British power and the provincial Loyalist heritage were active deterrents, for example.

The mercurial ideology of American expansionism, perhaps the most elusive factor in the equation, never really applied to the provinces, despite cultural similarities. And the movement of frontier settlers generally lay south and west, especially after 1815. In Texas or far Oregon, migratory frontiersmen formed expatriate settlements eager to shed their adopted governments and establish political links with the United States. That factor arose in the British provinces prior to 1812, but events demonstrated that by no means all ex-Americans would flock eagerly to an invading army from the republic to the south. American-provincial cultural similarities rendered assimilation easier for American migrants to the provinces. Dispersed and merged into local societies, they never formed the coherent blocs they did in Spanish Florida, Mexican Texas, or Hudson's Bay Company–controlled Oregon.

Internal politics in the United States also played a part at various times in discouraging expansion that might include the provinces. Southerners were reluctant to add potential free states, just as free soilers and other antislave men opposed adding territory that would become slave states. When provincial interest in annexation arose in 1849–50, expansion had become a divisive political issue. Besides, politicians were distracted by the debates that produced the Compromise of 1850. Just after the Civil War, when a few voices arose calling for annexation, Reconstruction proved another sponge for political interests and energies.

The provinces did not escape becoming extensions of the blossoming American commercial system of the 1830s, on the other hand, providing markets, sources of materials, goods to carry, and opportunities for investment. Many Americans concluded from such developments, as well as from internal provincial political changes, that the two societies would peacefully converge at some undetermined future date. Part rationalization and part article of faith, this expression of eventual union nurtured patience. Natural economic and historical forces would eventually make the provinces part of the United States. At the same time, other Americans concluded that a separate society had emerged in the provinces between 1783 and 1871 that had a right to its own political destiny, however it might resemble the United States and however much it might become integrated with the American economy.

The work of peace of 1783 created historical circumstances in which these factors arose and sorted themselves out in various juxtapositions over time. Through effort and habit, an undefended border did emerge. Mutual provincial and American perceptions were rooted in illusions and fears, but neither a concerted push nor an irresistible pull propelled American political power north, except in the limited circumstances of the War of 1812. Without question, many Americans wanted to see an eventual union of the provinces with the United States. But there was never a consensus about this at any time at either popular or official levels. These historical factors combined and reformed over time to translate the work of peace of 1783 into an American-Canadian reality. This story should remind us that the work of peace is truly work, as well as partly an accident of history. Peace, even between two broadly similar and sympathetic, although distinct, peoples, is perpetual labor.

NOTES

The staffs of the National Archives, the Library of Congress, The George Washington University Library, Harvard University Library, and the Robertson Library at the University of Prince Edward Island were all helpful. The work of my research assistant, Helen Gill, has been much appreciated along with the valuable critical advice of Robert Beisner of The American University of Washington, D.C., and of Thomas Spira of the University of Prince Edward Island.

1. Carl Berger discusses the major exception to this generalization in "Internationalism, Continentalism, and the Writing of History: Comments on the Carnegie Series on the Relations of Canada and the United States," in *The Influence of the United States on Canadian Development*, ed. R. A. Preston (Durham: Duke University Press, 1972), pp. 32–54. This series is dated now. C. P. Stacey, "The Myth of the Unguarded Frontier 1815–1871," *American Historical Review* 46 (October 1950):1–18.

2. The major works are Albert K. Weinberg, *Manifest Destiny: A Study of Nationalist Expansion in American History* (Baltimore: Johns Hopkins Press, 1935); Normal A. Graebner, *Empire on the Pacific: A Study in American Continental Expansion* (New York: Ronald Press, 1955); Frederick A. Merk, *The Monroe Doctrine and American Expansion 1843–1849* (New York: Alfred A. Knopf, 1966); William Goetzmann, *Exploration and Empire: The Explorer and the Scientist in the Winning of the American West* (New York: Alfred A. Knopf, 1966); and Reginald Horsman, *Race and Manifest Destiny: The Origins of American Racial Anglo-Saxonism* (Cambridge, Mass.: Harvard University Press, 1981).

3. Samuel F. Bemis, "Canada and the Peace Settlement of 1782–3," *Canadian Historical Review* 14 (September 1933):265–84; George Brown, "The St. Lawrence in the Boundary Settlement of 1783," *Canadian Historical Review* 9 (September 1928):223–38.

4. Edmund Randolph to John Jay, 18 August 1794, in *Diplomatic Correspondence of the United States: Canadian Relations 1784–1860*, ed. William R. Manning (Washington, D.C.: Carnegie Foundation, 1940–43), 1:78; James Madison to James Monroe and William Pinkney, 30 May 1806, in *Diplomatic Correspondence of the United States*, 1:174–75; House Committee on John Henry Intrigue, 19 March 1812, *American State Papers: Foreign Relations* (Washington, D.C.: Gales & Seaton, 1832), 3:454–55; Governor William Hull to William Eustis, 15 June 1811, in *Documents Relating to the Invasion of Canada and the Surrender of Detroit 1812*, ed. E. A. Cruikshank (Ottawa: Government Printing Bureau, 1911), pp. 1–3.

5. Jefferson to William Duane, 4 August 1812, in *The Works of Thomas Jefferson*, ed. Paul L. Ford (New York: G. P. Putnam's Sons, 1905), 11:265; Clay, "Speech," 22 February 1812, in *The Papers of Henry Clay*, ed. Mary Hargreaves and James Hopkins (Lexington: University of Kentucky Press, 1959–   ), 1:449–50; Monroe to Jonathan Russell, 26 June 1812, in *The Writings of James Monroe*, ed. S. M. Hamilton (New York: G. P. Putnam's Sons, 1901), 5:212–13.

6. The British Constitutional Act of 1791 divided Canada into upper and lower colonial jurisdictions to separate the French-Canadians from the influx of Loyalists, although many of these settled in what became the Eastern Townships of Quebec below the St. Lawrence River. The 1791 division corresponds roughly to the present Ontario-Quebec border.

7. Reginald C. Stuart, "Canada in the American Mind: The Era of the War of 1812," paper presented to the Canadian Historical Association, 6 June 1983, Vancouver, B.C.; J. C. A. Stagg, *Mr. Madison's War: Politics, Diplomacy and Warfare in the Early American Republic 1783–1830* (Princeton: Princeton University Press, 1983), chap. 1, believes that Madison invaded Canada to cut off that source of supply to the British West Indies and hence increase economic pressure on Great Britain. His evidence for a deliberate intention to conquer and keep Canada, however, is regrettably slender.

8. Woodward to Adams, 5 December 1818, in *Historical Collections*, Michigan Pioneer and Historical Society (Lansing: Darius Thorp, 1908), 36:346; Joseph Sansom, *Travels in Lower Canada* (New York: Kirk & Mercein, 1817), p. 571; Henry Dearborn to Daniel Webster, 19 February 1830, in *The Papers of Daniel Webster*, ed. Charles M. Wiltse and Harold D. Moser (Hanover, N.H.: University Press of New England, 1974–   ), 3:17–18. See also, John Quincy Adams to Abigail Adams, 30 June 1811, in *Writings of John Quincy Adams*, ed. Worthington C. Ford (New York: Macmillan, 1913), 4:128; and Andrew Jackson to William Lewis, 29 May 1839, in *Correspondence of Andrew Jackson*, ed. John S. Bassett (Washington, D.C.: Carnegie Institution, 1926), 6:16; Joe Patterson Smith, "A United States of North America—Shadow or Substance? 1815–1915," *Canadian Historical Review* 26 (June 1945):109–18.

9. Lewis Lin to R. Corbin, 16 December 1839, cited in M. C. Jacobs, *Winning Oregon: A Study of an Expansionist Movement* (Caldwell, Idaho: Caxton Printers, 1938), p. 117; *United States Magazine and Democratic Review* 17 (July 1845):9 (hereafter cited as *Democratic Review*); *New York Times*, 23 July 1852; Charles Sumner to Lord Morpeth, 8 January 1850, in *Memoir and Letters of Charles Sumner*, ed. Edward Pierce (Boston: Roberts Bros., 1893), 3:211.

10. For the Civil War Era, see James M. Callahan, "Americo-Canadian Relations Concerning Annexation, 1846–1871," *Studies in American History* (Bloomington: Indiana University Press, 1926), 6:187–214; Robin Winks, *Canada and the United States: The Civil War Years* (Baltimore: Johns Hopkins Press, 1960); Allen P. Stouffer, "Canadian-American Relations 1861–1871" (Ph.D. diss., Claremont Graduate School, 1971); James Snell, "The Eagle and the Butterfly: Some American Atttitudes towards British North America 1864–1867" (Ph.D. diss., Queens University, 1971).

11. E. H. Derby, *A Preliminary Report on the Treaty of Reciprocity with Great Britain to Regulate the Trade between the United States and the Provinces of British North America* (Washington, D.C.: Treasury Department, 1866), pp. 17–20; Snell, "Eagle and Butterfly," pp. 226–32; Bancroft to William H. Seward, 15 June 1867, cited in Snell, "Eagle and Butterfly," p. 155; Alvin Gluek, *Minnesota and the Manifest Destiny of the Canadian Northwest* (Toronto: University of Toronto Press, 1965); Brian Jenkins, *Fenians and Anglo-American Relations during Reconstruction* (Ithaca, N.Y.: Cornell University Press, 1969).

12. John Quincy Adams to Thomas Boylston Adams, 24 November 1812, *Writings*, 1:407; American to the British Commissioners, 9 September, 13 October 1814, Records of Negotiations Connected with the Treaty of Ghent 1813–15; Despatches of the American Commissioners, 29 August 1813–3 July 1815, RG 59, M 36, Department of State, National Archives, Washington, D.C., microcopy, reel 1; Alexander Dallas, *An Exposition on the Causes and Character of the Late War* (Washington, D.C.: Thomas Bangs, 1815), pp. 28–29.

13. Stacey, "Unguarded Frontier"; Stanley Falk, "Disarmament on the Great Lakes: Myth or Reality?" *United States Naval Institute Proceedings* 87 (December 1961):69–73; Howard Jones, *To the Webster-Ashburton Treaty: A Study in Anglo-American Relations 1783–1843* (Chapel Hill: University of North Carolina Press, 1977); A. B. Corey, *The Crisis of 1830–1842 in Canadian American Relations* (New Haven: Yale University Press, 1941); Lester B. Shippee, *Canadian-American Relations 1849–1874* (1939; reprint ed., New York: Russell & Russell, 1970).

14. John C. Calhoun, "Speech," 27 February 1815, in *The Papers of John C. Calhoun*, ed. Robert L. Meriwether and W. Edwin Hamphill (Columbia: University of South Carolina Press, 1959–   ), 1:277; Henry Clay, "Speech," 29 January 1816, *Papers*, 2:152; James Monroe to John Quincy Adams, 21 May 1816, *Diplomatic Correspondence*, 1:244; John Quincy Adams to William Eustis, 29 November 1815, *Writings*, 5:423; A. B. Corey, "Canadian Border Defence Problems after 1814 to Their Culmination in the 'Forties,' " in *Annual Report*, Canadian Historical Association (1938), pp. 111–20.

15. Lewis Cass, "On the Means and Measures Necessary for the Military and Naval Defences of the Country," 8 April 1836, *American State Papers: Military Affairs* (Washington, D.C.: Gales & Seaton, 1838), 6:366–67; J. R. Poinsett, "A Plan for the Protection of the North and Eastern Boundary of the United States," 10 January 1838, *American State Papers*, 7:985–98.

16. Orrin Tiffany, *The Relations of the United States to the Canadian Rebellions of 1837–1838* (Buffalo Historical Society Publications, no. 8, 1905); and Oscar Kinchen, *The Rise and Fall of the Patriot Hunters* (New

York: Bookman Associates, 1956), are the two major studies of this episode in American-Canadian affairs, although there are several articles on specific issues and locales.

17. David Lowenthall, "The Maine Press and the Aroostook War," *Canadian Historical Review* 32 (December 1951):315–36; *Diplomatic Correspondence*, 2:70–73; Henry Clay to S. B. Barrell, 19 November 1827, *Diplomatic Correspondence*, 2:141–43; Barrell's report of 11 February 1828, *Diplomatic Correspondence*, 2:148–60; Millard Fillmore, "Speech," 1 March 1839, in *Millard Fillmore Papers*, ed. Frank Severance (Buffalo: Buffalo Historical Society, 1906), 1:141–43.

18. Webster to David Ogden, 11 March 1839, *Papers*, 4:350–51; and see Nathan Hale in *American Almanac* (Boston, 1840), pp. 84–94; "The Northeastern Boundary Question," *Democratic Review* 3 (September 1838):49; Frederick Merk, *Fruits of Propaganda in the Tyler Administration* (Cambridge, Mass.: Harvard University Press, 1971).

19. James A. Field, Jr., *America and the Mediterranean World 1776–1882* (Princeton: Princeton University Press, 1969); Drew McCoy, *The Elusive Republic: Political Economy in Jeffersonian America* (Chapel Hill: University of North Carolina Press, 1980), chap. 8.

20. Horsman, *Race and Manifest Destiny*; Weinberg, *Manifest Destiny*, chap. 1, and pp. 12–14, 18, 25–31.

21. Weinberg, *Manifest Destiny*, pp. 53–64, 88–89, 109–12.

22. Tiffany, *United States to Canadian Rebellion*, pp. 1–147; Wilson P. Shortridge, "The Canadian-American Frontier during the Rebellion of 1837–1838," *Canadian Historical Review* 7 (March 1926):13–26; Kinchen, *Patriot Hunters*; Douglas Frank, "The Canadian Rebellion and the American Republic," *Niagara Frontier* (Winter 1969):96–104.

23. *Democratic Review* 1 (January 1838):218–19, 3 (December 1838):380–81, 4 (June 1838):103.

24. *North American*, 15 May 1840; *National Intelligencer*, 13 November, 27 November, 5 December, 7 December 1837; *Daily Albany Argus*, 12 December 1837; Eugene P. Link, "Vermont Physicians and the Canadian Rebellion of 1837," *Vermont History* 37 (Summer 1969):177–83; John Duffy and Nicholas Muller, "The Great Wolf Hunt: The Regular Response in Vermont to the *Patriote* Uprising of 1837," *Journal of American Studies* 8 (August 1974):153–69.

25. James C. Curtis, *The Fox at Bay: Martin Van Buren and the Presidency 1837–1842* (Lexington: University Press of Kentucky, 1970), pp. 171–74; Van Buren to Congress, in *Compilation of the Messages and Papers of the Presidents 1789–1908*, comp. James D. Richardson (Washington, D.C.: Bureau of National Literature and Art, 1908), 3:401, and documents appended, pp. 401–4; Howard Jones, "The *Caroline* Affair," *The Historian* 38 (May 1976):485–502.

26. *Albion*, docs. 9, 11–16, 19, in Public Archives of Canada, MG 24, B 157; Sansom, *Travels*, pp. 16, 68–72, 75; P. Stansbury, *A Pedestrian Tour of Two Thousand and Three Hundred Miles in North America* (New York: J. D. Myers & W. Smith, 1822), pp. 159–60; Benjamin Silliman, *Remarks Made on a Short Tour between Hartford and Quebec in the Autumn of 1819* (New Haven: S. Converse, 1824), pp. 214–15, 236–37, 391, 397; Theodore Dwight, *The Northern Traveller and the Northern Tour* (New York: Goodrich & Wiley, 1834), pp. 168–69; Theodore Dwight, *The Northern Traveller* (New York: John P. Haven, 1841), pp. 115, 121–22; Henry David Thoreau, *A Yankee in Canada* (Boston: Ticknor & Fields, 1866), pp. 23–34, 43, 62, 69, 83–84.

27. *National Intelligencer*, 4–7 December 1837; Proclamation by Governor of Vermont in *National Intelligencer*, 13 December 1837; *Daily Albany Argus*, 27 December 1837; *Niles' National Register*, 18 November 1837, p. 131, 13 January 1818, pp. 305–12, 20 January 1838, pp. 321–23, 10 March 1838, p. 19. A brief discussion of these events in Congress is in *The Congressional Globe*, 25th Cong. 2d sess., 1838 (Washington, D.C.: Globe Office), p. 79, 83, 195, 215.

28. *Daily Albany Argus*, 30 December 1837, reporting a meeting in Vauxhall Gardens, New York City; *Daily Albany Argus*, 5 January 1838; C. Dunkin, "British American Politics," *North American Review* 49 (October 1839):373–430; *National Intelligencer*, 15, 23, 27 January and 17 February 1838.

29. Graebner, *Empire on the Pacific*; David M. Pletcher, *The Diplomacy of Annexation: Texas, Oregon and the Mexican War* (Columbia: University of Missouri Press, 1973); Ernest Paolino, *The Foundations of American Empire: William H. Seward and American Foreign Policy* (Ithaca, N.Y.: Cornell University Press, 1973).

30. *American State Papers: Commerce and Navigation* (Washington, D.C.: Gales & Seaton, 1832), 1:641, 2:35, 442–43; H. N. Muller, III, "The Commercial History of the Lake Champlain–Richelieu River Route 1760–1815" (Ph.D. diss., University of Rochester, 1969); W. A. MacNutt, *The Atlantic Provinces: The Emergence of Colonial Society* (Toronto: McClelland & Stewart, 1963), chaps. 3–4.

31. F. Lee Benns, *The American Struggle for the British West Indian Carrying Trade 1815–1830* (Bloomington: Indiana University Studies No. 56, 1923), 10:67; W. E. Breening, "The Lumber Industry in the Ottawa Valley and the American Market in the Nineteenth Century," *Ontario History* 62 (June 1970):134–36; Harold Davis, *An International Community on the St. Croix (1604–1930)* (Orono: University of Maine Press, 1950); A. R. M. Lower et al., *The North American Assault on the Canadian Forest: A History of the Lumber Trade between Canada and the United States*

(Toronto: Ryerson Press, 1938), pp. 1–122; Peter Baskerville, "Americans in Britain's Backyard: The Railway Era in Upper Canada, 1850–1900," *Business History Reviews* 55 (Autumn 1981):314–36.

32. Sansom, *Travels*, pp. 72–73; Jesse Hawley, *An Essay on the Enlargement of the Erie Canal* (Lockport: Courier, 1840), p. 608; John Quincy Adams to Richard Rush, 30 July 1818, to Rufus King, 15 August 1822, *Writings*, 6:411, 7:293; "Report of the Committee of Foreign Affairs," 21 February 1823, House Report #96, *U.S. Serials Set*, no. 87, pp. 1–2; Henry Clay to Albert Gallatin, 22 September 1826, *Diplomatic Correspondence*, 2:106–11; Gallatin to Clay, 22 September 1826, *Diplomatic Correspondence*, 2:513.

33. "Statement Exhibiting the Trade between the British North American Colonies and the Districts of Passamaquoddy, Portland, Boston, and New York, during the Years ending December 31, 1828 and 1837," Secretary of the Treasury to the House of Representatives, 4 April 1838, 25th Cong., 2d sess., House Document #300, *U.S. Serials Set*, No. 329, pp. 218–19; *American Almanac*, 1835, pp. 300–2, 1841, p. 247, 1849, pp. 218–19; *Albany Argus*, 1825–45; *Niles' Weekly Register*, 1815–1850; *National Intelligencer*, 1815–18.

34. Department of State, Despatches from United States Consuls, National Archives, Washington, D.C., RG 59, microcopy T 469, Halifax; T 485, St. John; T 222, Montreal.

35. Andrews to State Department, 16 and 20 April, 5 July 1846, 15 January 1848; Despatches from United States Consuls, T 485, St. John, reel 1.

36. House Report, "British North American Products," House Report #258, 30th Cong., 1st sess., *U.S. Serials Set*, No. 525, pp. 108; Report of the Secretary of the Treasury, 8 February 1851, Senate Executive Documents, #24, 31st Cong., 2d sess., pp. 2–3; and see also, *Merchants' Magazine and Commercial Review* 3 (1948):216–26; 4 (1841):96–97; 6 (1842): 538–54; 10 (1844):16–20, 38–47, 354–59. On illicit trade, see T. L. Thompson's letters to the Secretary of the Treasury, July 1843–December 1844, Department of the Treasury, RG 56, Entry 248, National Archives, Washington, D.C.; Joint Special Committee on the Railroad Celebration, 17–19 September 1851, *Tabular Representation of the Present Condition of Boston . . . Also a Few Statements Relative to the Commerce of the Canadas* (Boston: J. H. Eastburn, 1851), p. 23.

37. D. C. Masters, *The Reciprocity Treaty of 1854* (London: Longman's Green & Co., 1937); Charles C. Tansill, *The Canadian Reciprocity Treaty of 1854* (Baltimore: Johns Hopkins Press, 1922); Lawrence H. Officer and Lawrence B. Smith, "The Canadian-American Reciprocity Treaty of 1855 to 1866," *Journal of Economic History* 28 (December 1968):598–623.

38. See Officer and Smith, "Canadian-American Reciprocity Treaty"; and Roy F. Nichols, *Franklin Pierce: Young Hickory of the Granite Hills* (Philadelphia: University of Pennsylvania Press, 1958), pp. 263–65; the discussion in the *Congressional Globe*, 30th Cong., 2d sess., pp. 46, 182–85, 327–32; 31st Cong., 1st sess., pp. 261, 701–2, 1009–11, 1908; 33d Cong., 1st sess., pp. 2212, 2219; Alan Dowty, *The Limits of Isolation: The United States and the Crimean War* (New York: New York University Press, 1971), pp. 35–38, 143–44.

39. Adams to Abigail Adams, 30 June 1811, *Writings*, 4:128; "Backwoodsman," *Military Monitor and American Register*, 21 June 1813, pp. 340–41; James Monroe to John Taylor, 13 June 1812, *Writings*, 5:207; Alexander McLeod, *A Scriptural View of the Character, Causes and Ends of the Present War* (New York: Eastburn, Kirk & Co., 1815), pp. 224–25; Christian Schultz, *Travels on an Inland Voyage 1807 and 1808* (New York: Gregg Press, 1968), pp. 50, 55, 59, 96–97.

40. Review of Haliburton's work in *North American Review* 30 (January 1830):134–35; see also, Edward Everett in *North American Review* 30 (January 1930):235–36, and 33 (October 1831):454–55; *National Intelligencer*, 27 November, 5 and 6 December 1837; see also Sansom, *Travels*, p. 571; E. A. Theller, *Canada in 1837–38* (Philadelphia: Henry F. Anners, 1841), 2:277.

41. Duane, *Canada and the Continental Congress* (Philadelphia: Edward Gaskill, 1850), p. 19; Henry Dearborn to Daniel Webster, 19 February 1830, *Papers*, 3:17–18; *Democratic Review* 16 (July-August 1845):9–10.

42. Bancroft to Clayton, 9 March 1849, *Diplomatic Correspondence*, 4:252; Andrews to Secretary of State, 28 June 1849, Department of State, Special Agents (1849), vol. 16, RG 59, Entry 38, National Archives, Washington, D.C.; Andrews to Secretary of State, 31 July 1849, 19 August 1849, Department of State, Special Agents (1849), vol. 16, RG 59, Entry 38, National Archives, Washington, D.C.; Thomas Le Duc, "Israel Andrews," *Dictionary of American Biography* (New York: Charles Scribners, 1944), Supplement 1:29–30; and William Overman, "I. D. Andrews and Reciprocity in 1854: An Episode in Dollar Diplomacy," *Canadian Historical Review* 15 (September 1934):248–63, provide the only substantial studies of Andrews.

43. Clayton to Secretary of State, 9 February 1850, Consular Despatches, Montreal; Andrew's dispatches in Special Agents (1849) records, and "I. D. Andrews on the British North American Colonies and United States Trade," 6 February 1851, Senate Executive Documents, #23, 31st Cong., 2d sess., *U.S. Serials Set*, no. 590, pp. 14–23; B. Hammatt Norton, U.S. Consul, Pictou, Nova Scotia to John Clayton, 21 November 1849, *Diplomatic Correspondence*, 4:319–21; C. Dorwin to William Marcy, 1 November 1855, Consular Despatches, Montreal.

44. *Merchants' Magazine*, June 1852, p. 681; *New York Times*, 24 September, 27 October 1852; Laura Poor, ed., *Life and Writings of John Alfred Poor* (New York: G. P. Putnam's Sons, 1892), pp. 166, 173–75, for Poor's views written in 1850; *North American Review* 79 (October 1854): 483; *American Railroad Journal* 25 (March 1852):154; (10 July 1852): 439–40; (2 October 1852):626–27; ibid., 27 (12 August 1854):507; *National Intelligencer*, 26 July 1854; William H. Seward, "The Destiny of America," 14 September 1853, in *The Words of William H. Seward*, ed. George E. Baker (Boston: Houghton, Mifflin & Co., 1884), 4:123–24.

45. William Marcy to Israel Andrews, 12 September 1853, *Diplomatic Correspondence*, 4:82; Nichols, *Franklin Pierce*, pp. 343–44; Pierce, "First Annual Message," 5 December 1853, *Messages and Papers*, 5:208–12, and "Second Annual Message," 4 December 1854, *Messages and Papers*, 5:277; Marcy to James Buchanan, 11 March 1854, William Learned Marcy Papers, Library of Congress, Washington, D.C., vol. 48.

46. Masters, *Reciprocity*, pp. 119–28; Officer and Smith, "Canadian-American Treaty"; Snell, "Eagle and Butterfly," pp. 21–45.

47. E. H. Derby, "Report on British Trade," 19 February 1867, Senate Executive Documents, #30, 39th Cong., 2d sess., *U.S. Serials Set*, no. 1277, pp. 18–25; John Potter to William H. Seward, 26 June 1865, Consular Despatches, Montreal; David Thurston to Seward, 23 February 1865, Consular Despatches, Toronto, T 491; Seward's speeches in Baker, *Works*, 5:567–70; Paolino, *Foundations of Empire*, pp. 1–16.

48. Joshua Giddings to Charles Sumner, 9 October 1863, 5 April 1865, in George Julian, *The Life of Joshua R. Giddings* (Chicago: A. C. McClung & Co., 1892), pp. 390, 394; *American Railroad Journal* 39 (June 1866):537–38, 540.

49. J. P. Smith, "Republican Leadership and the Movement for Annexation of Canada in the Eighteen Sixties," Canadian Historical Association, *Annual Report*, 1935, pp. 65–75; Ronald D. Tallman, "Annexation in the Maritimes? The Butler Mission to Charlottetown," *Dalhousie Review* 53 (Spring 1973):97–112; Arthur H. DeRosier, "American Annexation Sentiment toward Canada 1866–1871" (M.A. thesis, University of South Carolina, 1955), pp. 62–74.

50. Adams to Seward, 16 March 1865, cited in Snell, "Eagle and Butterfly," pp. 271–72; *New York Tribune*, 7 April 1865; speech of J. Johnson of Milwaukee at Detroit Convention, in E. H. Derby, *A Preliminary Report on the Treaty of Reciprocity with Great Britain to Regulate the Trade between the United States and the Provinces of British North America* (Washington, D.C.: Treasury Department, 1866), p. 82.

51. *New York Times*, 27 February 1867; Snell, "Eagle and Butterfly," covers American responses to Confederation in detail; Alice R. Stewart,

"The State of Maine and Canadian Confederation," *Canadian Historical Review* 33 (June 1952):158–64; Seward, "Speech," at Sitka, Alaska, 12 August 1869, and "The Pacific Northwest," speech at Victoria, B.C., August 1869, *Works* 5:568, 570.

52. *Rochester Daily Union and Advertiser*, 25 September 1866; Joseph Larned, *Report on the State of Trade between the United States and the British Possessions in North America* (Washington, D.C.: U.S. Government Printing Office, 1871), pp. 25–27.

53. William Darby, *A Tour from the City of New York to Detroit* (New York: Kirk & Mercein, 1819), pp. 76–77, 84–86, 189; Stansbury, *Pedestrian Tour*, pp. 215–16, 233–34; Silliman, *Remarks*, pp. 210–15, 236–37, 391–97.

54. *Northern Traveller*, pp. 81–90, 162–78; Dwight, *Northern Traveller*, pp. 115–22; Thoreau, *Yankee in Canada*, pp. 20–24, 27–28, 43, 62, 83–84, 104–7, 126; William S. Hunter, *Hunter's Panoramic Guide from Niagara Falls to Quebec* (Boston: John P. Jewett & Co., 1857); Frederick Cozzens, *Acadia: Or, a Month with the Blue Noses* (New York: Derby & Jackson, 1859), pp. 90, 95.

55. *National Intelligencer*, 27 November, 5 and 7 December 1837; Linus Miller, *Notes of an Exile to Van Diemen's Land* (Fredonia: W. McKinstry & Co., 1846), pp. 2–3; Edward Theller, 19 June 1838, letters in Public Archives of Canada, MG 24, B 42; Andrews to Secretary of State, 15 January 1848, Despatches from Consuls, St. John; John Clayton to Secretary of State, 9 February 1850, Despatches from Consuls, Montreal.

56. William Marcy to Israel Andrews, 24 March 1855, Instructions to Consuls, Series 5, vol. 7, pp. 153–59, Department of State Archives, National Archives, Washington, D.C., RG 59, E 54; Marcy to Andrews, 12 September 1853 and 15 September 1854, *Diplomatic Correspondence*, 5:82, 89–90; John Appleton to W. B. S. Moore, 12 October 1857, Instructions to Consuls, Series 1, vol. 7, pp. 212–14.

57. *Merchants' Magazine*, June 1852, pp. 660–62, 680–81, March 1853, pp. 277–80; *American Almanac*, 1854–61, passim; Conkling in *De Bow's Review*, January 1859, pp. 97–99; and see also, *New York Times*, 22 October 1851 and 24 September and 27 October 1852; *Boston Courier*, 15 January 1866.

58. *National Intelligencer*, 2 March, 5 April, 8 June 1867, 17 June 1868; *Merchants' Magazine*, November 1865, p. 361, and December 1869, pp. 430–31; A. Pillsbury, "British North America," *De Bow's Review*, New Series 3, February 1867, pp. 156–66.

59. James Snell, "A Foreign Agent in Washington: George W. Brega, Canada's Lobbyist, 1867–1870," *Civil War History* 26 (March 1980):53–70; see also, Instructions to Consuls, Series 1, vol. 13, 467–68, vol. 15, 174–

75, 354, 375; David Thurston to William H. Seward, 31 March 1863, Despatches from Consuls, Toronto.

60. Adrian Cook, *The Alabama Claims: American Politics and Anglo-American Relations 1865–1872* (Ithaca, N.Y.: Cornell University Press, 1975); Maureen Robson, "The Alabama Claims and the Anglo-American Reconciliation, 1865–1871," *Canadian Historical Review* 42 (March 1961):1–22; Doris Dashew, "The Story of an Illusion: The Plan to Trade the Alabama Claims for Canada," *Civil War History* 15 (December 1969):322–48; the text of the treaty is in *Treaties and Agreements Affecting Canada in Force between His Majesty and the United States of America with Subsidiary Documents 1814–1925*, comp. External Affairs (Ottawa: King's Printer, 1927), pp. 37–49.

61. W. L. Morton, "British North America and a Continent in Dissolution, 1861–1871," *History* 47 (June 1962):139–56.

6 RUSSELL F. WEIGLEY

The Anglo-American Armies and Peace, 1783–1868

Throughout most of the years of British-American peace since the Treaty of Paris of 1783, the primary symbol of the absence of conflict has been the undefended border between the United States and Canada. Yet the undefended border has been founded upon a paradox. The American-Canadian frontier could become free of fortifications only after there was an indisputable preponderance of military power residing on one side of the Great Lakes and the forty-ninth parallel.

Until the United States achieved such a preponderance, the border, contrary to myth, was never undefended. Once the preponderance was attained, international amity's dependence on United States superiority posed for Canada nice problems in how to maintain sufficient force to assure internal law and order, particularly in dealing with *métis* and Indians, without generating enough force to disturb the peaceful equilibrium inseparable from the military supremacy of the United States in North America. Along the American-Canadian frontier, peace and safety became to a remarkable degree the offspring of an imbalance of military power—a result made possible, to be sure, because that military power was usually wielded for benign purposes.

To review the historical role of the military in preserving the peace between the United States on the one hand and the United Kingdom and her North American progeny on the other, however, first requires a glance at the circumstances of two hundred years ago when there existed an utter absence of American military preeminence. At the time of the Treaty of Paris, the day when American military power might overshadow the ability of what was then the world's greatest empire to project strength into its American possessions could scarcely be imagined. In 1783, the political disunity and economic weakness of the United States caused the Continental Army to fall into an advanced condition of decay long before the ratification of the peace settlement. The puny American Confederation had grasped independence by the narrowest of margins, through a convergence of extraordinary strokes of luck that snatched the victory of Yorktown from the debris of a Revolutionary War otherwise fast sinking into confusion, apathy, and defeat.

After Yorktown the American government of the Articles of Confederation possessed neither the means nor the will to preserve a respectable measure of armed strength even until the formal termination of the war. Most of the Continental Army was disbanded before peace was assured. Following the Treaty of Paris, Congress on 2 June 1784, mustered out the last regiment of the Continentals, retaining only eighty men and a proportionate number of officers, none above the grade of captain, to guard military stores at West Point and Fort Pitt.[1]

The following day, it is true, Congress recommended that Connecticut, New York, New Jersey, and Pennsylvania contribute quotas of militia to create a seven hundred–man military force for twelve months. Periodically renewed, this force became the First American Regiment, in effect the army of the Confederation, and it endured until after the ratification of the Constitution of 1787; but the regiment was chronically understrength, perpetually short of supplies, and incapable of keeping peace even in a small segment of the Indian country of the Old Northwest. The First American Regiment posed so little challenge to the garrison retained in North America by Great Britain after the Treaty of Paris that London could reduce the establishment in the province of Canada to fewer than two thousand men and still feel sure of an ample margin of superiority. Not only could Canada be readily reinforced, but British regulars could count on a wide margin over the Americans in military discipline and skills.[2]

To be sure, the population of the United States in 1783 already dwarfed that of British North America, some two and a half million people south of the new border to fewer than half a million above it. On its face, the population disparity might have implied a British weakness at the outset—"except," as the British military historian Sir John Fortescue was to put it a century later, "against so unmilitary a nation as the Americans."[3] Citing American noncompliance with those clauses of the peace treaty providing for restitution to Loyalists, the British army felt free, against so unmilitary a nation, to maintain detachments in territory nominally surrendered to the United States at Paris. These were the "Western Posts" soon to be notorious: two forts at the head of Lake Champlain; Oswegatchie, present Ogdensburg, New York, on the upper St. Lawrence; Oswego, on the route from Lake Ontario to the Mohawk River; Niagara, where the Niagara River enters Lake Ontario; Presque Isle, the sheltered Lake Erie harbor at the site of Erie, Pennsylvania; Sandusky, dominating the routes between Lake Erie and the Ohio River; Detroit, on the straits between Lake Huron and Lake Erie; and Michilimackinac, on the straits between Lake Michigan and Lake Huron. The British authorities did not contemplate retaining these Western posts forever; they were intended primarily to permit the merchants of Montreal and Quebec to use suitable leisure in liquidating their trade routes running through the new United States, gradually shifting the fur trade to all-British channels. For a full decade after the British acknowledgment of American independence, nevertheless, the Americans could muster no military force posing any semblance of a threat to hasten evacuation of the detachments; meanwhile the British also used them to cultivate such friendly relations with the Northwest Indians as might make of the aborigines a permanent barrier against the possibility that the superior numbers of the American population could one day annoy Canada. Taking shape was a British dream of a Northwest Indian Confederacy, autonomous but dependent upon Great Britain, an enduring instrument to protect the Canadians from the white Americans and to stunt the growth of the United States.[4]

This military predominance of a European power on the principal intra–North American frontier proved to assure, however, not peace but strife, and it was to do so as long as it persisted. Unmilitary a nation though the Americans might be, the persisting military predominance of a European power on their northern frontier and the concomitant threat of an Indian buffer state appeared to them an intolerable combination of impediments to the westward expansion of the United States. If they lacked the military power to overcome the alien predominance and compel the removal of the Western posts, the Americans could at least rail against their fate, and relations between them and the British would thus remain poisoned. The Americans could also attempt to rally the potential strength represented by their population into a modicum of military reality. Their desire to do so was no small motive for the framing of the Constitution of 1787. Under that Constitution, the administration of President George Washington mounted expeditions into the Northwest to overawe and pacify the Indians in both 1790 and 1791, the one using the First American Regiment and militia auxiliaries, the other combining a newly raised Second Regiment with the First and the militia. Unfortunately for the Americans, both expeditions ended in humiliating defeats for the infant United States Army.[5]

Congress then utilized the military and financial powers of the new Constitution to authorize the recruiting of five 960-man regiments, and Washington commissioned one of the most successful military leaders of the Revolution, Anthony Wayne, as major-general commanding. As desired by Washington and Secretary of War Henry Knox and permitted by statute, Wayne reorganized the army into a "Legion of the United States," comprising four sublegions each of which was a combined-arms infantry, cavalry, and artillery team. Between early 1792 and the spring of 1794, Wayne drilled the Legion into the first, albeit miniature, American approximation of a European professional army. While he did so, he also reported to the War Department from the Northwest frontier his assessment of the consequences of British military ascendancy along the Canadian border:

Previously to entering into a detail or plan of Operations against the Hostile tribes of Indians: I beg leave to offer a few general observations, why I think the War must progress, the Savages have become confident haughty & insolent from reiterated success, which they have evinced by a Wanton & deliberate Massacre of our *flags* an enormity that can't be permitted to pass with impunity unless the U S of America will sacrifice National Character & Justice to Mistaken prejudice & mean Economy in order to patch up a temporary peace which can neither be honorable expedient or permanent, under present circumstances and impressions, particularly whilst

British are in possession of our posts on the Lakes—for altho' they may not *directly*—I am convinced that they do *indirectly* stimulate the savages to continue the War, nor can all the sophistry, of British Embassadors Agents or states spies convince me to the contrary until they surrender up those posts.[6]

Wayne believed that Indian war would prove interminable until the United States could force British evacuation of its rightful territory, and that peace accordingly depended upon some mobilization of American power. Foreshadowing the pattern of subsequent American-British-Canadian relations, he proceeded to demonstrate the accuracy of his perceptions.

The Indians, not fully appreciating the extent of Wayne's ability to create a disciplined and effective army, but nevertheless apprehensive by June 1794 of his careful probing northward and westward from the Ohio River, attacked his advance guard at Fort Recovery on the last day of the month. The fort, built on the site of the Americans' 1791 defeat near the present Celine, Ohio, was garrisoned by somewhat under two hundred of Wayne's troops. Striking with about ten times that number, the Indians found themselves unable to overcome the newly confident and tactically skillful American regulars. Wayne thereupon resumed a northward advance with the main body of the Legion, augmented by fifteen hundred Kentucky mounted volunteers. On 20 August 1794, he brought the Indians to battle across fields where a tornado had felled a grove of trees, and with disciplined tactical skill Wayne's soldiers routed the Indians in an hour and a half.

The Indians had felt obliged to fight at Fallen Timbers because the British army had closed against them the gates of a stockade just to their rear. This was Fort Miamis, an addition to the Western posts built on the banks of the Maumee River under the direction of Lieutenant Governor John Graves Simcoe of Upper Canada to curb Wayne's progress toward the approaches to Detroit. The garrison of Fort Miamis had appraised Wayne's advance, however, as more formidable than anticipated. They decided that circumspection toward the Americans was therefore in order despite a recent speech by Governor-General Guy Carleton, Baron Dorchester, seeming to assure the Indians of British military protection. Consequently the

British had barred the retreating Indians from the fort and consigned them to Wayne's mercies.[7]

Similar circumspection in the face of reports of rising American military preparedness helped persuade London to sign Jay's Treaty two months later, on 19 November 1794, agreeing to evacuate all the Western posts by 1 June 1798. This concession was not prompted so much by General Wayne's military activities directly as by a reluctance to face trouble in America if war resumed with France in Europe. Nevertheless, the temporal coincidence of the forts' evacuation and the birth of the Regular Army of the United States in the form of Anthony Wayne's Legion was significant for the future of American-British-Canadian relations. Increments of American military strength tended to bring proportionate relaxations of the kinds of British policies calculated to spawn ill-feeling.[8]

But the United States did not yet possess the will or the resources to maintain permanently an army of the quality of Wayne's Legion. General Wayne died soon after winning the battle of Fallen Timbers and negotiating with the Indians the Treaty of Greenville, which opened much of the Old Northwest to American settlement. Wayne's passing left Brigadier-General James Wilkinson the senior officer of the American army. Wilkinson is best remembered as the consummate scoundrel of the early frontier, but his simple incompetence was to have more devastating effects on the army than his rascality. Training, discipline, and morale all plummeted under a self-important but lazy leader. Because the mood of the Indians was relatively chastened, however, and the British were fulfilling their agreement to evacuate the Western posts, the United States government lacked sufficient motivation to sack Wilkinson and seek to restore the army by finding another Wayne.[9]

The undeclared war with France in 1798–1800 brought impressive increases in the congressionally authorized military strength of the new Republic, and Washington's return from retirement to the highest rank in the army, along with the recall to active duty of several other Revolutionary War officers, seemed to promise relief from Wilkinson's direction. Yet the changes were slight and ephemeral. The increase in personnel occurred mainly on paper; real enlistments lagged amid the deep partisan divisions provoked by the war. A tired Washington did not greatly exert himself, and his most energetic deputy, Inspector-General (Major-General) Alexander

Hamilton, busied himself largely in aggravating partisan bitterness by assuring the allegiance of newly commissioned officers to the Federalist faction. At least, there was no threat to the peace along the Canadian-American border; Hamilton and his fellow Federalist Anglophiles had no intention of using the army in any way that might offend Great Britain, a tacit ally in the current American troubles with France. For the most part the army of the Quasi-War with France was irrelevant to British-American relations. In any event, military preparedness soon passed into discard, when the Francophile President Thomas Jefferson reduced the army once again to minuscule numbers—fewer than three thousand soldiers by 1802—and to the command of the egregious General Wilkinson.[10]

The subsequent renewed troubles with Great Britain and her Indian allies that led toward the War of 1812 caused a gradual enlargement of the Regular Army. By the eve of war in 1811 it had grown to 5,608. Military preponderance in North America remained with the British, however, because London responded to the same troubles by increasing the North American garrison from thirty-four hundred men in 1804 to eight thousand by 1809.[11] As usual, superior training and discipline made British preeminence much greater than the numbers alone suggested. The United States Military Academy at West Point was founded in 1802, but as yet it had little corrective impact upon American military inefficiency. When calls for the conquest of Canada became strident accompaniments to the drift toward a second Anglo-American war, only the ignorant can have entertained any serious expectation that the United States could generate the strength to achieve such a conquest.

Although the War of 1812 opened with American attacks on Canada, the aims were relatively modest. President James Madison, hardly an outstanding war president but not without a certain sense of military realism, did not strike against Canada in the hope of achieving a general conquest, but rather on the chance that his troops might be able to deliver blows painful enough to make the British feel at least some measure of punishment for their violations of American maritime rights that had precipitated the war. Even this limited goal proved beyond the American army's grasp. American attacks on Canada were just threatening enough to stimulate Canadian nationalism.

Those attacks having been repelled, the central military issue of the War of 1812 changed. Admittedly on the defensive, Americans aimed at fighting effectively enough to frustrate British counterinvasions that threatened to rob the United States of the bargaining power needed to prevent the British from finally establishing an autonomous Indian confederacy as a client state and a permanent buffer against the Americans. Despite the necessity to focus on Napoleon as the principal current enemy, the British and Canadians in their turn resolved to inflict punishment on the Americans; London eventually put 25,975 soldiers into Canada and threatened the United States from other directions as well. Fear goaded the American Congress into increasing the authorized strength of the Regular Army to an extraordinary 62,274 by February 1814, a figure not to be matched again until 1898. As in the Quasi-War with France, however, recruiting lagged far behind paper strength; at most, the actual numbers of nominal Regulars climbed to some thirty-five thousand by late 1814. Nevertheless, with militia increments bringing maximum wartime strength up to about seventy thousand toward the end of the same year, sheer quantity at last allowed the Americans to blunt a series of British incursions and thus stave off the Indian buffer state when that issue arose in the peace negotiations.[12]

On the defensive, the United States eventually not only enlisted respectable numbers, but made impressive logistical exertions, such as those that gave Commodore Oliver Hazard Perry a fleet with which to gain naval superiority on Lake Erie and those that, in the absence of leadership equal to Perry's, attained at least a balance of naval power on Lake Ontario. Toward the end, American numbers also began to be joined with somewhat surprisingly competent military leadership on land: that of Brigadier-General Winfield Scott and Major-General Jacob Brown along the Niagara frontier; of Major-General Samuel Smith, Maryland State Militia, in front of Baltimore; and of Major-General Andrew Jackson at New Orleans. The British finally had to conclude that the military exertions necessary to achieve any appreciable advantage over the Americans would be disproportionate to any possible lasting gains, and they became willing to negotiate a compromise peace.[13]

This outcome signified that although no fundamental change had diminished Britain's military predominance in North America at the close of the War of 1812, at least a subtle shift in the balance of power had developed along the Canadian-American border. The

Americans had demonstrated the beginning of a capacity to translate their overall population advantage into military strength. There was an erosion of British preponderance just sufficient to end the war on terms not altogether unfavorable to the Americans—and also to permit a series of further agreements to foster Anglo-American amity after the war. Once again, even slight increments of American military power proved to have the effect not of worsening, but of improving, Anglo-American relations.

Among the postwar agreements, the one that has remained best known was specifically military in nature: the convention signed in 1817 by Richard Rush, acting secretary of state of the United States, and Charles Bagot, British minister in Washington, to assure the termination of the naval-building race that had begun on the Great Lakes during the war. An exchange of notes stipulated that neither the United States nor Great Britain should maintain armed naval forces on the lakes except for certain small revenue cutters. Significantly, this convention concerned the one border area where the United States had scored a clear-cut victory during the war, Commodore Perry's triumph on Lake Erie. Still again, harmony along the border evolved in direct proportion to the American capacity to achieve any degree of military advantage.[14]

On land, the Americans had attained no wartime advantage comparable to Perry's naval victory, and the Rush-Bagot Agreement did not prohibit maintaining and expanding fortifications on the frontier. Here something of a fortress-building race took shape, though a sense of inferiority instilled considerably more energy into American efforts than the British and Canadians displayed. While the memory of British amphibious expeditions against Washington, Baltimore, and New Orleans moved the United States to prepare a new generation of ambitious casemated masonry fortifications all along the Atlantic and Gulf coasts, the similar memory of overland invasions from Canada during both the Revolution and the War of 1812 caused the Americans to include the Canadian border in the program as well. Expensive because it was highly ambitious, the new "permanent system" of American fortifications was conceived in the years immediately following 1815; but appropriations lagged, and construction occupied much of the skill and labor available to the tiny American Corps of Engineers for more than a generation. The forts were still uncompleted when the American Civil War put several of those along the seacoast to unexpected uses. In the course of the prolonged building program, four major strongholds were built along the Canadian frontier: Fort Ontario at Oswego, New York, was reconstructed in 1839; Fort Wayne at Detroit took shape in the 1840s as a square, four-bastioned, casemated pile of brick and mortar; Fort Montgomery at Rouses Point, New York, emerged in the same decade as the intended principal defense of the border, commanding the historic Lake Champlain–Richelieu River route; and even old Fort Niagara was kept in repair at the mouth of the Niagara River, with new casemates added as late as the Civil War. Across the frontier, the British applied their main efforts to Quebec and to Kingston, the outlet of the Great Lakes into the St. Lawrence. Plans to fortify Montreal never made much progress.[15]

Renewed construction activity along the border during the 1840s was stimulated by troubles in the late 1830s. Rebellions led by Louis Joseph Papineau in Lower Canada and William Lyon Mackenzie in Upper Canada against the oligarchical colonial government flashed across the border, threatening to explode into a third Anglo-American war. One dangerous climax was the *Caroline* affair. The *Caroline* was a steamboat that sometimes carried munitions supplied by American supporters of the rebels from Fort Schlosser, New York (the site of an old French post no longer in fact a fort), across the Niagara River to Navy Island in Canadian territory. On the island some of Mackenzie's faction had declared the independence of Canada and prepared for military action on behalf of that object. On 29 December 1837, a Canadian government force under Captain Andrew Drew, Royal Navy, crossed to Fort Schlosser, took possession of the *Caroline*, and sent her drifting in flames over Niagara Falls. In the process of capturing the boat, Drew's men shot and killed at least one American citizen, Amos Durfee. This violation of United States sovereignty precipitated a shrill outcry for armed retaliation that President Martin Van Buren feared might become irresistible.[16]

The episode also reflected the continuing contempt of British and Canadian authorities for the military capacities of the United States. That those capacities were not altogether undeserving of contempt was promptly demonstrated by the inability of the American government to halt the unneutral activities that had provoked the attack on the *Caroline* and also by the inability of Van Buren to include the dispatch of a strong military force among his efforts to defuse the crisis. The Regular Army of the United States happened to be badly strained at the time by the frustrating events of the counter-guerrilla struggle known as the Second Seminole War (1835–1842). Most of the militia of the states along the northern border were so much disposed to sympathize with the Mackenzie rebels that calling them to arms was more likely to intensify than to muffle the dangers. Fortunately for peace, however, the Americans—if they could not send troops to the border—could at least send an exceptional general in the stout, majestic, brilliantly uniformed person of Brigadier-General and Brevet Major-General Winfield Scott.

Scott had first won fame in the very neighborhood of the *Caroline* affair, along the Niagara frontier. During the War of 1812 he created those superbly disciplined regiments of United States Regulars that stood toe to toe against British veterans of Field-Marshal Arthur Wellesley, Duke of Wellington's Peninsular Campaign in the battles of Chippewa and Lundy's Lane. Scott's men had been the first American soldiers to prove themselves equal to British regulars in discipline and tactical skill on open, European-style battlefields where numbers and advantages of position were approximately equal—a milestone in the evolution of the military balance on the Canadian border, but one on which the Americans were as yet no more ready to capitalize permanently than they had been on Anthony Wayne's achievements. No one could doubt Winfield Scott's bravery, his military abilities, or his dedication to the interests of the United States; no one therefore could have been a better choice than he to carry from President Van Buren to William L. Marcy and Charles H. Paine, the governors of New York and Vermont, messages urging restraint and patience while diplomacy might resolve the *Caroline* crisis and to employ his own efforts in the same direction.[17]

Through the winter months of early 1838, in fact, General Scott traveled tirelessly up and down the border, journeying by sleigh back and forth from Fort Niagara to Monroe, Michigan, to quiet passions on both sides of the frontier with assurances of responsible American conduct for the Canadians and of defense of the national honor for the Americans. No one, furthermore, could better have raised second thoughts in British minds about American military respectability. When two British armed schooners operating in

American waters stood off Black Rock in the Niagara River prepared to fire on yet another steamboat, the *Barcelona*, which they thought guilty of gunrunning to rebels, Scott materialized posing defiantly atop Black Rock in full uniform with several American guns and cannoneers at his side; the British did not molest the *Barcelona*. (This incident, it must be acknowledged, would have been less perilous if Scott had clearly informed all the relevant British authorities of the very pertinent facts that he had purchased the *Barcelona* to keep it from mischievous hands and that the boat carried no munitions; his failure to do so was apparently inadvertent.)[18]

The violation of the letter of international law notwithstanding, a considerable measure of justification lay with the British in the matter of the *Caroline*. As the distinguished American diplomatic historian Samuel Flagg Bemis was to describe the policy of the British prime minister, Henry John Temple, Viscount Palmerston, "Lord Palmerston took the same attitude toward American protests that John Quincy Adams would have taken if this had been a case of Andrew Jackson and Florida."[19] By that token, there was also a degree of merit in a long letter that Sir Francis Bond Head, lieutenant governor of Upper Canada, wrote to the British minister in Washington taking issue with General Scott's insistence that the first principle of restraint to be observed was a ban on any further violation of the international border whatever, by either side. It was less justifiable that the letter was soon made public in the *Toronto Patriot*. In any event, Head observed, Scott conceded that with only himself and a handful of cannoneers and other soldiers on hand in place of an army, the United States could offer no guarantees against rebel incursions into Canada from the States. Therefore, Head complained, "One would have supposed that the invisible boundary line through the waters of the Niagara might well have been permitted to be passed over [by the British], without adverting even to the question of absolute right to do so by the Law of Nations."[20] Nevertheless, Scott's stress on absolute rights under international law may well have been essential in calming American emotions. The lieutenant governor's very complaint, by reflecting the British authorities' decision that they must respect Scott's wishes, confirmed that when the United States could not dispatch an army to allay crisis, Winfield Scott was a reasonably close equivalent.

After a summer interlude dealing with the unpleasant, but not internationally sensitive, business of removing the Cherokees from the Appalachian Mountains to the west, General Scott again functioned as a substitute for an army to keep the peace on the border during the following winter, 1838–39. The 1783 Treaty of Paris had left the location of the international boundary unclear as it ran through the woods south of the St. Lawrence River and west of the St. John River. Amid priceless stands of timber and in the fertile valley of the Aroostook River, a tributary of the St. John, rival Maine and New Brunswick settlers were now plunging into an informal conflict called the "Restook War." The Maine legislature unanimously directed Governor John Fairfield to station a military force on the Aroostook, voted $800,000 for the purpose, and instructed the governor to call upon the United States for assistance. On 9 March 1839, Congress responded by authorizing the president to call out the militia and to enlist 50,000 volunteers in the army, voting a credit of $10,000,000 for the purpose. Sir John Harvey, lieutenant governor of New Brunswick, called upon his own militia to repel aggression within the province.

Fortunately for peace, President Van Buren again preferred the exertions of General Scott over those of the militia. Scott benefited from the circumstance that, following the American burning of York (from 1834 Toronto) during the War of 1812, he had returned to Harvey, then a staff officer, a captured trunkful of uniforms and a miniature of Harvey's wife. Scott also employed to shrewd advantage on the American side of the border the fact that he was a Whig in politics, but dispatched by a Democratic president, so that cooperating with him in the cause of peace should harm neither political party. Above all, his imposing presence again exerted the ultimate influence in extracting from the parties to the dispute mutual disclaimers of an intent to seize the contested territory by military force. On the Maine–New Brunswick border as on the Niagara frontier, Winfield Scott secured the suspension of hostilities and the easing of tensions that opened the way for the subsequent broad resolution of American-British-Canadian border disputes and other differences by Secretary of State Daniel Webster and the British special plenipotentiary Alexander Baring, Baron Ashburton, in their treaty and exchange of notes of 1842.[21]

The Webster-Ashburton Treaty opened a period of better feelings between the United States and Canada, assisted by John George

Lambton, Earl of Durham's proposals of responsible government for the British North American provinces and thus easing of the internal troubles that had spawned Papineau's and Mackenzie's rebellions. More to the point here, the good feelings were reinforced also because the 1840s and 1850s represented a time of transition in the military balance between the United States on the one hand and Great Britain and British North America on the other. Never again after 1839 would the United States have to rely on the strength of an individual like General Scott to substitute in British-American relations for the power of an army. Never again would American military strength on the northern border be so lacking as it was when the Regular Army was preoccupied by the Second Seminole War. It was a growing sense of power of the United States that led the government of Sir Robert Peel in 1846 to concede to the Americans a division of the Oregon country along an extension of the forty-ninth parallel westward to the Straits of Fuca, despite the strong historic claim the activities of the Hudson's Bay Company gave Great Britain at least as far south as the Columbia River. It was the same awareness that led the Liberal opposition to Peel, under the usually more militantly nationalist Lord Palmerston, to acquiesce in this settlement.[22]

To be sure, we are speaking of a time of transition. It was not actual American military strength, but the potential posed by the weight of American population, including American settlers in Oregon, that convinced London to forego a struggle for territory otherwise British by impressive traditional claims. Nevertheless, the contempt for American military capacity so evident before the War of 1812 and lingering even in Sir Francis Bond Head's attitude toward General Scott's conduct on the Niagara frontier was evidently evaporating. It could hardly have survived the American military exploits of the Mexican War of 1846–48. Indeed, the Reciprocity Treaty of 1854 sprang, on the British and Canadian side, from the hope that increased Canadian-American commerce might minimize the dangers of sentiment favoring the annexation of Canada, of which growing American military might was a possible stimulant.[23]

The American Civil War ended the transition and opened a new and lasting era, the time of peace assured by complete American military predominance. The completeness of the change and of the American predominance were not immediately recognized, and

even historians writing with the advantage of hindsight have sometimes been imperceptive. But the change occurred.

The population and resources of the United States had grown so
rapidly by 1861 that, notwithstanding the secession of eleven southern states, Congress could meet the challenge of Civil War by voting
in July of that year for two successive increases in the American
army of half a million men each and by the beginning of December
have over 660,000 actually under arms; while a general who had
served with the French army could testify that the force was so well
supplied that a French army half its size could subsist on what it
wasted. The military professionalism of the American officer corps,
nurtured by West Point and proven in the Mexican War, permitted
the enormous new United States Army to be organized, administered, and trained with an efficiency at least equal to that displayed
by the British, French, and Russian armies that had waged war less
than a decade earlier in the Crimea. By the time the Civil War
ended in 1865, some two and a half million men had passed through
the United States Army at one time or another, and the actual
strength of the army at war's end was about a million men.[24]

In late 1861, at a time when the United States Army had already
gone well over the half-million mark, a British-American diplomatic
crisis erupted over the American Captain Charles Wilkes's seizure
of the Confederate emissaries James M. Mason and John Slidell
from the Royal Mail steamer *Trent*. The British government regarded the violation of neutral rights under international law as
serious enough to require preparation for war. The Cabinet, headed
by Lord Palmerston, dispatched an ultimatum to Washington de-
manding an official apology for the actions of the United States sloop-
of-war *San Jacinto* and its commander. Her Majesty's Government
also expected the surrender of Mason and Slidell to British custody
within seven days of delivery of this demand by the British minister,
Richard Bickerton Pemell Lyons, Earl Lyons. Meanwhile, the British army embarked 13,730 soldiers, 706 officers, and 207 horses,
along with appropriate weapons and equipment, for Canadian ports
and readied the Home Fleet for war. About forty-three hundred
British troops were already in British North America.[25]

News of official British anger and of popular enthusiasm for war
in London cast a pall over American celebrations of Captain Wilkes's
twisting of the lion's tail. At an emergency meeting of President

Lincoln's cabinet on Christmas Day, the president and Secretary of State William H. Seward resolved that the Unitd States must yield the apology and the prisoners as demanded by Great Britain, though seeking to redeem America's public position by contending that the concession was really a triumph for the "old, honored, and cherished American cause" of freedom of the seas, for which the nation had fought England in 1812.[26]

The *Trent* affair was a dangerous hour in British-Canadian-American relations—but never quite so dangerous as it seemed amidst the emotions of the hour itself. The fourteen thousand troops hastened by Great Britain to Canada as a gesture of force suggest why the danger was not so overwhelming. The reinforced Canadian garrison of eighteen thousand remained dwarfed many times over by the United States Army of 660,000. The Canadian militia had fallen into decay and would have represented a dubious reserve force behind the British regulars. Very obviously, the United States forces were busy on another front as well, against the Confederacy. But the Confederates were never able to enlist more than a total of about eight hundred thousand against the two and a half millions who at one time or another in the war served in the Union armed forces, and the Union never approached a total mobilization of its manpower. It would not have been easy for the United States to fight a two-front war, but it had manpower and resources to spare for the purpose.[27]

Great Britain, in contrast, would by the 1860s have confronted insoluble military problems in a war against the United States. The military prestige that was a primary element in Britain's preeminence as a world power rested largely on the contributions the British army and navy had made to the defeat of Napoleon. But in the decades since 1815 the substance of British military power had perilously melted away. The Royal Navy retained the appearance of maritime supremacy principally because it existed in a naval vacuum, with no serious rivals except for halfhearted and sporadic challenges from the French. At that, the British navy would have had a difficult time making itself felt on the coast of the United States. The coming of steam power had destroyed the ability of its most modern warships to cruise indefinitely in American waters as blockading squadrons had done in 1812. Even with the base at Halifax, or possible aid from Confederate ports, the British navy would have found it a precarious venture to try to keep steamers on station near United States ports. No steam navy would successfully operate against any reasonably formidable enemy at distances from home a transatlantic war would have imposed on the British fleet until the United States Navy fought the Japanese in World War II. The Royal Navy of the 1860s was a hidebound and inefficient service that could not have begun to approximate the American logistical effort of the 1940s, while the Union navy of the 1860s was a formidable adversary near its own coastline even at the end of 1861 and it was growing rapidly stronger.[28]

As for armies, a British newspaper correspondent such as William H. "Bull Run" Russell might sneer at the American volunteers, but the British, their officers' commissions for sale to the competent and incompetent alike, spent the middle years of the nineteenth century demonstrating the ineptitude of their own army in a series of colonial military disasters from Afghanistan to Zululand. In the Crimea, the British had also shown that it was almost impossible for their badly officered and administered army to maintain itself at any distance from the home islands. The British force in the Crimea had shrunk from twenty-six thousand in September 1854 to a bare eleven thousand by the end of January 1855, mostly from disease and other manifestations of logistical mismanagement.[29]

Indeed, the Crimean War had already gone all too far toward revealing that British military power was an illusion and thus toward jeopardizing Britain's very status as a great power. A war with America in the 1860s would have presented the grave peril of destroying the illusion altogether. Bluster though he might, Palmerston knew enough about military realities to sense the risk. It would have been too much to expect the British government to recognize that the foundations of British economic primacy were also tottering, though in retrospect historians can perceive that the rate of growth of the British economy began to slow and Britain's industry began to lose its inventive and progressive energies from about the middle of the nineteenth century onward. The British government did appreciate something of the economic peril latent in a war with the United States, apart from such manifest dangers as a new wave of Yankee raiders preying upon British shipping as in 1812–15.

When not long after the *Trent* affair, Palmerston tried to assert British influence in the Schleswig-Holstein crisis, Bismarck brusquely ignored him, and the British role in the eventual resolution of the crisis turned out to be, humiliatingly, nil.[30] The shrewd statesman Otto von Bismarck had taken an accurate measurement of the power behind British pretensions. Lincoln would have been well advised to do the same. A British military challenge to the United States within North America was no longer in the cards. The peace of the Canadian-American frontier was already assured by America's military unchallengeability.

Further Anglo-American frictions grew out of the Civil War, well after the *Trent* affair, especially those caused by Confederate commerce raiders built in the British Isles and actually or potentially to be released to attack United States shipping. But always the outcome of the difficulties was conditioned by the same essential principle that shaped the *Trent* affair. British statesmen could still bluster imperiously, but Great Britain could no longer afford to fight the United States. Thus was the American Civil War the decisive turning point in the history of British-Canadian-American relations. If Britain could not risk war with the United States even when the American Union was divided, still less could she do so after the restoration of the Union in 1865.[31]

Henceforth, to prevent the British North American provinces from gravitating into the American orbit, only those provinces' own sense of separateness from the Americans together with such American goodwill as might be cultivated could suffice. In the face of unquestionable United States military predominance, the British and Canadians during the 1860s abandoned all pretense of mounting a military challenge to the Americans, turning instead to the resources of Canadian nationalism and the nurturing of American goodwill. The British North America Act stimulated and fortified Canadian nationalism while allaying lingering Canadian discontent with British rule. Enacted in 1867, it gave legislative reality to the concept of dominion status and united the North American provinces into a self-governing confederation. This confederation was intended to see to its own defense, as much as military defense was possible; and in 1869–71 the British army withdrew from Canada. At the same time, the Treaty of Washington of 1871 settled the *Alabama* claims, as well as eliminated other sources of Anglo-American friction left over from the American Civil War, with a British generosity toward the United States that could only signify that cultivating

American goodwill had taken first priority in London's view of Anglo-American relations.[32]

The withdrawal of Britain's legions proceeded notwithstanding the new Dominion of Canada's need to flex at least a modicum of military muscle in dealing with the first Riel Rebellion in 1869–70 as well as with persistent threats of Fenian intrusions from south of the border. The United States' ungenerous attitude toward Canada's use of American locks on the Great Lakes and American railroads in subduing the Riel Rebellion was ominous; if wooing American benevolence was to be the keystone of British-Canadian foreign policy, Canada dared not go far at all in any military activities carrying the slightest semblance of challenge to American predominance. Yet somehow Canada had to maintain law and order among Indians and settlers on the dominion's Far Western frontier in a manner partially analogous to the patrolling of the United States Cavalry below the forty-ninth parallel.[33]

On the heels of the Riel and Fenian troubles, the murder of some Assiniboine Indians by white men—allegedly Americans—in 1873 dramatized this requirement. It has even been stated that Ottawa initially thought to respond by creating Mounted Rifles directly resembling the American cavalry, but that the fear of seeming to challenge the Americans was running so high, Canada turned instead to the North West Mounted Police (N.W.M.P.). Susceptibility to American sensibilities did not operate quite so simply; various internal considerations also shaped the N.W.M.P. Yet it remains significant that Canada felt obliged to create a force deliberately and self-consciously different from the United States Cavalry and deliberately and self-consciously not a military body. South of the border, the cavalry was regarded, along with the rest of the United States Army, primarily as an instrument of the country's international policy; the preoccupation of its most intelligent, conscientious, and dedicated officers was with preparation for foreign war, while constabulary duties were considered distinctly a secondary purpose even if they consumed day-to-day life. In Canada, the priorities were at least the opposite, and there was no doubt that the North West Mounted Police were first and foremost a constabulary.[34]

More than that, except for the N.W.M.P. the Dominion of Canada chose to have no standing army of any consequence. The withdrawal of the legions, the removal of the last of the British garrison from

Canada, was completed when the 60th King's Royal Rifle Corps marched out from the Citadel of Quebec on 11 November 1871. Thereafter Canada relied on a citizens' militia for such military strength as she chose to possess. Only the most minimal of cadres was established for the administration and training of the militia; as late as 1914 the permanent force numbered only about two thousand. The basic military statute, the Militia Act of 1868, divided the citizen-soldiery into two categories. The Reserve Militia consisted of all able-bodied men between the ages of sixteen and sixty, but possessed neither training nor organization nor mobilization plan; it was not even worthy of being called a paper force. The Non-permanent Active Militia had an authorized strength of forty thousand and could claim somewhat greater substance, but not much. When the British army departed there were forty-three thousand officers and men on the rolls of the Active Militia, of whom only thirty-four thousand had participated in prescribed training programs. By the late 1870s, the number of participants in training camps fell off to twenty-three thousand. At best, Canada's Active Militia resembled the volunteer militia companies south of the border, which during the period at hand were evolving into the American National Guard. No one would have mistaken either militia force for the United States Regular Army. Though still small by European standards, the United States Army had by now completed its professionalization not only through the Civil War experience, but through the postwar rise of professional societies and of professional schools on the graduate level beyond West Point.[35]

To be sure, some Canadians deluded themselves that because their militia had performed well in defense of the country against the embryonic United States military forces in the War of 1812, the same could happen again. No well-informed soldier or statesman on either side of the border believed any such thing. After 1871, Canada was for practical purposes without an army. The country deliberately chose to possess only a police force to maintain order along its Indian frontier and no real military force whatever to guard its international frontier. The latter boundary, for decades until the 1860s the scene of troubles and alarums, had grown infinitely more quiet and infinitely more secure. It had done so following the emergence of the unquestionable military preponderance of the United States along the boundary. Wisely, an independent Canada did nothing to challenge the preponderance of the United States Army. Wisely, by dealing with Indian problems through a constabulary rather than a military force, Canada avoided even the semblance of a challenge to the American military.

Not until the Boer War did the Canadian militia begin to rise from impotence. Notwithstanding the stimulus of the Boer War, the Active Militia still enrolled only about forty-five thousand on the eve of World War I.[36] It required the military trials of the British Empire and Commonwealth in the twentieth century to prompt the creation of Canadian armed forces. By that time, however, larger shifts in world politics had assured that Canadian forces would be associates and allies, not rivals, of the American military.

Throughout the years of the rise of United States military predominance in North America, the Americans had remained a sufficiently unmilitary people to be remarkably unselfconscious about the muscle they became able to flex. As late as the Civil War, in fact, President Abraham Lincoln and his administration seem to have exaggerated the military perils if Britain should have intervened. American statesmen boasted of the vastness and resources of their country, but they were generally not inclined to boast about its armed strength. While it was preponderant in North America, the actual, mobilized armed strength of the United States remained minuscule by European standards, except during the brief period of the Civil War. If Americans had been more self-conscious about their military predominance vis-à-vis Canada, they might possibly have been more inclined to wield the power aggressively. The cynical might say that they hardly needed to do so, because the expansion of United States influence through all of North America could rely on economic and cultural, rather than military, means. The less cynical would point out that after the 1783 Treaty of Paris Anglo-American friendship had gradually flowered—enough to prevent a preponderance of military power from turning aggressive.

For the latter reason, caution seems in order as far as generalizations based on the American-British-Canadian military experience are concerned. Geoffrey Blainey has advanced the thesis that imbalances of military power between neighbors and rivals are, contrary to conventional opinion, less likely to issue in war than near-equalities. Wars develop when both sides think they can win.[37] The American-British-Canadian story appears to bear out Blainey's thesis. Nevertheless, too many additional sources of lasting peace among the English-speaking people grew up after 1783 to make the North American military imbalance an altogether satisfactory test of the thesis. At the same time, it remains true that, all qualifications notwithstanding, in North America a preponderance of United States military power did breed peace, not war. Armed strength is not always a source of mischief and destruction. Peacekeeping is sometimes its consequence.

NOTES

1. William Addleman Ganoe, *The History of the United States Army*, rev. ed. (Ashton, Md.: Eric Lundgren, 1964), p. 90; Robert K. Wright, Jr., *The Continental Army, Army Lineage Series* (Washington, D.C.: Center of Military History, United States Army, 1983), pp. 179–82.

2. Worthington, C. Ford et al., eds., *Journals of the Continental Congress, 1774–1789*, 34 vols. (Washington, D.C.: U.S. Government Printing Office, 1904–37), 27:530–31; Wright, *Continental Army*, p. 182; James Ripley Jacobs, *The Beginning of the U.S. Army, 1783–1812* (Princeton: Princeton University Press, 1947), pp. 16–39; Richard H. Kohn, *Eagle and Sword: The Federalists and the Creation of the Military Establishment in America, 1783–1802* (New York: Free Press, 1975), pp. 60–72; William H. Guthman, *March to Massacre: A History of the First Seven Years of the United States Army, 1784–1791* (New York: McGraw-Hill, 1975); Charles P. Stacey, *Canada and the British Army, 1846–1871: A Study in the Practice of Responsible Government*, rev. ed. (Toronto: University of Toronto Press, 1963), p. 10. For Canadian military policy, the latter work includes much background information preceding its opening date; another book offering an overview from the beginning, while focusing on late nineteenth- and twentieth-century military contingency planning, is Richard A. Preston, *The Defense of the Undefended Border* (Montreal: McGill-Queen's University Press, 1977). An overview of most of the period covered by this chapter, written from the Canadian perspective, is John Mackay Hitsman, *Safeguarding Canada, 1763–1871* (Toronto: University of Toronto Press, 1968).

3. Sir John Fortescue, *A History of the British Army* (London: Macmillan & Co., 1899–1930), 9:326–27, quoted in John K. Mahon, *The War of 1812* (Gainesville: University of Florida Press, 1972), p. 15.

4. John Bartlet Brebner, *North Atlantic Triangle: The Interplay of Canada, the United States and Great Britain* (New York: Columbia University Press, 1945), p. 60, including a listing of the Western posts; Gerald M.

Craig, *The United States and Canada* (Cambridge: Harvard University Press, 1965), pp. 99–100; Reginald Horsman, "American Indian Policy in the Old Northwest, 1783–1812," *William and Mary Quarterly* 3d series, 28 (January 1961):35–53. For an overview of diplomatic policy in the early years, see Alfred L. Burt, *The United States, Great Britain, and British North America from the Revlution to the Establishment of Peace after the War of 1812* (New Haven: Yale University Press, 1940).

5. Jacobs, *Beginning of the U.S. Army*, pp. 40–123; Kohn, *Eagle and Sword*, pp. 95–124; Guthman, *March to Massacre*, pp. 173–244.

6. Wayne to Knox, 24 August 1792, in *Anthony Wayne: A Name in Arms: Soldier, Diplomat, Defender of Expansion Westward of a Nation: The Wayne-Knox-Pickering-McHenry Correspondence*, ed. Richard C. Knopf (Pittsburgh: University of Pittsburgh Press, 1960), pp. 71–72. See also, the remainder of this letter, pp. 72–78; Jacobs, *Beginning of the U.S. Army*, pp. 124–68; Kohn, *Eagle and Sword*, pp. 124–27, 142–56.

7. Jacobs, *Beginning of the U.S. Army*, pp. 168–75; Brebner, *North Atlantic Triangle*, p. 76.

8. The standard work remains Samuel Flagg Bemis, *Jay's Treaty: A Study in Commerce and Diplomacy*, rev. ed. (New Haven: Yale University Press, 1962). See also, Jerald A. Combs, *The Jay Treaty: Political Battleground of the Founding Fathers* (Berkeley: University of California Press, 1970).

9. Jacobs, *Beginning of the U.S. Army*, pp. 189–235. See also, the biographies of the morbidly fascinating Wilkinson: Thomas Robson Hay and Morris R. Werner, *The Admirable Trumpeter: A Biography of General James Wilkinson* (Garden City, N.Y.: Doubleday, Doran & Co., 1941); James Ripley Jacobs, *Tarnished Warrior: Major-General James Wilkinson* (New York: Macmillan, 1938); and Royal O. Shreve, *The Finished Scoundrel: General James Wilkinson* (Indianapolis: Bobbs-Merrill Co., 1933).

10. Jacobs, *Beginning of the U.S. Army*, pp. 189–266; Kohn, *Eagle and Sword*, pp. 170–303; U.S. Bureau of the Census with the Cooperation of the Social Science Research Council, *Historical Statistics of the United States, Colonial Times to 1957* (Washington, D.C.: U.S. Government Printing Office, U.S. Department of Commerce, Bureau of the Census, 1960), p. 737, Tables Y 764–66. For a revisionist interpretation of Jefferson's attitude toward the military, holding that Jefferson firmly valued the professionalism of the Regular Army, see Thomas J. Crackel, "Jefferson, Politics, and the Army: An Examination of the Military Peace Establishment Act of 1802," *Journal of the Early Republic* 2 (April 1972):21–38.

11. *Historical Statistics of the United States*, p. 737, Tables Y764–66; Stacey, *Canada and the British Army*, p. 11.

12. On troop strengths, Mahon, *War of 1812*, p. 384, for the British; for the Americans, Russell F. Weigley, *History of the United States Army*

(New York: Macmillan, 1967), p. 121. On Madison's policy, John C. A. Stagg, "James Madison and the Coercion of Great Britain: Canada, the West Indies, and the War of 1812," *William and Mary Quarterly* 3d series, 38 (January 1981):3–34. On the War of 1812 from Canada's perspective, Morris Zaslow, ed., *The Defended Border: Upper Canada and the War of 1812* (Toronto: Macmillan Canada, 1964); and John Mackay Hitsman, *The Incredible War of 1812: A Military History* (Toronto: University of Toronto Press, 1965).

13. See especially Mahon, *War of 1812*, pp. 165–76, 266–84, 305–16, 354–72.

14. Samuel Flagg Bemis, *John Quincy Adams and the Foundations of American Foreign Policy* (New York: Alfred A. Knopf, 1950), pp. 230–31; James Morton Callahan, "Agreement of 1817: Reduction of Naval Forces upon the American Lakes," *Annual Report of the American Historical Association for the Year 1895* (Washington, D.C.: U.S. Government Printing Office, 1896), pp. 369–92; and idem, *The Neutrality of the American Lakes and Anglo-American Relations* (Baltimore: Johns Hopkins University Press, 1898), pp. 1–199; Stanley L. Falk, "Disarmament on the Great Lakes: Myth or Reality?" United States Naval Institute *Proceedings* 87 (December 1961):69–73; Bradford Perkins, *Castlereagh and Adams: England and the United States, 1812–1823* (Berkeley: University of California Press, 1964), pp. 240–44.

15. On American defenses, Willard B. Robinson, *American Forts: Architectural Form and Function* (Urbana: University of Illinois Press, 1979), pp. 85–89, 123; Emanuel Raymond Lewis, *Seacoast Fortifications of the United States: An Introductory History* (Washington, D.C.: Smithsonian Institution Press, 1970), pp. 37–39, 42–45. On Canadian defenses, Albert B. Corey, "Canadian Border Defense Problems after 1814 to Their Culmination in the 'Forties," *Report* of the Annual Meeting of the Canadian Historical Association Held at Ottawa, 23–24 May 1938 (Toronto: University of Toronto Press, 1938), pp. 110–20; and Stacey, *Canada and the British Army*, pp. 13–25.

16. On the *Caroline* affair and its background, Albert B. Corey, *The Crisis of 1830–1842 in Canadian-American Relations*, Carnegie Endowment Series, The Relations of Canada and the United States (New Haven: Yale University Press, 1941), especially pp. 34–38 for the immediate events of the *Caroline* incident; Howard Jones, "The *Caroline* Affair," *The Historian* 38 (July 1976):485–502; Wilson P. Shortridge, "The Canadian-American Frontier during the Rebellion of 1837–1838," *Canadian Historical Review* 7 (March 1926):13–26; Orrin E. Tiffany, "The Relations of the United States to the Canadian Rebellion of 1837–38," *Buffalo Historical Society Publications* 8 (1905):1–49.

17. Charles Winslow Elliott, *Winfield Scott: The Soldier and the Man* (New York: Macmillan, 1937), passim, and especially pp. 335–40; Corey, *The Crisis of 1830–1842*, pp. 48–49.

18. Elliott, *Winfield Scott*, pp. 334–44; Corey, *The Crisis of 1830–1842*, pp. 62–67.

19. Samuel Flagg Bemis, *A Diplomatic History of the United States*, 3d ed. (New York: Henry Holt & Co., 1950), p. 259.

20. Elliott, *Winfield Scott*, p. 343, from Head to Henry Fox, British Minister at Washington, March 1838, in *Toronto Patriot*, 23 March 1838.

21. Elliott, *Winfield Scott*, pp. 357–66, *The Crisis of 1830–1842*, pp. 114–15, and for the treaty, Chap. 11, "The Webster-Ashburton Treaty," pp. 159–84; Henry S. Burrage, *Maine in the Northeastern Boundary Controversy* (Portland, Me.: Marks Publishing Co., 1919); Howard Jones, "Anglophobia and the Aroostock War," *New England Quarterly* 48 (December 1975):519–39; Thomas LeDuc, "The Maine Frontier and the Northeastern Boundary Controversy," *American Historical Review* 53 (October 1957):30–41. For a comprehensive view of the background, Howard Jones, *To the Webster-Ashburton Treaty: A Study in Anglo-American Relations, 1783–1843* (Chapel Hill: University of North Carolina Press, 1977).

22. John S. Galbraith, *The Hudson's Bay Company as an Imperial Factor, 1821–1869* (Berkeley: University of California Press, 1957); Frederick Merk, *The Oregon Question: Essays in Anglo-American Diplomacy and Politics* (Cambridge, Mass.: Harvard University Press, 1967); Melvin C. Jacobs, *Winning Oregon* (Caldwell, Idaho: Maxton Press, 1938); Joseph Schafer, "The British Attitude toward the Oregon Question, 1815–1846," *American Historical Review* 16 (January 1911):273–99; Lester B. Shippee, *Canadian-American Relations, 1849–1874* (New Haven: Yale University Press, 1939), is a guide to the period following the Oregon controversy.

23. On motives for the Reciprocity Treaty, see Gerald M. Craig, *The United States and Canada* (Cambridge, Mass.: Harvard University Press, 1968), p. 134. I have inferred the military ingredient in the motives.

24. Weigley, *History of the United States Army*, pp. 200, 206; *The War of the Rebellion: A Compilation of the Official Records of the Union and Confederate Armies . . .* , 4 series (Washington, D.C.: U.S. Government Printing Office, 1880–1901), Series Three, 1:380–84, 455–56. Brigadier-General Irwin McDowell made the comment about the French Army; U.S. Congress 37th Cong., 3d Sess., *Report of the Committee on the Conduct of the War*, 4 vols. (Washington, D.C.: U.S. Government Printing Office, 1866), 1:139.

25. For British reinforcements, see Stacey, *Canada and the British Army*, p. 122; and for British troops in America before reinforcement, ibid., p. 118. For a thorough review of almost all aspects of the *Trent* affair, albeit

with emphasis on the role of France in effecting a settlement, see Lynn
M. Case and Warren F. Spencer, *The United States and France: Civil War
Diplomacy* (Philadelphia: University of Pennsylvania Press, 1970), pp. 190–
249.

26. Quotation from Seward from David Donald, *Charles Sumner and
the Rights of Man* (New York: Alfred A. Knopf, 1970), p. 39, no specific
citation given.

27. For total Union and Confederate army strength, see E. B. Long with
Barbara Long, *The Civil War Day by Day: An Almanac, 1861–1865* (Garden
City, N.Y.: Doubleday, 1971), p. 703. My own estimates differ slightly from
the Longs' and are based on my own studies of Civil War history.

28. For a general discussion of the impact of steam power on naval
cruising range and therefore strategy in the middle of the nineteenth century, see Bernard Brodie, *Sea Power in the Machine Age* (Princeton: Princeton University Press, 1941), pp. 90–93, 98–115.

29. Cyril Falls, *A Hundred Years of War, 1850–1950* (New York: Collier
Books, 1962), p. 29, for initial force of twenty-six thousand; Theodore Ropp,
War in the Modern World, rev. ed. (New York: Collier Books, 1962), p.
167, for eleven thousand men by January 1855. From November 1854 to
February 1855, nine thousand British soldiers died, mostly from sickness;
Falls, *A Hundred Years of War*, p. 34. In contrast, the French, Britain's
ally, began with twenty-eight thousand troops in September 1854 (ibid.,
p. 29) and increased their force to seventy-eight thousand by January 1855
(Robb, *War in the Modern World*, p. 167).

30. For a brief account, see Arthur J. P. Taylor, *The Struggle for Mastery
in Europe, 1848–1918* (Oxford: Clarendon Press, 1954), pp. 146–50.

31. For an overview, see Robin W. Winks, *Canada and the United States:
The Civil War Years* (Baltimore: John Hopkins Press, 1960).

32. For the movement toward creating the Dominion of Canada, see
especially William L. Morton, *The Critical Year: The Union of British North
America, 1857–1873* (Toronto: McClelland & Stewart, 1964); and Peter B.
Waite, *The Life and Times of Confederation, 1864–1867* (Toronto: University of Toronto Press, 1962). The military aspects are considered, in
addition to military histories of Canada previously cited, in Richard A.
Preston, *Canada and "Imperial Defense": A Study of the Origins of the
British Commonwealth's Defense Organization, 1867–1919* (Durham, N.C.:
Duke University Press, 1967); and Donald C. Gordon, *The Dominion Partnership in Imperial Defense, 1870–1917* (Baltimore: Johns Hopkins University Press, 1965).

33. On the Riel Rebellions, see George F. G. Stanley, *Louis Riel* (To-
ronto: University of Toronto Press, 1963); and idem, *The Birth of Western
Canada: A History of the Riel Rebellions*, rev. ed. (Toronto: University of
Toronto Press, 1961).

34. The histories of the North West Mounted Police are disappointing, except for Roderick C. MacLeon, *The North-West Mounted Police, 1873–1905* (Toronto: University of Toronto Press, 1976). Others are Ronald Atken, *Maintain the Right: The Early History of the North West Mounted Police, 1873–1900* (Toronto: Macmillan Canada, 1973); and the old standard, John P. Turner, *The North West Mounted Police*, 2 vols. (Ottawa: King's Printer, 1950). Some worthwhile essays appear in Hugh A. Dempsey, ed., *Men in Scarlet* (Calgary: Historical Society of Alberta and McClelland & Stewart West, 1974). A superb comparison of the North West Mounted Police and the United States Cavalry, with comments on the internal Canadian factors that led to the choice of a constabulary rather than a military force, is Desmond Morton, "Comparison of U.S./Canadian Military Experience on the Frontier," in *The American Military on the Frontier: The Proceedings of the 7th Military History Symposium United States Air Force Academy 20 September–1 October 1976*, ed. James P. Tate (Washington, D.C.: Office of Air Force History, Headquarters USAF and United States Air Force Academy, 1978), pp. 17–35. See also, Samuel W. Horill, "Sir John A. Macdonald and the Mounted Police Force for the Northwest Territories," *Canadian Historical Review* 53 (June 1972):179–99; Charles P. Stacey, "The Military Aspect of Canada's Winning of the West, 1870–1885," *Canadian Historical Review* 21 (March 1940):1–24.

35. Gordon, *Dominion Partnership*, pp. 41–42; Desmond Morton, *Ministers and Generals: Politics and the Canadian Militia, 1865–1904* (Toronto: University of Toronto Press, 1970); George F. G. Stanley in collaboration with Harold M. Jackson, *Canada's Soldiers: The Military History of an Unmilitary People*, rev. ed. (Toronto: Macmillan of Canada, 1954). Emphasizing more recent Canadian military history is Desmond Morton, *Canada and War* (Toronto: Butterworth, 1981). For further readings, see Oliver A. Cooke, comp., *The Canadian Military Experience, 1867–1967: A Bibliography/Bibliographie de la vie militaire au Canada, 1867–1967* (Ottawa: Department of National Defence, Directorate of History, 1979).

36. *Encyclopaedia Britannica*, 11th ed., s.v. "Canada," by George Robert Parkin. By that time there were an additional five thousand in the permanent military force; ibid.

37. Geoffrey Blainey, *The Cause of War* (New York: Free Press, 1973).

7 MICHAEL A. LUTZKER

The Precarious Peace: China, the United States, and the Quemoy-Matsu Crisis, 1954–1955, 1958

As we reflect on the past two centuries of our national history, we find a mixed legacy of armed conflict as well as the pursuit of peace. Historians have engaged in spirited debates over the causes and consequences of our several wars; less attention, however, has been accorded to systematic analyses of wars that *might* have occurred, but did not.

In future crises the United States is likely to confront, it would be useful to draw upon the lessons of wars we have *avoided* as well as those we have fought. What issues brought us and other nations to the brink of hostilities; and what considerations have caused one or both to draw back? There are enough such instances in recent years to warrant careful analysis. Anyone who remembers the thirteen harrowing days of the Cuban Missile Crisis will recognize how high the stakes are when major powers confront each other in the nuclear age. The delicate decisions that must be made, frequently under great stress, are worthy of intensive examination, particularly as we ponder the world's current trouble spots. If any of our present disputes becomes critical, and if a single one beomes uncontrollable to the point where nuclear weapons are used, we may not be around to analyze what went wrong. Thus we are well advised to study the crucial factors operating in crisis situations *beforehand*, while trusting that policymakers will take some account of our research.

Two such crises were the near-war between the United States and Communist China in 1954–55 and again in 1958. This case study is a particularly interesting one. The former crisis was checked without resort to armed conflict, only to have substantially identical conditions bring both sides to the brink again three years later. We can all agree that it is difficult for nations to resolve disputes under the immediate stress of crisis; but we might ask why diplomacy was so ineffective in the intervening three years. To answer that question we might consider the earlier confrontation and, in particular, the way in which each antagonist perceived the outcome.

One testament to the nonviolent result of the confrontation between the United States and China is that few Americans have any but a vague memory of Quemoy and Matsu. The two Quemoys lie about two miles off the Chinese mainland, just outside the port of Amoy. The Matsu group is located about ten miles from the port of Foochow. By contrast, Formosa (Taiwan) is approximately one hundred miles from China and the Pescadores, islands in the Formosa Straits, are about sixty miles from the mainland. All these territories were occupied by Chiang Kai-shek's Nationalist forces as they retreated from the mainland following the victory of Mao Tsetung and the Communist-led revolution in 1949.[1]

Where one chooses to begin discussing the chain of events that brought the United States and China to the brink of war constitutes a form of interpretation. For instance, President Dwight D. Eisenhower's memoirs open the account with the Chinese Communist bombardment of Quemoy on 3 September 1954, clearly portraying the Chinese as disrupters of a relatively peaceful status quo.[2] Chiang's forces, however, had used the islands for conducting commando raids on the mainland and harassing and sinking Chinese Communist ships. To Mao, of course, the Quemoy bombardment was one more chapter of civil war with the Nationalists, waged with greater or lesser intensity for twenty years.[3]

The crisis assumed worldwide significance less from the Communist threat to capture the offshore islands than from the U.S. involvement on the side of Chiang; thus it is the roots of the *American* commitment that require exploration.

Following the postwar collapse of National resistance to Mao's forces and Chiang's retreat from the mainland in 1949, President Harry S. Truman seemed to have accepted the verdict of battle. In a statement issued 5 January 1950, he announced that the United States would not interfere in that ongoing civil war. This hands-off policy underwent a sharp shift with the North Korean attack on South Korea in June 1950. When Truman ordered American forces to Korea, he accepted Secretary of State Dean Acheson's recommendation that the U.S. Seventh Fleet be interposed between the Chinese mainland and Formosa, effectively renewing American involvement in the Chinese civil war. Once Mao's troops entered the Korean conflict, Chiang was increasingly sought by the United States as an ally.[4] In 1952, after the Korean fighting had dragged on for two years, the Republican Party promised a "forward" policy stressing liberation from communism, not merely its containment. The campaign rhetoric helped create expectations that would later bedevil the newly elected preisident, Dwight Eisenhower.

The Republican administration's decision to "unleash Chiang" (while continuing U.S. protection of Formosa) was hardly cause for immediate alarm in Peking, but it presaged a new buildup of Chiang's forces. In July 1953 a truce was finally agreed upon in Korea. Though it was a major achievement of the Eisenhower administration to bring an end to the frustrating, stalemated bloodletting between Americans and Chinese, the truce left in its wake a legacy of bitterness between the two nations.[5]

During the spring of 1954, American leaders faced a dilemma. They had vowed to roll back communism, yet in Indochina the French military position against the Communist-led Vietminh had deteriorated to the point of near collapse. After considerable agonizing, Eisenhower overruled those advisors who favored direct U.S. military intervention; but this decision reinforced his determination that no other territory be lost.[6]

In late July 1954, South Korea's President Syngman Rhee visited the United States and in an address to a joint session of Congress called for an invasion of the Chinese mainland by a two million-man Asian army made up of Koreans and Nationalist Chinese, with the support of U.S. naval and air forces. He conceded that such an action might lead to intervention by Soviet forces, a contingency that did not deter him. Rather, he viewed their involvement as justifying bombing the Russian centers of production before their hydrogen bombs could be produced in quantity.[7] Many members of Congress were unhappy with the speech, but declined to say so publicly.[8] One wonders at the limits of hospitality. The lack of congressional response must have puzzled the Chinese. President Eisenhower tried to smooth things over, noting that the two countries had occasional differences over the "methods and means." Such words could hardly have been reassuring to Peking, which repeatedly denounced U.S. interference in Chinese internal affairs and reiterated its intention of liberating Taiwan from the grip of Chiang.[9]

In early September 1954, as shells began falling on the Nationalist forces holding Quemoy, Eisenhower and his top advisors met to assess the situation. The Joint Chiefs of Staff, headed by Admiral Arthur Radford, had recommended that the offshore islands be defended by the United States, not, curiously, because they were essential to the defense of Formosa (the Chiefs said they were not), but because their loss would be a severe psychological blow to the Chiang regime. Only General Matthew B. Ridgeway dissented. They all agreed, however, that if the Chinese Communists attacked, the islands could not be held without direct American assistance, which meant U.S. bombing of the mainland.[10] But the president held the view that if America became militarily involved, the conflict could not be confined to Quemoy.

We're not talking about a limited brush-fire war. We're talking about going to the threshold of World War III. If we attack China, we're not going to impose limits on our military actions as in Korea. Moreover . . . if we get into a general war, the logical enemy will be Russia, not China, and we'll have to strike there.[11]

Secretary of State John Foster Dulles cautiously suggested that the issue be taken to the United Nations Security Council in an effort to get a cease-fire. At this point Eisenhower chose to reject the prospect of U.S. military involvement and instead sought to gain a diplomatic advantage at the United Nations.[12]

Tension increased in late November when the Chinese announced that thirteen Americans shot down over Korea near the end of that conflict had been convicted of espionage and sentenced to long prison terms. Senator William Knowland, Republican majority leader, called for a blockade of the China coast. Eisenhower opposed such a move.[13]

The signing of a bilateral defense agreement between Washington and Taipei, in December 1954, mollified supporters of the Nationalists in the United States. Given Chiang's numerous announcements of an imminent attack on the mainland, Peking was inclined to view the treaty as an endorsement of those aims and, consequently, a threat to her security. Though Dulles sought to portray the treaty as defensive, the parties chose to keep secret for more than a month an exchange of letters specifying that the Nationalists would not use force against the mainland without U.S. concurrence. Meanwhile, the Soviets issued a statement voicing "full support" for their Chinese ally.[14]

In January 1955 the crisis intensified. Chiang's New Year's message forecast war to liberate the mainland.[15] The Communists responded with raids involving about one hundred planes against the Tachen Islands, which are scattered about two hundred miles north of Formosa. On 18 January Mao's forces quickly seized, from Nationalist irregulars, Yikiang (Ichiang) Island in the Tachens. The island, like the other Tachens farther south, had no relation whatever to the defense of Formosa; but more seizures could have had a serious impact on an administration deeply concerned about Nationalist morale. Thus Eisenhower took a cautionary step. Aware that even Chiang saw little value in holding the Tachens, he ordered the U.S. Navy to assist in their evacuation, while making it clear that a line would be drawn after that point. Once again overruling the Joint Chiefs, who wanted the islands retained, the president sought to repair the psychological damage by rallying the country to the defense of Formosa.[16]

The president's strategy was designed to demonstrate to the Chinese Communists (and perhaps to America's skeptical allies as well) that the administration had the nation's support in backing Chiang. On 24 January he asked Congress for authority to use U.S. forces, if necessary, for the defense of Formosa, the Pescadores, and "related areas." Adroitly worded, the resolution would have allowed Eisenhower to repel an invasion of Quemoy and Matsu if he believed such an attack was a prelude to an assault on Formosa.[17]

The House fell into line in a single day, voting 410–3 for the resolution. In the Senate, some Democrats voiced criticism, with opposition encompassing a wide political spectrum from Wayne Morse, who feared the United States would be dragged into a war with China over the offshore islands, to Russell Long, for whom holding the islands was like "defending the doormat in front of your enemy's home." Estes Kefauver sought an amendment that would have specifically excluded Quemoy and Matsu, but it was roundly defeated 75–11. Following a three-day debate, the Senate passed the Formosa Resolution, giving Eisenhower a clear congressional mandate to use American forces in an area halfway around the world.[18] (With one stroke he had disarmed the criticism that President Truman had encountered late in the Korean War by not having sought congressional approval for intervention in the summer of 1950.) Two weeks later, the Senate reiterated its support for the Nationalists by ratifying the mutual defense treaty 65–6.[19]

It grew increasingly clear that the United States had drawn the line at yielding any further territory. To emphasize the point, Dulles journeyed to Formosa and stated publicly that if an attack on Quemoy and Matsu were viewed as an attack on Formosa, the aggressor would not have immunity in the staging area.[20] On his return from the Far East, the secretary admitted at a private White House meeting that the situation was more serious than he had thought earlier. Dulles stressed the determination of the Chinese Communists to capture Formosa. "If we defend Quemoy and Matsu, we'll have to use atomic weapons. They alone will be effective against mainland airfields." Eisenhower agreed. "Before this problem is solved," Dulles concluded, "I believe there is at least an even chance that the United States will have to go to war."[21]

On 16 March Eisenhower stated at his press conference that, if necessary to repel an attack, he would authorize the use of atomic weapons against strictly military targets, that is, shore batteries or airfields. This warning, the *New York Times*'s James Reston wrote, "sent a shudder through almost every ambassador in the capital and the diplomatic cables were full of it."[22] Earlier, British Foreign Secretary Anthony Eden had called for Nationalist withdrawal from the offshore islands and negotiations by those concerned. Canada's Lester Pearson was more blunt. His country would not fight over Quemoy and Matsu, he stated.[23]

The next dire prophecy, spread across the nation's front pages, began to stir public debate. On 26 March headlines appeared quoting a "high administration official" that a Chinese attack would come by mid-April and that the United States would have to respond. Admiral Robert Carney, chief of Naval Operations, had invited a select group of Washington reporters to a private dinner and given them his own assessment of the crisis. Apparently he sought to prepare the public for the conflict he viewed as imminent. The following day those reporters not so favored by the admiral had identified him as the source of alarm, which prompted some worried senators to ask who was in charge.[24]

Eisenhower tried to calm the situation by authorizing his press secretary to tell reporters that the president "did not believe war was upon us."[25] The widespread sense of impending war remained despite Eisenhower's attempt of reassurance. On 26 March for the first time, some loyal supporters of the president's policies began to voice doubts. Senator Walter George of Georgia, who as chairman of the Foreign Relations Committee had carefully steered the Formosa Resolution through the upper house, told James Reston of his fears. "We are burning daylight," he said, "the darkness is coming on from the Far East." Talk of using atomic weapons deeply distressed the senator, as did the isolation of the United States from its foremost allies.[26] The following week Senators Wayne Morse and Herbert Lehman introduced a resolution excluding the offshore islands from U.S. protection. The vote, however, showed only slightly more support than it had received in January.[27] Though defeated 74–13, the resolution helped prolong the public debate and served as the "extreme" position against which others could show their "moderation" while expressing misgivings over the administration's policy. By early April press comment and voices from the pulpit began to express strong criticism of the idea of fighting a war over Quemoy and Matsu. Senator Alexander Wiley of Wisconsin, a senior Republican, shifted his position, stating that he would favor withdrawal of American protection of the offshore islands provided the Western allies would aid the defense of Formosa.[28]

Meanwhile, a few days earlier Eisenhower had abandoned his personal appeals to Prime Minister Winston Churchill to back U.S. policy and, profoundly disturbed over the choices he faced, directed the State Department to explore every possible action that might offer a peaceful outcome.[29]

A meeting of top State Department officials on 28 March produced wide-ranging discussion. An account of the meeting, recently declassified, is remarkable for revealing a lack of clear policy objectives in a crisis that had persisted for six months—one in which, if attack came, the need to use atomic weapons was widely assumed. Dulles expressed concern that the islands not become a psychological symbol as in the case of Dien Bien Phu. If they came under attack, how could the United States allow them to fall without risking the charge of rewarding aggression on the one hand, or becoming engaged in a much larger war on the other hand? Yet, compelling Chiang to withdraw from the islands risked a psychological blow that could lead to the loss of Formosa by subversion. The discussion clarifies the meaning of this oft-used term. American officials feared that some Nationalist commander might desert Chiang, order his forces to depose the generalissimo, and then proceed to negotiate with the mainland government. Substantial U.S. ground forces, therefore, might have to be stationed on Formosa to deter or, if necessary, fight the army of a rebel commander.

If the communists attacked Quemoy or Matsu, possible responses included a blockade of the China coast, which, it was noted, constituted an act of war, or intensive bombing of China's interior, which raised the possibility of Soviet intervention. At one point Dulles wondered whether Chiang could understand that the use of atomic weapons would "be a poor way to gain the support of the Chinese people for his cause." It was one of the more illuminating comments in the entire discussion. The meeting ended without a clear consensus.[30] Eisenhower could not have been reassured upon reading the account of the discussion.

Sometime between that meeting of 28 March and 5 April, the president reached a decision that the United States should *not* become involved directly in defending the offshore islands. In a strongly worded memo to Dulles, Eisenhower made it clear that he wanted Chiang to convert Quemoy and Matsu to "outposts" for the defense of Formosa. Instead of a "full out" defense of the islands, in the event of a Communist attack, they would be contested only to a point; after inflicting heavy losses on the attackers, the Nationalists should carry out a planned withdrawal. This plan would mean a reduction of the existing troop concentrations on the islands. Thus, no matter what the outcome of an attack on the islands, they would not become symbols that, in Eisenhower's words, threatened the "collapse of the free world position in the region."[31]

Such a proposal, if implemented, would have removed the possibility of U.S. involvement in a war over the islands without support from its major allies. Indeed, some officials believed such a policy might induce allies to join in guaranteeing Formosa. But, as Eisenhower was well aware, his proposal would checkmate Chiang's strategy of gaining U.S. military support for a war against the mainland. Therefore, the problem was by what combination of the carrot and stick the generalissimo could be made to agree.

To palliate Chiang the president was prepared to assure him of additional military assistance. Moreover, all changes in military planning would be made at Taipei's initiative, to avoid any suggestion of U.S. coercion. However, in one of the most puzzling moves of the entire crisis, Eisenhower chose two of Chiang's strongest partisans, Admiral Radford and Assistant Secretary of State for Far Eastern Affairs Walter Robertson, to persuade him. Since both believed the United States should help the Nationalists in every possible way to bring down the Communist regime, it is not surprising that their mission failed.[32] In the meantime, other developments dramatically changed the situation.

The Peking government had been rethinking its position, perhaps in response to threats of atomic war or in preparation for the first conference of Asian and African nations scheduled for Bandung, Indonesia. Convened at the invitation of the major Asian neutrals, the conference drew leaders of twenty-nine nations encompasssing 1.6 billion people. Premier Chou En-lai made a bid for leadership of the emerging nations with a skillful address that emphasized their common colonial heritage.

Toward the end of the conference, the Chinese delegation issued a statement whose conciliatory tone, coming after months of threats over the Formosa Straits, made headlines everywhere.

The Chinese people are friendly to the American people. The Chinese people do not want to have a war with the United States of America. The Chinese government is willing to sit down and enter into negotiations with the United States government to discuss the question of relaxing tensions in the Far East and especially the question of relaxing tension in the Taiwan area.[33]

The State Department's initial response suggests how out of touch the administration was with world opinion. It insisted that Nationalist China must participate as an equal in all discussions. The *London Times* commented: "Most unfortunately, Washington's brusque reply to Mr. Chou En-Lai's fair seeming offer is likely to supply the final touch to China's brilliantly successful wooing of Asian opinion."[34]

Under increasing pressure from its allies as well as domestic critics, the administration reversed its position: talks at the ambassadorial level were scheduled for Geneva on 25 July. Chou's offer considerably reduced the sense of immediate crisis. The Chinese had made it clear that, however fixed their long-term goals might be, in the short run they had changed their policy. By mid-May there was an informal cease-fire in the Straits.

The immediate threat of war had dissolved, and the crisis soon disappeared from the front pages. Although all the issues that produced the tension awaited resolution, negotiating them privately while the guns were stilled and the invective diminished should have held promise. Even if the talks became deadlocked, Eisenhower's outpost strategy offered the possibility of U.S. disengagement.

The resolution of issues would depend, in large measure, on the way in which each side interpreted the crisis. In his memoirs Eisenhower recounts how his administration had steered a course

with watchfulness and determination, through narrow and dangerous waters between appeasement and global war . . . we refused to retreat, and the enemy, true to his formula, for a while tried harrassment but refused to attack. The crisis had cooled; it would not heat up again for three years. The hard way is to have the courage to be patient.[35]

What the president did not say is that had he been willing to implement his own outpost plan, it is unlikely that the United States and China would have teetered on the brink three years later.

From 1955 to 1957 the U.S. and Chinese ambassadors at Geneva held informal talks without making any substantive progress to resolve the issues that divided them. When the American ambassador was transferred and not replaced, the talks were suspended.[36] Meanwhile Chiang had continued to increase his forces on the offshore islands until they totaled nearly one hundred thousand by the summer of 1958. In late August the Communists began a massive bombardment of Quemoy. The storm had arrived and was no surprise to the barometer.

The act that may have contributed most to raising tension in the Straits came from the United States. One year earlier, in May 1957, a page-one story in the *New York Times* announced that atomic missile units with a range of six hundred miles were being emplaced on Formosa. A statement by the Defense Department that the missiles were "adding to rather than creating a new 'atomic punch' " for the United States could hardly have been reassuring to the Chinese.[37] We now have some perspective on that event. Since the episode of Soviet missiles ninety miles off the U.S. mainland in 1962, Americans have a better understanding of how Peking probably viewed those weapons one hundred miles from its shores.

In the year that passed between the missile announcement and the bombardment of Quemoy, Formosa newspapers carried stories of military exercises involving Nationalist and U.S. forces, inspection tours by high-ranking American military leaders, reconnaissance overflights of the mainland, and clashes near the offshore islands. The Communists, for their part, tried to harass Nationalist forces during their buildup on Quemoy and Matsu.[38]

On 3 May 1958, the American press carried accounts of the test firing of the U.S. missiles on Formosa.[39] In early July, Taipei newspapers reported that the head of the U.S.-Taiwan Defense Command had told an audience of Nationalist naval officers:

The task you bear of counter-attacking the mainland is absolutely certain to succeed—there is no need to have the slightest doubt—because your training has reached the highest standards. Add to that your admirable spirit and awesome determination—these are conditions for the success of [Nationalist] China's new navy.

A State Department publication of August cited signs of "dissatisfaction and unrest" to support the view that "communism's rule in China is not permanent and that it will one day pass."[40]

Notwithstanding the threats directed against the mainland, U.S. intelligence reports indicate that not until July 1958 did a significant increase occur in the level of Communist military activity opposite the offshore islands. The Peking government had been deeply involved in domestic issues surrounding the "Great Leap Forward" in economic production.[41]

Once the Quemoy bombardment was underway, small-craft naval clashes took place off the coast as the Communists sought to blockade the island. Meanwhile, the U.S. Seventh Fleet patrolled nearby. The U.S. destroyer *Hopewell* observed the sinking of some Nationalist landing boats and radioed for instructions. The *Hopewell* was ordered to aid the damaged vessels, but not to fire unless fired upon. The Communist torpedo boats circled the *Hopewell*, but then departed. Following this incident U.S. warships were authorized to "drive off or destroy surface craft firing on friendly [i.e., Nationalist] ships in international waters." This was a new departure, for it meant that U.S. ships could become directly involved in the fighting even in the absence of a full-scale attack on Quemoy.[42]

A small-scale landing on one of the tiny islands in the Quemoy group was repulsed. Meanwhile, Chinese bombers struck the beaches of Quemoy. In just a few days following the Quemoy artillery bombardment, the situation had assumed grave proportions.

On 25 August Eisenhower personally authorized new orders to the Pacific Defense Command alerting them for possible use of not only conventional weapons, but also atomic weapons in case of an attack on the offshore islands.[43] The Seventh Fleet was to be reinforced with two additional aircraft carriers, one from the Mediterranean, the other from Hawaii. These naval moves, which would surely be monitored by the Russians, were designed to signal the seriousness of U.S. intentions. The augmented Seventh Fleet, with its nuclear capabilities, would constitute the mightiest armada ever assembled.[44] The president also ordered that the Nationalists *not* be informed of U.S. readiness. Even at the height of the crisis, he continued to be almost as concerned about Chiang's adventurism as about Mao's aggressiveness.[45]

It should be emphasized that no American leader seriously expected a direct attack on Formosa even if Quemoy were captured. As in 1955, Chinese torpedo boats and junks were hardly a match for the U.S. Navy. Washington's fears continued to center on the psychological blow the loss of the islands would represent to the Chiang regime.[46]

While Eisenhower was alerting American forces, the Communists moved at least three armies into the area opposite the Straits and also augmented their air and naval forces.[47] Meanwhile, the Soviets issued a warning through the authoritative "Observer" byline in

Pravda. They would give China "moral and material aid" and cautioned that any U.S. aggression would only lead to an expansion of the war.[48]

On 3 September a top secret position paper prepared by the secretaries of state and defense, as well as the Joint Chiefs of Staff, was presented to Eisenhower. The president's approval, in the words of historian Tang Tsou, "brought the U.S. to the brink of war."[49] This evaluation succeeded in tying the fate of Quemoy and Matsu to the entire U.S. defense position in the Far East. If the islands fell, the blow would be such as to put Formosa under the threat of falling by subversion. This would

seriously jeopardize the anti-communist barrier consisting of . . . Japan, Republic of Korea, Republic of China, Republic of the Philippines, Thailand and Vietnam. Other governments in Southeast Asia such as those of Indonesia, Malaya, Cambodia, Laos and Burma would probably come under communist influence . . . and Japan with its great industrial potential would probably fall within the Sino-Soviet orbit. These events would not happen all at once but would probably occur over a period of a few years.[50]

Therefore (the report continued), atomic weapons might be used to save the offshore islands despite "a strong popular revulsion against the U.S. in most of the world. It would be particularly intense in Asia and particularly harmful to us in Japan." But there was a silver lining to this cloud. Said the report:

If relatively small detonations were used with only air bursts, so that there would be no appreciable fallout or large civilian casualties, and if the matter were quickly closed, the revulsion might not be long-lived or entail consequences as far reaching and permanent as though there had occurred the series of reversals . . . [described above].[51]

A close reading of this remarkable document, which was private and therefore frankly expressive of its signers' views, shows how far the president had diverged from his 1955 position. The offshore islands *had* become symbols that would have to be defended at all costs regardless of their actual importance. It was a singular triumph for Chiang, for American leaders had apparently accepted the geopolitical analysis long held by their client state and were ready to act upon it.

As tensions rose, domestic opposition to fighting for Quemoy and Matsu encompassed a wider spectrum than in 1954–55. Republican Senators George J. Aiken and John Sherman Cooper gave public voice to their doubts. Leading Democrats Mike Mansfield, Theodore Green, J. William Fulbright, and John Kennedy were publicly critical. Mail to the State Department ran heavily against the administration. There were calls for a special session of Congress if a decision involving U.S. forces had to be made. James Reston commented: "Do we have to fight 600 million Chinese to demonstrate that the Republicans are tougher on Communists than the Democrats?" Walter Lippmann summed up the critics' concerns best, calling American relations with Chiang "a classic example—the most far reaching in our history—of an entangling alliance."[52]

The private comments of administration leaders show them well aware that they lacked public support. Dulles confided to Vice President Nixon that the situation was difficult "because everybody says why fight for Quemoy and Matsu."[53]

Former President Truman rallied to the support of the administration. "The situation in Quemoy and Matsu cannot be isolated into a local issue," he stated. "It is part of a world crisis and should be treated as a major element in a global struggle for survival." But his former secretary of state, Dean Acheson, took the contrary view, arguing that neither the offshore islands nor Formosa was worth a war.[54]

On 6 September, with tension continuing high, Chou En-lai proposed resumption of talks with the United States at the ambassadorial level. Dulles quickly accepted and was hopeful that they would begin without undue delay.[55]

The situation in the Straits made it clear that Peking was not acting out of weakness; its blockade of Quemoy had reduced supplies to the beleaguered garrison by about 80 percent. Discussions among high U.S. officials reflected their concern that Nationalist troops might be completely cut off by the massive artillery fire. Surrender of the embattled forces was a possibility without an actual attack, and Peking's propaganda broadcasts sought to persuade Nationalist soldiers that, in the end, the United States would desert them: their best hope lay in peaceful unification with the mainland.[56]

No less worrisome, particularly to Air Force General Nathan

Twining, was some adventurous act by Chiang such as wholesale bombing of the China coast that would draw in U.S. forces.[57]

By mid-September, U.S. naval craft risked mainland fire while escortng Nationalist supply ships to within three miles of Quemoy. This dangerous maneuver helped penetrate the blockade. When Communist jet fighters rose to interdict the supply ships, Nationalist Sabrejets using U.S.–supplied Sidewinder air-to-air missles exacted a heavy toll and retained command of the air.[58] Throughout this critical period, Peking refrained from sending bombers over the Quemoy beaches to destroy supplies as they were landed. Finally, in one more step in the war of nerves, the United States announced that it was supplying eight-inch howitzers, capable of firing atomic shells, to the Quemoy garrison. Despite the risks being taken by the United States, Chiang continued to take a dim view of the situation and pressed Washington with threats to initiate wholesale bombing of the mainland.[59]

The siege mentality in the White House was evident during the late stages of the crisis. On 29 September Senator Theodore Green, head of the Senate Foreign Relations Committee, sent a private letter to the president expressing his deep concern. He feared the United States risked becoming involved "at the wrong time, in the wrong place, and on issues not of vital concern to our security, and all this without allies, either in fact or in heart." Other critics called publicly for Congress to return and debate the issue of war over the islands.

When the contents of the letter became known, Eisenhower launched an angry attack on the senior Democrat. Said the president, "I deeply deplore the effect upon hostile forces of a statement that if we become engaged in battle, the U.S. would be defeated because of disunity at home." Several prominent newspapers rallied to the president.[60] Dulles complained privately that the senator had come close to treason in his criticism.[61]

In the meantime, however, the secretary of state responded to the critics with a change of emphasis, even offering a public rebuke to Chiang. He stated at his 30 September news conference: "If there were a cease fire in the area which seemed to be reasonably dependable, I think it would be foolish to keep those forces on these islands. We thought it was rather foolish to put them there."[62]

By early October it was becoming increasingly clear that the blockade had been broken. Peking acknowledged this by announcing a one-week cease-fire during which it would allow the Nationalists to ship supplies as long as there was no escort by the U.S. Navy. Thus, tension was substantially reduced.[63]

With the issue removed from the front pages, Dulles, General Maxwell Taylor, and Walter Robertson were dispatched to deal once again with Chiang and, following some very frank negotiations, a joint communique renounced the use of force to regain the mainland. Despite his mighty efforts to embroil the United States in a war on his behalf, Chiang had finally been obliged to acknowledge that direct American involvement in the conflict—which almost certainly meant the use of atomic weapons—was not the way he would win the hearts and minds of his countrymen on the mainland.

Months later, after the tension had receded, U.S. government analysts concluded that American policy had been successful because the administration had stood firm.[64] That interpretation poses grave risks as we face the possibility of future confrontations with major powers. During each of the offshore islands crises, decisions made by the other side—decisions over which we had no control—could have forced the United States into a major war over areas unconnected to the nation's vital interests. Since we cannot assume that in future crises a powerful antagonist will always respond rationally when confronted by the threat of force, the crucial matter is one of determining in each instance whether the nation's survival is truly at stake.

There is no substitute for a searching analysis of the policies that precede a crisis. With regard to the offshore islands, we must endeavor to put ourselves back into the context of the 1950s to appraise fairly the decision-making process. Yet even in that fear-ridden era, many questioned whether the United States had a vital stake in Quemoy and Matsu. There were opportunities for disengagement. In persuading Chiang to evacuate the Tachen Islands, far to the north of Formosa, in January 1955, the United States could have disavowed the importance of the offshore islands. If, simultaneously, President Eisenhower, the popular leader and military expert, had appeared on national television with a map showing the location of Quemoy and Matsu in relation to the mainland and Formosa, he very likely could have dissolved the isssue overnight.

Even the hard-line Joint Chiefs acknowledged that the islands were not militarily necessary for the defense of Formosa, arguing instead that their loss would be a psychological blow to Chiang's regime. Eisenhower accepted this view and tried mightily in 1955 to enlist British support. Harking back to his World War II friendship with Churchill, he made a strong personal appeal, writing of his fears that a collapse of the Nationalist regime would "doom the Philippines and eventually the remainder of the region." He evoked memories of the 1930s, arguing that the Communist sweep since World War II was more relentless than that of the Axis powers. The spectacle of the American president trying to persuade the venerable author of the "iron curtain" speech of the dangers of Communist expansion is an indication of how alarmed Eisenhower was. Perhaps it was his failure to convince Churchill that finally led Eisenhower to conclude in April 1955 that the United States should not be directly involved in defending the offshore islands.

Most intriguing is the question of why no concerted effort was made after the 1955 crisis to compel Chiang's adherence to making the islands outposts rather than risking an all-out defense. Despite the generalissimo's rejection of suggestions that he reduce the Quemoy garrison, his intransigence seemed to be rewarded by increased military and economic aid.[65]

In fact there was more than one way of exerting pressure on the Nationalists. Between 1955 and 1957, U.S. and Chinese ambassadors pursued their informal talks in Geneva. Any hints of progress in these discussions, any minimal agreements on cultural exchanges, would have been a message to Chiang. Instead, it was the generalissimo who seemed particularly adept in hinting at the possibility of a deal with the mainland, a tactic that continued to produce U.S. support.[66]

In the final analysis, the Eisenhower administration was a captive of its own rhetoric. The Republican campaign of 1952 promised more than it could deliver. Under the heading of moving from containment to liberation, it gave new life to the belief in Chiang's power. This myth was a slender reed on which to base a policy. The generalissimo had escaped to Formosa in 1949 with the remnants of a vast army defeated on the mainland. There they joined the poorly disciplined Nationalist troops that had taken over Formosa following the Japanese surrender. The Nationalists soon alienated the indigenous population, so much so that in early 1947 there had been a revolt with reports of nearly ten thousand Formosans killed. After 1949 the ten million native Formosans became the subjects of the two million émigré Chinese. They were given no voice in the government; their leaders remained under the surveillance of Chiang's secret police.[67] This was the government and the army the Chinese people on the mainland were supposed to rally to. It is hardly surprising that Chiang, who had made a career out of exaggerating his power, should make such excessive claims; but the real anomaly is that American diplomats and military men should have given credence to his words. We are, of course, dealing with the State Department of the 1950s, whose ranks of analysts were decimated by the loyalty program and the slanders of Senator Joseph McCarthy.

During the course of each crisis, the danger was real enough. Peking declared its intention of liberating the offshore islands and Formosa as well. The possibility of a quick strike at the offshore islands could not be discounted. Since American leaders had not used the opportunities between 1955 and 1958 to disengage themselves from an admittedly difficult situation, there was little room for maneuver once the Communists began their artillery bombardment in August 1958. Eisenhower admitted privately that he did not like to fight on ground chosen by others and that the United States was at a great disadvantage in the view of world opinion. But in September 1958 he thought the United States had no choice but to take a firm stand.[68]

Crises by their nature are characterized by diminished options, but it remains sobering to read accounts of discussions in which participants virtually assumed that atomic weapons would be used if the Communists attempted a landing. American leaders were aware that these weapons were many times more powerful than the bomb dropped on Hiroshima, yet somehow they seemed capable of convincing themselves that "revulsion might not be long lived," as their statement put it. They also knew that under certain atmospheric and wind conditions, atomic fallout would menace friendly forces on Quemoy and could threaten Formosa itself.[69] Yet the standby orders remained. It was up to Peking to back down.

Some analysts have viewed the decision-making process in psychological as well as political terms. Irving Janis, for example, has emphasized the solidarity of the group and its inability to weigh alternatives if they challenge group norms.[70] What is notable in the discussions over the offshore islands is what may be called the illusion of moderation. Eisenhower, Dulles, and their colleagues believed that they were steering a moderate course between two extremes. They rejected a preemptive attack on the mainland as called for by Chiang. On the other hand, they refused to risk the charge of appeasement by leaving the Nationalists to fend for themselves on the islands. Thus, U.S. leaders could see their actions in each crisis as the middle course. By their perceived moderation they have won the plaudits of some deterrence advocates and, in truth, there was no war. Lest one be tempted to conclude that this represents a vindication of the policy pursued during the crisis, a brief enumeration of the risks involved is in order. There was, for example, the possibility in 1958 that Chinese artillery fire might accidentally (or deliberately) strike a U.S. escort ship as it guided supplies to Quemoy. Communist bombers might have tried to destroy supplies as they were landed on the beaches. If successful, the blockade either would have starved the island or, more likely, necessitated direct U.S. involvement to break it. All these might have occurred without an actual landing on the island. As if there was not risk enough, there remained the possibility that a militant faction would gain ascendancy in the Peking leadership and decide on an all-out assault. Moreover, U.S. warships were authorized to engage Communist naval craft if they sank Nationalist supply ships in international waters, and an incident could have led to a wider war. U.S. planes were permitted to engage in hot pursuit over the mainland if harassed by MIGs, a policy which could have triggered a major air battle. Although Eisenhower was careful to keep the ultimate decision for war in his own hands—and the same was likely true of Mao and Chou in Peking—the possibility of a local commander acting on his own should not be discounted. Finally, there was the distinct possibility that Chiang would make some move of desperation that would draw retaliation and ultimately bring about U.S. involvement. None of these was beyond the realm of possibility: each might have led to a general war and the use of atomic weapons.

One must conclude that America's national interest was not well served by its leaders' policies relating to the Formosa Straits. If vital security had been truly endangered, the Eisenhower administration would have been justified in taking risks. But when its most trusted allies could not be convinced, when the major nations of Asia, the region most directly affected, were out of sympathy, and when skepticism was rife at home—the support from a handful of small Asian client states provided no basis for risking nuclear war.

The 1950s prefigured what subsequent decades were to demonstrate, that the time was passing when the Western powers could decisively influence the course of events in Asia with military force. That this reading of history was not entirely lost on American leaders can be seen from an internal administration document from the 1955 crisis. Writing of the need to avoid direct U.S. involvement in any battle over the offshore islands, the analysis states:

It is . . . of the utmost importance that the issue should not take on the appearance of a struggle between races. . . . It is important that if there is fighting around Taiwan, it should be primarily a fight between the Chinese Nationalists and the Chinese Communists, and not a fight between the "white" Westerners and the "yellow" Chinese.[71]

There is tragedy in the failure to heed this insight. The other Western imperial nations—the British, French, and Dutch—had gradually, painfully recognized their diminshed power in Asia. Even the Soviets seemed to be coming to this realization as the Sino-Soviet rift widened. After a century of Western imperial rule over these proud, ancient civilizations, the Asians were increasingly determined to follow their own path, China differently from India, Indonesia differently from Burma.

But the United States, misreading the outcome of the Quemoy-Matsu crises, continued to believe that client states, backed by American military power, could stem the tide of nationalism in Asia. Americans would—perhaps—finally learn the bitter lesson in the steamy jungles and rice paddies of Vietnam.

NOTES

1. Dwight D. Eisenhower, *Mandate for Change, 1953–1956* (Garden City, N.Y.: Doubleday, 1963), pp. 460–61.

2. Ibid., p. 459.

3. Chi Yung Lin, "The Quemoy Matsu Crisis: A Study of American

Policy" (Ph.D. diss., Southern Illinois University, 1969) (University Microfilms, 1978), p. 2; Stewart Alsop, "The Story Behind Quemoy: How We Drifted Close to War," *Saturday Evening Post*, 13 December 1958, p. 86; O. Edmund Clubb, "Formosa and the Offshore Islands in American Policy, 1950–1955," *Political Science Quarterly* 74 (December 1959): 521–22. Eisenhower said that the guerrilla raids had been discontinued by the summer of 1953; *Mandate for Change*, p. 461. This is open to some question. See Alsop, "The Story Behind Quemoy," p. 87. For an on-the-scene account of the role of the CIA and its cover organization, "Western Enterprises," see the account by Fernand Gigon, "Formose Ou Les Tentations de la Guerre," *Le Monde*, 23–24 January 1955. This is one of a series of six articles on the Formosa crisis.

4. Dean Acheson, *Present at the Creation* (New York: New American Library, 1970), p. 481. Acheson says the purpose of the Seventh Fleet was to quarantine the fighting within Korea, not to encourage its extension. Though this directive is open to criticism, coming as it did at the outbreak of the Korean conflict, in fact it became virtually inevitable once the United States decided to cross the 38th parallel and the Chinese intervened in Korea.

5. Townsend Hoopes, *The Devil and John Foster Dulles* (Boston: Little, Brown, 1973), chaps. 9–10.

6. For a clear account of the Indochina crisis, see Herbert S. Parmet, *Eisenhower and the American Crusades* (New York: Macmillan, 1972), pp. 353–81. But it is puzzling to find how little space Parmet devotes to the offshore islands crisis.

7. *New York Times*, 29 July 1954, pp. 1–2.

8. *The Times* (London), 29–30 July 1954.

9. *New York Times*, 30 July 1954. The day following Rhee's speech, an air battle was fought just off the China coast. A British civilian airliner was shot down off Hainan island by Chinese Communist fighters. Some Americans were aboard the plane. Eleven U.S. Skyraiders from the aircraft carrier *Philippine Sea* were engaged in searching for survivors and were attacked by two Chinese planes, both of which were shot down. The battle took place, Vice Admiral W. K. Phillips said, "14–1/2 miles offshore." The Chinese apologized immediately to the British and denounced the intrusion of the U.S. planes. See *New York Times*, 31 July 1954.

10. J. H. Kalicki, *The Pattern of Sino-American Crises* (New York: Cambridge University Press, 1975), pp. 128–29.

11. Eisenhower, *Mandate*, pp. 463–64.

12. Ibid.; Kalicki, *Pattern*, p. 137.

13. Eisenhower, *Mandate*, p. 465.

14. As Kalicki points out:

Washington tended to consider its commitment [under the treaty] as relatively modest, defensive and constructive in nature. To Peking, however, these moves were very ominous indeed, in view of Dulles' apparent failure to rule out the use of force—while the Dulles-Yeh correspondence was kept secret for a month (*Pattern*, p. 140).

15. Ibid., p. 151.

16. Ibid., p. 142; Leon V. Sigal, "The 'Rational Policy' Model and the Formosa Straits Crises," *International Studies Quarterly* 14 (June 1970):130.

17. Eisenhower, *Mandate*, pp. 466–67. It should be noted that Chiang would agree to implement the evacuation of the Tachens only after passage of the proposed Formosa Resolution and after informal assurance that Quemoy and Matsu would be defended. See Karl Lott Rankin, *China Assignment* (Seattle: University of Washington Press, 1964), pp. 220–21. Two months later it was still a matter of dispute among top State Department officials whether that guarantee was still in force. See "Memorandum of Meeting Held in the Secretary's Office, March 28, 1955," "Top Secret" declassified 2 August 1982. Copy in John Foster Dulles Papers, Princeton University, White House Memoranda Series, Box 2, White House Memoranda, 1955—Formosa Straits.

18. *New York Times*, 24–26 January 1955; Chi Yung Lin, "The Quemoy Matsu Crisis," pp. 236–37. In opposing the resolution on the Senate floor, Senator Wayne Morse said that it authorized preventive war; *Congressional Record*, 101:736ff. Senator Herbert Lehman was one of three senators to vote against the final resolution (Morse and William Langer were the others). An examination of Lehman's constituent mail reflects strong feelings on both sides of the issue. It divides approximately 60 to 40 percent in favor of his vote. Many letters came from outside of New York state as well, some quite lengthy. A number expressed the fear of war. Said one letter: "We are indeed pursuing a dangerous policy. We actually turn the leadership over to the Red Chinese to decide on war or peace." (D. D. Barta to Lehman, 13 March 1955, Lehman Papers, Columbia University, Correspondence Re: Formosa, C66, 24.)

19. Chi Yung Lin, "The Quemoy Matsu Crisis," p. 242. It is noteworthy that while the Democratic National Committee favored defending Formosa, it took a position opposing the Mutual Defense Treaty. Its statement contended that the United States should seek the independence of Formosa based upon the self-determination principle of the United Nations Charter. The treaty had been negotiated without regard to the wishes of the Formosan people. Thus, twenty-five senators abstained on the treaty vote. See Lin, "The Quemoy Matsu Crisis," pp. 286–95.

20. Clubb, "Formosa and the Offshore Islands." Says Clubb of the sit-

uation: "The United States now stood at its closest approach to the brink of war" (p. 256).

21. Eisenhower, *Mandate*, pp. 476–77. In response to Dulles's assessment, the president sent his top aide, Colonel Andrew Goodpaster, to confer with Admiral Felix Stump, commander of the Pacific Fleet. A report came back that the period of greatest danger for an attack on the offshore islands was the period 15–25 March, while the Nationalist buildup proceeded; Eisenhower, *Mandate*, p. 477.

22. Ibid.; *New York Times*, 7 April 1955. Eisenhower may have been seeking to gain time for the Nationalists with this statement and little more than that.

23. Eisenhower, *Mandate*, p. 478. Earlier, a meeting of the British Commonwealth prime ministers had urged that the Nationalists evacuate Quemoy and Matsu along with the Tachen islands. See *Wall Street Journal*, 1 February 1955. *The Economist* (London) commented that public opinion outside the United States would not support military action in the offshore islands. Cited in Chi Yung Lin, "The Quemoy Matsu Crisis," pp. 323ff.

24. *New York Times*, 26–27 March 1955.

25. Eisenhower, *Mandate*, p. 479. Years later in his memoirs Eisenhower calmly recounted the incident; but a truer measure of his feelings at the time was suggested by Hanson Baldwin, the *Times*'s military analyst, who quoted a Pentagon official on the famous Eisenhower temper. The president, the official noted, had very strong views on the service chiefs' advocating their own positions in the press. "Every time [mention of] a guided missile gets in the papers he blows his top." Baldwin wrote that there had been a lot of "guided missiles and parochial service views" in the press recently; *New York Times*, 7 April 1955. See also *New York Times*, 3 April 1955, sec. IV, and 10 April, sec. IV.

26. See account of James Reston's interview with Senator George, *New York Times*, 27 March 1955.

27. For an analysis of rising opposition to defending the offshore islands, see James Reston's analysis, *New York Times*, 7 April 1955; also *Times*'s survey of national public opinion, 3 April 1955, sec. IV. On Senator Wiley's shift, see *New York Times*, 5 April 1955. Chi Yung Lin discusses public opinion in "The Quemoy Matsu Crisis," pp. 283–96. Elsewhere he notes that as both the 1955 and the 1958 crises became prolonged, the opposition in the United States grew.

28. Chi Yung Lin, "The Quemoy Matsu Crisis," pp. 319–21.

29. For Eisenhower's correspondence with Churchill, see *Mandate*, pp. 472–74. His letter to Churchill of 29 March 1955 is in the Eisenhower Papers, Ann Whitman File, DDE Diary Series, Box 6, with a copy in the Dulles Papers, Princeton University. It was "Eyes Only—Top Secret," declassified 15 November 1977.

30. "Memorandum of Meeting," 28 March 1955, declassified 2 August 1982, Dulles Papers, Princeton University.

31. Extracts of Eisenhower's Memo are printed in Appendix P in *Mandate*, pp. 611–12. Portions of it appear in "Draft, Formosa," a position paper dated 8 April 1955, which sought to implement Eisenhower's 5 April memo. A copy is in the John Foster Dulles Papers, White House Memoranda Series, Box 2, Secret, declassified 9 December 1981. See also, Memorandum with comments on the draft by Robert R. Bowie, 9 April, Dulles Papers, White House Memoranda Series, Box 2, Secret, declassified 8 June 1982. These memoranda taken together constitute some of the strongest arguments against U.S. involvement in defending the offshore islands.

32. Stewart Alsop, "The Story Behind Quemoy."

33. Quoted in Tang Tsou, *The Embroilment over Quemoy: Mao, Chiang, and Dulles*, International Study Paper No. 2 (Salt Lake City: University of Utah, Institute of International Studies, 1959), pp. 8–9.

34. Ibid.

35. Eisenhower, *Mandate*, p. 483.

36. Melvin Gurtov, "The Taiwan Straits Crisis Revisited: Politics and Foreign Policy in Chinese Motives," *Modern China* 2 (January 1976):68–70.

37. *New York Times*, 7 May 1958, p. 1. For the range of Matador missiles, see James Baar and William E. Howard, *Spacecraft and Missiles of the World* (New York: Harcourt Brace & World, 1962), pp. 74–75.

38. Gurtov, "The Taiwan Straits Crisis Revisited," pp. 71–73. Gurtov has a listing of reported Nationalist military activity in the Straits from January–July 1958.

39. *New York Times*, 3 May 1958, p. 4.

40. Gurtov, "The Taiwan Straits Crisis Revisited," p. 72.

41. Ibid., p. 74.

42. [Morton Halperin], RAND Corporation Research Memorandum, "The 1958 Taiwan Straits Crisis: A Documented History," December 1966, pp. 158–59. This is an unpublished study, parts of which have been declassified. I am grateful to my colleague McGeorge Bundy for sharing his copy with me.

43. Dwight D. Eisenhower, *Waging Peace* (Garden City, N.Y.: Doubleday, 1965), Appendix O, "Memorandum re Formosa Strait Situation," 4 September 1958, pp. 691–93, item 10. This memo was top secret at the time. For Eisenhower's approval of it, see ibid., p. 295.

44. RAND Research Memorandum, p. 159.

45. Ibid., pp. 112–15.

46. Ibid., pp. 120–21.

47. Ibid., pp. 162–63.

48. Ibid., p. 167. This warning was dated 31 August 1958. As a number of writers have pointed out, the strongest warnings by the Soviets came *after* the crisis had begun to recede. See Gurtov, "The Taiwan Straits Crisis Revisited," pp. 85–86.

49. Tsou, "The Embroilment over Quemoy," p. 19.

50. Top Secret Memo, 4 September 1958, Ann Whitman File, DDE Diary, Box 22, DDE Papers, Eisenhower Library.

51. Eisenhower, *Waging Peace*, pp. 691–93.

52. Marian D. Irish, "Public Opinion and American Foreign Policy: The Quemoy Crisis of 1958," *Political Quarterly* 31 (April–June 1960): 151–62.

53. Dulles's telephone conversation, 25 September 1958, Dulles Papers, Box 9.

54. Irish, "Public Opinion and American Foreign Policy," pp. 152–53.

55. Tsou, "The Embroilment over Quemoy," p. 22.

56. Telephone conversation, Dulles and Christian Herter, 16 September 1958, 12:11 P.M., Dulles Papers, Box 9.

57. Telephone conversations, Dulles and Herter, 16 September 1958, 3:16 P.M., and 18 September, 8:47 P.M. Dulles was also concerned about the danger of "Chiang going off on his own."

58. Eisenhower, *Waging Peace*, pp. 302–3; Tsou, "The Embroilment over Quemoy," p. 22–23.

59. Ibid., p. 23.

60. Irish, "Public Opinion and American Foreign Policy," p. 158.

61. Telephone conversation, Dulles and Nixon, 2 October 1958, Dulles Papers, Box 9.

62. Kalicki, *Pattern*, p. 197.

63. RAND Research Report, pp. 518–32.

64. Ibid., p. 550.

65. Two knowledgeable students of the issue find the explanation in bureaucratic inertia and the many issues the president must cope with in the short run. See Morton H. Halperin and Tang Tsou, "United States Policy toward the Offshore Islands," *Public Policy* 15 (1966):119–38.

66. Tsou, "The Embroilment over Quemoy," pp. 29–30.

67. Chi Yung Lin, "The Quemoy Matsu Crisis," pp. 8–11. See also, "Tyranny in 'Free' Formosa," *The Progressive*, December 1967, pp. 32–35.

68. General Andrew J. Goodpaster, "Memorandum of Conference with The President," 29 September 1958, Eisenhower Papers, declassified 17 November 1971.

69. "Draft, Formosa," 8 April 1955, p. 8, Dulles Papers.

70. Irving L. Janis, *Victims of Groupthink* (Boston: Houghton Mifflin Co., 1972).

71. "Draft, Formosa," 8 April 1955, p. 12, Dulles Papers.

PART IV

Peace through the Obsolescence of War?

Finally, in chapter 8, the noted British military historian John Keegan addresses the future of war—and thus, implicitly, the prospects for peace.

Here he speculates that war may have become obsolescent in our own era of "high-tech" military hardware. He insists that war involves sustained and systematic killing. Tension, conflict, and "cold war" are all forms of peace, and the duty of statesmen is to prevent these from being translated into the battle-killing that is war. Should they fail, he suggests, war itself may nonetheless be aborted because "the emotions and emotional props that are the essential and ultimate impulses of the battlefield" will no longer sustain men in contemporary combat.

8 JOHN KEEGAN

The Evolution of Battle and the Prospects of Peace

The conference that occasioned this chapter was dedicated to peace-making—in a celebration of the peace that brought the War of American Independence to an end—but also an event devoted to the hope that peacemaking may flourish in our own times and in the future. This chapter may seem an anomaly since its subject—battle—is antithetical to peace. It is, nevertheless, an appropriate subject because it is indeed battle rather than anything else that signifies when peace is absent. Although writers have said that peace is a state which can be defined only *relatively*, not absolutely, I suggest they do not mean relative to *war*.

For the state of war only becomes recognizably distinct from the state of peace when people fall to killing each other—and killing each other in a sustained and systematic rather than merely inter-mittent and haphazard way. That seems to me true at a variety of levels. Legally, of course, a state of war may exist between countries without one doing a whit of harm to the other over a period of many years. By diplomatic oversight, for example, the Isle of Man, tech-nically a polity distinct from that of the United Kingdom, was not included among the signatories of the Treaty of Versailles in 1919 and so remained legally at war with Germany throughout the twen-ties and thirties, a situation only regularized by the outbreak of the Second World War in 1939.[1] Needless to say, the oversight made

not a ha'porth of difference to life on the Isle of Man, or inside
Weimar Germany, during the appropriate period.

But even if the governments in Berlin and the city of Douglas,
Isle of Man, had been aware of the legal irregularity, I cannot believe
that they would have been greatly disturbed or would have thought
that the situation needed urgent regularization. Germany had done
the Isle of Man no harm between 1914 and 1918, and the contrary
was also true. In short, there was no *subjective* recognition of hostility between the two countries. And it is such *subjective* recognition
which very largely, in the modern world, distinguishes war from
peace. For if we examine what it is about a "war effort" that truly
differs from the conditions of peace, we can point to really very
little. War calls forth, it is true, an extraordinary upsurge in arms
production. But so, too, does the activity we call an arms race which,
while it disturbs relations between the competing parties, by no
means commits them to war or exposes them to its experience. War
conscripts the manpower of nations to military service; but con-
scription is, in many countries, a normal ingredient of civic duty.
War heightens the economic activity of a country—but heightened
economic activity is something eagerly sought by every state and
regarded by all as a highly desirable condition.[2] War enlarges the
powers which the state exercises over individuals and greatly re-
stricts their liberty—particularly of movement, expenditure, and
expression. But it is an unfortunate fact that those liberties have all
been greatly restricted by governments, even of the democracies,
during the twentieth century, and the restriction has been justified
as the price to be paid for social equalization and domestic order.

When we move from the subjective experience of populations to
the subjective experience of individuals, the differentiation of war
from peace in the modern world becomes even more difficult to
establish. War gets young men into uniform. But of the millions of
Americans and Britons—and Germans and Russians—who wore uniforms during the Second World War, the number who actually
confronted each other across the barrel of a gun was proportionally
quite small. For the majority war meant work rather than fighting—
driving a truck, shifting stores, filing paper, repairing machines—
work no different from that performed in peacetime; and perhaps
for the individual, given an army's understandable desire to avoid

the burden of training men unnecessarily, exactly the same work as performed in peacetime.[3]

An obvious objection to emphasizing the absence of any social abnormality associated with modern war derives from the unusual danger and privation which blockade, shortages, and aerial bombardment bring to civilians. And it is certainly true that the Russian, German, and Japanese populations did suffer greatly in these ways during the Second World War. But we must still enter provisos. The aerial bombardment of Germany and Japan was confined to the cities and was concentrated into comparatively short periods—about six months for Japan and, effectively, about eighteen months for the Germans. The Russian population experienced acute shortages of foodstuffs and necessities during 1941–45, but it would be interesting to attempt an equation of the degree of privation experienced then with that undergone during collectivization of agriculture and crash industrialization in the early thirties.[4] The United States population, of course, was spared aerial attack altogether during 1941–45, a period of enormously enhanced economic activity and unparalleled personal prosperity. In Britain, which was both bombed and blockaded from 1940 to 1944, the population was actually better fed as a whole in those years than it had ever been before. By any measure used—incidences of infant mortality, malnutrition, disease of deprivation, even mental illness—social conditions during the Second World War showed a marked improvement over those prevailing in the twenties and thirties, indeed, in any period of the country's history.[5]

If we are looking, at the subjective level, for what makes war different from peace, therefore, we have to turn from the collective to the individual experience—from merely belonging to a population which is legally at war, to experiencing the thing which in peace has no counterpart—to, that is, the deliberate killing of other human beings in the name of one's own people. But here, again, I must mark an interruption, though this time a cultural rather than a subjective one. War is a cultural activity. I am tempted to say biological rather than cultural, but it does seem that we know of a few cultures in which nothing like warfare exists. Warfare is, apparently, unknown to the Eskimos, and perhaps to a few other human groups whose struggle for existence in an overwhelmingly harsh environ-

ment precludes the luxury of struggle against fellow humans.[6] Elsewhere, even among peoples whom we call primitive in the starkest
sense, warfare is a universal phenomenon. But the warfare of primitives today, where we can still observe it, as in the mountains of
New Guinea, and the warfare of humankind everywhere until perhaps five thousand years ago, is now entirely different from the
warfare we know today. Our wars are marked by a formal opening
and closing of hostilities in time, and, while in progress, by the
search for decision. Our wars have, or are given, a purpose. The
warfare of primitives is, or appears to be, an end in itself.

The typical means of exchanging hostility in primitive war are the
raid and the ambush—forms of fighting in which one antagonist
attacks another without warning, without formality, and without any
result that precludes the possibility of tit-for-tat. Indeed, such means
positively encourage and provoke tit-for-tat, interminably repeated.
Raiding and ambush do occasionally lead to the staging of battles.
But battles between primitives are carefully organized to avoid the
possibility of one side decisively defeating the other. Battles are
rituals, usually fought at extreme missile range, which a death or
even a serious wounding bring immediately to an end.[7]

What happened five thousand years ago to transform primitive
warfare into the purposive business we now call war is deeply ob-
scure. Rising population pressure on territory is the most generally
accepted explanation—and some anthropologists discern a gradual
redistribution of territory among primitives resulting from their
habit of incessant, if unlethal, fighting. But it may equally have been
through the envy of less civilized people for more civilized people's
wealth—particularly irrigated land in the Middle East—or it may
again have been the outcome of a quantum advance in technology
or the harnessing of resources. The invention of the chariot by steppe
peoples on the fringe of the cultivated lands of the Middle East
about 1700 B.C. is one such leap to which historians point; another
is the breeding of horses strong enough to bear a man's weight,
again in the same region about 900 B.C.[8] These resulting chariot
and cavalry revolutions, as they are called, may have encouraged
the transformation of primitive warfare into purposive war simply
through the potentiality for victory and conquest which the two
successively offered.

Frankly, we do not know; and the origins of battle, as opposed to endemic fighting, remains one of the most mysterious of all historical problems—truly mysterious, for, if we could dissect it, we should be a great deal nearer than we are to understanding and so reforming the societies to which we ourselves belong. Let us accept, since we must, that about two hundred generations ago, out of the 120,000 generations through which humanity has lived, our ancestors abandoned sporadic, low-intensity quarreling with weapons and began to kill each other in a deadly and systematic way for stated political purposes.

War, in short, ceased to be primarily a cultural activity and became *primarily* a political activity, of which the principal transaction was the battle. As it happens, the first battle which we can certainly date in time and place in space occurred in the fifteenth century B.C. at Armageddon, near Haifa in modern Israel, between the Pharoah Rameses II and some of his rebellious subjects.[9]

So it is upon battles like Armageddon, and the many thousands which have followed it, that I think students of peace ought to concentrate their study. There are many ways to do so—in terms of the technology which the exigencies of warfare have so strongly stimulated, of the social forms which effective military organization has generated, of the economic and industrial activity to which battle and its threat have so consistently lent urgency. But to do so is to plunge into a field of such complexity and variety that time would defeat us before we had begun to draw even the outlines of a comprehensible pattern. My subject is the *evolution* of battle, and I propose to concentrate upon that area in which battle's evolution has made itself most dramatically and strikingly felt: the consciousness of those who take part directly in battle, rather than stage its happening or live with its results.

I return to the point I made earlier: much in warfare differs little from much of peaceful and normal existence. It is battle which sets the soldier apart from the rest of a population merely engaged in warfare, and so it is the emotions of the soldier which most truthfully reflect the evolutionary process.

What emotions are we discussing? Battle generates many emotions, and it would be foolish to think that some are not pleasurable. Men feel exhilaration on the battlfield, excitement, pride, curiosity, hatred occasionally, and quite commonly boredom. But unquestionably the universal and most intense emotion that human beings feel is fear.[10]

So, "how do men bear fear?" seems to me the most important of all military questions. But it assumes another one: what sort of fear are men asked to bear? Neither, it seems to me, can be asked in the abstract. They have to be related to real time, because fear is the product of a concrete threat and the bearing of fear is to some extent a function of preconditioning, and *both*—the concrete threat and the preconditioning—issue from a particular social and economic context. The concrete threat is offered by weapons, which are the products of a more-or-less developed technology, the preconditioning by a social climate. To be precise rather than vague, let us look at the difference between a medieval and a modern battlefield. The clothyard arrow offered a different threat from that offered by poison gas—both arouse a very proper fear. But while the soldier of the First World War could to some extent prepare himself emotionally and even equip himself to face poison gas, at least after 1915, the medieval warrior could never have done so. He, on the other hand, though rightly anxious about the effect of archery, would at least have been able to judge when and when not archers had him within range, how quickly arrows would arrive, what would provide shelter against them, and the like. A modern soldier, on the other hand, would be likely to react to attack by a clothyard arrow with an acute sense of personal outrage.

Starting with this rather simple idea, I propose another one: the principle of convergence and divergence of civilian and battlefield experience. Roughly what I argue is as follows: if one looks at a medieval battle, say, Agincourt, one sees a number of very horrible things going on, what a modern private soldier would no doubt call "bloody murder"; but, while contemplating this bloody murder and wondering why men expose themselves to it, one has got to remember (a) that bloody murder was a very common ingredient of *civil* life in the medieval world,[11] and (b) that a high proportion of the men on the battlefield, at least among the common soldiery, would have been guilty of bloody murder before joining up and had indeed done so in order to escape civil punishment. Nor should we think of the armored man-at-arms as a peace-loving civilian turned soldier for the duration. Practice for war was, after all, what the well-brought-up child received from his earliest moments of mobility, while make-believe war became in the later middle ages the principal amusement of the aristocracy.[12] It is not indeed too far-fetched to regard a medieval battle as a sort of social occasion, to which the activity of the common soldiery, though often decisive, was tangential—the central activity being the individual duels between the notables of both sides, who often called out to each other by name in order to fix an engagement. Moreover, if the social engagement proved tiresome, or too much of a crush, or threatened to drag on, escape was literally close at hand. Medieval battlefields were tiny and—at Agincourt, for example—many of the mourned knights lost themselves in the surrounding woods immediately after they received the first English arrow strikes. In any case, medieval battles did not drag on. They were alwaays short, a few hours at most; and while the danger during those hours could be intense, it did not acquire that relentless and interminable character which soldiers of the twentieth century were to find so depressing and enervating.[13]

Indeed, once this is said, the drift of my argument will become apparent. Modern war offers danger on a different time scale from medieval war, a very much more protracted one, producing problems of nervous exhaustion and collapse which the medieval soldier did not experience. It also offers danger in an invisible and silent form. The medieval soldier could see and hear the weapons which threatened him—they were indeed scarcely different from the tools of everyday life—and dodge or retreat to avoid their effect, while the modern soldier must live with the fear of being killed or wounded by a projectile he will *not* see or hear. His fears thus become internal, fears of the imagined rather than the perceived; and the courage he must muster is over his nerves rather than his reflexes. This point has been graphically made by a French soldier-writer of the First World War, Galtier-Boissiere: "The soldier of antiquity," he said, "took strength from his courage. If he was braver than the enemy, he would triumph. But what use is courage today? Is it any good to show courage to a Volcano?"[14]

Paradoxically, while the modern soldier is prey to the fear of silent or unheard killing agents, he is also assaulted by noise of an intensity and duration which no medieval soldier experienced or could imagine; almost all modern soldiers testify to the fear-inspiring and depressing effect of battlefield noise.

But despite the much narrower divergence of civil and battlefield experience in earlier times, it would be specious to argue that the medieval soldier bore his fear without difficulty. Indeed, it is apparent that many fought because they had no alternative, because the conditions of the battlefield impelled them into situations where to fight was the only way to save their lives. A medieval battle—to paraphrase Stephen Crane—was like a football scrimmage, and the analogy was exact.[15] Whatever the competition for the post of honor at the front before the battle began, once it began those in front had to fight, like it or not, because those behind held them in place. And here I advance on the first of my universals in explaining how men bear their fear: they are given no alternative; they are compelled or coerced. Compulsion on the medieval battlefield gives way to direct, calculated coercion on the battlefields of the eighteenth and nineteenth centuries, where properly organized armies had the hierarchy of officers and NCOs to prevent the soldiers from running away—the battlefields were still small and rapid escape possible if permitted—by open threat and physical effort, pushing, thumping, and hitting. Nor does coercion disappear as we approach our own times. The danger above ground in the First World War confined soldiers to the trenches, the exits of the trenches were patrolled during battle by specially detailed battle police, and there was no realistic alternative to going forward when ordered to do so.[16] Of the role of coercion or compulsion on the contemporary battlefield, I will speak later.

There are other universals in the bearing of fear; an important one is—or was—the hope of enrichment. Ransom in medieval warfare offered the chance of fortune-making overnight, an almost unique event in a cashless economy; and even as late as the nineteenth century, when the absence of military banks required soldiers to carry their valuables on their bodies, the prospect of loot was a powerful inducement in keeping men close to the point of action.

A third universal in the bearing of fear, I would suggest, is narcosis. Soldiers in battle have traditionally used liquor. They have drunk before battle and during battle and often they have been fighting drunk in battle. In other cultures they have used drugs and, when exposed to drug culture though not from one themselves, they have adopted drugs. The American army's indulgence in drugs in Vietnam ought not, I think, to be seen as evidence of a unique moral breakdown, but as a particular manifestation of a general reaction to military danger.[17]

A fourth universal is a recourse to spiritual consolation. "There are no atheists in foxholes" is not the most elegant exhortation to religious belief, but it has to be remarked how strongly and widespread is the expression of the religious impulse in some form among men threatened by death on the battlefield; it may be only that they seek to repair a friendship or to rationalize their expected death (in terms of some purpose higher than the immediate present) in a letter home; but often the approach of battle does seem to kindle in soldiers a rebirth or strengthening of spiritual belief, experienced as a necessity and not a mere expedient.[18]

The most important universal—though I would want to weigh it against coercion—is, however, my last, and one now generally recognized. It was first proposed in its explicit form by the American army during and after the Second World War and is usually described as "small group loyalty." I will not labor an analysis, because it is well known. What the Americans found is that loyalty in the battlefield is not given in its plenitude by the individual to country, a cause, army, or general, but to his immediate comrades; and it is given, in General S.L.A. Marshall's words, because he fears losing the one thing that he is likely to value more highly than life—his reputation as a man among other men.[19] To appear a coward to one's friends is, in short, the ultimate shame. Regular armies, though practicing coercion, have always recognized this and have always bent their efforts to encouraging small group loyalty, though never more so than today. Indeed, if one wants a definition of what armies are for and what wars are about, the shortest and most popular definition I can give would go something like this: in peace, armies seek to create their own loyalty groups; in war, they seek to destroy the enemy's.[20]

The phenomenon we have been describing is clearly an extraordinary one. What we have seen is an experience which generates the most profound and intense of all known emotions—fear, at times reaching the proportions of terror—produced by an acute divergence between the experience of the battlefield and anything in civil life which anticipates it. The battlefield and civil life are not, of course, entirely separate and distant places, since prevailing technology and social forms connect the one with the other. But *existentially* they are worlds apart. So separated are they existentially that individuals are only sustained in their presense on the battlefield by the operation of extraordinary inducements and sanctions. Narcosis contracts the chemical impulsion to depart. Coercion, perhaps loaded with inducement, impedes involuntary flight. The cultivation of intense personal bonds overcomes the natural instinct to self-protection.

Step by step, and in the face of threats to the safety and sanity of the individual which an ever-more-refined technology of death has come to offer, societies have found means to keep the battlefield populated and to prolong the utilitqy of battle as a political act in the settlement of social disputes. Humanity has shown itself more successful in the management of battle as a form of social and political communication than in almost any other activity.

This sustained and continuing success does not bode well for peace—its making or maintenance—since it is, as I have suggested, by the absence of battle rather than by the mere existence of a legal "state of war" that peace is defined. Is humanity's ingenuity in this field to continue? Will battles go on forever?

Fortunately, there are hopes, I believe, that it will not. The ultimate form of battle to be waged directly by heads of state against each other's territories and populations, the form of battle we denote by the term "central strategic nuclear exchange" seems—we pray and hope—to preclude itself by mutual fear of the consequences. If we are wrong, that is an end of it. But we must proceed as if our hopes and prayers will be realized.

Traditional or conventional war is all too much with us—we have several in progress in the world today, for example, between Iraq and Iran, approaching in lethality anything seen since the Second World War. But here, too, I believe there are grounds for hoping that the phenomenon is in decline—certainly as it might effect what we call the first and second as opposed to third worlds. For today's warfare, while suffered almost exclusively by the third world, is fought with weapons produced in the others. And while the wars of the third world are small and intermittent enough to be fueled by the dribs and drabs of our military production, a war between the industrialized powers, even if fought only with conventional weapons, would be likely to exhaust their arsenals long before it would have achieved any point worth fighting for. This hope was held out before, in a slightly different form, by Norman Angell before the Great War of 1914–18.[21] Angell's depressing disproof of optimistic forecasts to the contrary, I believe that the extraordinary inflation of weapon costs, which precludes any chance of accumulating stocks sufficient to sustain a long war beforehand, allied with production lead times which prevent output keeping pace with the phenomenal rate at which equipment is now mutually consumed in battle, makes the prospect of conventional war unlikely, for a combination of financial and economic factors.

But the best prospects for peace lie, I believe, neither in deterrence, nor in the probability of rapid economic exhaustion, but in those factors I have most emphasized—the emotions and emotional props that are the essential and ultimate impulses of the battlefield.

Man is a resilient and adaptive creature. Five thousand years ago he taught himself to do that against which his nature rebelled—to confront his enemy face-to-face, rather than fall upon him by stealth and surprise, and fight for a decision to the finish. Somehow he has found the means to suppress the fears which this discovery of a new social form brought with it. Now, I suspect, he has reached the point where the emotional props he contrives are no longer equal to the experience he can create. He has made battle more than flesh and blood can bear and will break himself if he persists in the struggle against his own nature.

Such a suggestion may sound unrealistic and overoptimistic. But what has been learned may be unlearned. Forms of behavior found useful in one age may be abandoned in another if their usefulness is lost. With one minor exception, in 1812–14, the British and American peoples decided after the Peace of Paris that nothing in their relationship—and it has abounded in differences—might be usefully served by going to the battlefield. The example they have given is a hope to the world.

NOTES

1. R. H. Kinvig, *The Isle of Man* (Liverpool: Liverpool University Press, 1977), pp. 166–69.

2. Alan Milward, *War, Economy and Society, 1939–45* (Berkeley: University of California Press, 1977), pp. 2–6.

3. John D. Millett, *The Organization and the Role of the Army Service Forces* (Washington, D.C.: Office of the Chief of Military History, Department of the Army, 1954), p. 160. By 1943 the combat arms had declined in strength from 52.4 percent (1941) to 32.8 percent, while service troops then represented 36.5 percent of the Army (including the Army Air Force).

4. See Harrison Salisbury, *The Siege of Leningrad* (London: Secker & Warburg, 1969), pp. 515–16; Robert Conquest, ed., *Agricultural Workers in the USSR* (London: Bodley Head, 1968), pp. 28–29. Between eight hundred thousand and one million civilian Leningraders died in the siege of 1941–44; by comparison, the population of the Ukraine, a focus of collectivization, declined from thirty-one to twenty-eight million, from 1926 to 1939.

5. Richard M. Titmuss, *Problems of Social Policy* (London: H.M. Stationery Office, 1950), p. 531, especially. This work is in the British official history series.

6. Ritchie Calder, *Men against the Frozen North* (London: Allen & Unwin, 1957), pp. 247–59.

7. W. T. Divale, *Warfare in Primitive Societies*, rev. ed. (Santa Barbara, Calif.: ABC-Clio, 1973), pp. xxi–xxii.

8. William H. McNeill, *The Pursuit of Power* (Oxford: Blackwell Publishers, 1983), pp. 10–20.

9. P. H. Newby, *Warrior Pharoahs* (London: Faber & Faber, 1980), p. 23.

10. S. L. A. Marshall, *Men against Fire* (New York: William Morrow, 1947), pp. 145–50, especially.

11. J. B. Given, *Society and Homicide in Thirteenth Century England* (Stanford, Calif.: Stanford University Press, 1977), ch. 2, particularly. In the mid-thirteenth century, homicide rates in English countries varied between 4 and 147 per 100,000 population; in England in 1959 the rate was 0.4 per 100,000.

12. M. H. Keen, *Chivalry* (New Haven: Yale University Press, 1984), pp. 83–101.

13. John Keegan, *The Face of Battle* (New York: Viking, 1976), pp. 302–4.

14. J. Galtier-Boissiere, *Un hiver à Souchez* (Paris: Berger-Serrault, 1917).

15. Stephen Crane in *Dictionary of Military and Naval Quotations*, ed. Robert Debs Heinl (Annapolis: U.S. Naval Institute Press, 1966), p. 348.

16. John Ellis, *Eye-Deep in Hell* (Breckenham, Kent: Croom Helm, 1976), ch. 7, passim.

17. Guenter Lewy, *America in Vietnam* (New York: Oxford University Press, 1978), p. 154.

18. Alan Wilkinson, *The Church of England and the First World War* (London: Society for the Promotion of Christian Knowledge, 1978), particularly the introduction.

19. Marshall, *Men against Fire*, p. 153.

20. Josephine Klein, *The Study of Groups* (London: Routledge & Paul, 1956).

21. Norman Angell, *The Great Illusion* (London: Heinemann, 1911).

Bibliographical Essay

An examination of the authors' endnotes will reveal the sources on which they relied most heavily in writing these original essays. Here we discuss those secondary sources most significant in shaping the authors' views, as well as other secondary accounts that, though not cited in the essays themselves, readers should consult if they wish to pursue the subject matter further.

Only recently have historians explored the role of women in the revolutionary era. Besides her chapter in this volume, readers should begin with Linda K. Kerber's *Women of the Republic: Intellect and Ideology in Revolutionary America* (Chapel Hill: University of North Carolina Press, 1980; paperback edition, New York: W. W. Norton, 1986), especially chapters 2 and 3, for an analysis of the relationship of women to the new political order ushered in by the American Revolution. Also essential reading is Mary Beth Norton, *Liberty's Daughters: The Revolutionary Experience of American Women* (Boston: Little, Brown, and Co., 1980). Lawrence D. Cress, *Citizens in Arms: The Army and the Militia in American Society in the War of 1812* (Chapel Hill: University of North Carolina Press, 1982), includes an evaluation of the relationship of military service to the rights of citizenship in the early republic. An indispensable history of the conceptualization of citizenship, which pays some attention to the distinctive position held by women, is James

H. Kettner, *The Development of American Citizenship, 1608–1870* (Chapel Hill: University of North Carolina Press, 1978), especially chapters 6 to 8. An influential book, J. G. A. Pocock, *The Machiavellian Moment: Florentine Political Thought and the Atlantic Republican Tradition* (Princeton: Princeton University Press, 1975), includes a sensitive discussion of the traditional relationship between military service and civic identity.

Barton C. Hacker's "Women and Military Institutions in Early Modern Europe: A Reconnaissance," *Signs: A Journal of Women in Culture and Society* 6 (1981): 643–71, is a pioneering review of women's participation in armies from the Renaissance to the French Revolution. Though outdated in many respects, Waldo Emerson Waltz's *The Nationality of Married Women: A Study of Domestic Policies and International Legislation* (Urbana: University of Illinois Press, 1937), especially chapter 2, contains a useful summary of early U.S. laws.

Readers of David F. Musto's essay will wish to consult other psychological analyses of revolutionary and post-revolutionary America. These include C. G. Burrows and M. Wallace, "The American Revolution: The Ideology and Psychology of National Liberation," *Perspectives in American History* 6 (1974): 167–306, where the American Revolution is considered as a stage in the evolution of a parent-child relationship that Americans accepted until about 1760 and then angrily resented; and Steve R. Pieczenik, "Some Psychological Consequences of International Dependency," *American Journal of Psychiatry* 132 (1975): 428–43, a creative application of psychological principles to the relationships between nations written by a psychiatrist also trained as a political scientist. Musto has earlier inquired into the psychological impact on the Adams family of revolutionary and republican imagery in "The Adams Family," *Proceedings of the Massachusetts Historical Society* 93 (1981): 40–58. An intriguing and plausible attempt to explore the relationship between Thomas Paine's personality and his role in catalyzing American hostility toward George III appears in Winthrop D. Jordan, "Thomas Paine and the Killing of the King, 1776," *Journal of American History* 60 (1973): 294–308.

Essential for a grounding in the period of Musto's chapter is Bernard A. Bailyn, ed., *Pamphlets of the American Revolution, 1750–1776*, vol. 1 (Cambridge: Harvard University Press, 1965).

The introduction to this work provides a discussion of the gradual development of a mutual suspicion between the Americans and the British; ultimately, neither could trust the intentions or promises of the other. Bailyn's *The Ordeal of Thomas Hutchinson* (Cambridge: Harvard University Press, 1974) is a modern account of Governor Hutchinson's life and actions: the author emphasizes the gross distortions about Hutchinson that were so important in sustaining the American revolutionists' belief in British perfidy and corruption. Philip Greven, Jr., *Four Generations: Population, Land, and Family in Colonial Andover, Massachusetts* (Ithaca: Cornell University Press, 1970), a detailed examination of the records of a New England town, provides indications that Americans were ready for national independence in the 1770s. John Duffy, *The Healers: The Rise of the Medical Establishment* (New York: McGraw-Hill, 1976), is an account of the medical background of the Revolutionary period and of the role of Benjamin Rush, who foresaw remarkable changes as a result of republican virtues. A sound overview of the entire period is Ralph Ketcham, *From Colony to Country: The Revolution in American Thought, 1750–1820* (New York: Macmillan, 1974).

The subject of early American trade with the Far East, especially with India, discussed in Harold D. Langley's essay, can be examined in greater detail in G. Bhagat, *Americans in India, 1784–1860* (New York: New York University Press, 1970). The bicentennial of the first American contacts with India called forth an updated summary in Bhagat's "Americans and American Trade in India, 1784–1814," *The American Neptune* 46 (1986): 6–15. Additional information on early trade will be found in several documentary publications, especially C. H. Philips and B. B. Misra, eds., *Fort William-India House Correspondence and Other Contemporary Papers Relating Thereto: Foreign and Secret, 1782–1786*, vol. 15 (Delhi: Controller of Publications, Government of India, Civil Lines, 1963); vol. 18 of the same series, ed. by H. Heras (1974); and Worthington C. Ford, ed., *Commerce of Rhode Island, 1726–1800, Proceedings of the Massachusetts Historical Society*, 7th Series, vol. 2 (Boston: Massachusetts Historical Society, 1895). Two individuals who knew a great deal about American trade with Asia and hoped to develop even greater commercial ties between the new republic and the east may be studied in Richard Haskayne McKay, Jr., "Elias Hasket

Derby, Merchant of Salem, Massachusetts, 1739–1799" (Ph.D. dissertation, Clark University, 1961), and Hans Huth and Wilma J. Pugh, trans. and eds., *Talleyrand in America as a Financial Promoter, 1794–96*, vol. 2 of the *Annual Report of the American Historical Association for the Year 1941* (Washington: Government Printing Office, 1942).

Two older works still useful as introductions to the beginning of contacts with Asia are Tyler Dennett's classic, *Americans in Eastern Asia* (New York: Macmillan, 1922), and Charles O. Paullin, *American Voyages to the Orient, 1690–1856* (Annapolis, Md.: U.S. Naval Institute, 1971). James Kirker covers activities in the South Atlantic, Australasia, Polynesia, Fiji, and the southeastern Pacific, as well as Canton and the Indian Ocean, in *Adventures in China: Americans in the Southern Oceans, 1792–1812* (New York: Oxford University Press, 1970). An excellent book supplanting all previous work on the beginnings of American trade with China is Philip Chadwick Foster Smith, *The Empress of China* (Philadelphia: Philadelphia Maritime Museum, 1984). Early American contacts with Japan are examined in Lee Houchins, "The Early American Experience in Japan, 1791–1809: A Reexamination" (unpublished paper, 1973), and William L. Neumann, *America Encounters Japan: From Perry to MacArthur*, paperback edition (New York: Harper & Row, 1963). Important articles on the subject of this chapter include A. Toussaint, "Early American Trade with Mauritius," *Essex Institute Historical Collection* 87 (1951): 353–87; Sharom Ahmat, "Some Problems of the Rhode Island Traders in Java, 1799–1836," *Journal of Southeast Asian History* 6 (1965): 94–117; and John H. Reinoehl, ed., "Some Remarks on the American Trade: Jacob Crowninshield to James Madison, 1806," *William and Mary Quarterly*, 3d Series, 16 (1959): 103–18.

An excellent foundation for the chapter by James A. Field, Jr., can be found in Felix Gilbert, *To the Farewell Address: Ideas of Early American Foreign Policy* (Prineton University Press, 1961), which described the diplomatic implications of "republicanism" before the current scholarship on this subject (none of which addressed the subject of foreign affairs) became fashionable. Field's own book, *America and the Mediterranean World, 1776–1882* (Princeton: Princeton University Press, 1969), expands the concept, discussing the commercial, naval, missionary, and modernization endeavors of

Americans in the Mediterranean, activities that provided a school for later American involvement in the Far East.

Works that consider various aspects of the history of the American maritime frontier and open leads to further investigation include J. G. E. Hutchins, *The American Maritime Industries and Public Policy, 1789–1914* (Cambridge: Harvard University Press, 1941); Charles O. Paullin, *Diplomatic Negotiations of American Naval Officers, 1778–1883* (Baltimore: Johns Hopkins University Press, 1912); Vincent Ponko, *Ships, Seas, and Scientists* (Annapolis, Md.: U.S. Naval Institute, 1974); and Lance C. Buhl, "Maintaining an American Navy, 1865–1889," in Kenneth J. Hagan, ed., *In Peace and War: Interpretations of American Naval History, 1775–1978* (Westport, Conn.: Greenwood Press, 1978). Vernon G. Setser, *The Commercial Reciprocity Policy of the United States, 1774–1829* (Philadelphia: University of Pennsylvania Press, 1937), is the best available work on a subject of great importance. With respect to missionaries, Clifton J. Phillips, *Protestant America and the Pagan World* (Cambridge: Harvard University Press, 1969), takes the story of the American Board of Commissioners to 1860; for a view of the greatly expanded effort at the century's end and a reflection of late nineteenth century attitudes, see James S. Dennis, *Christian Missions and Social Progress*, 3 vols. (New York: Fleming H. Revell Co., 1898–1906).

For a summary of the history of the generalized American effort to help the human race, see James A. Field, Jr., "Philanthrophy," in Alexander DeConde, ed., *Encyclopedia of American Foreign Policy*, 3 vols. (New York: Scribners, 1978). For American technical and scientific advice and assistance to the outer world and the spreading of "every useful art," see Merle Curti and Kendall Birr, *Prelude to Point Four: American Technical Missions Overseas, 1838–1938* (Madison: University of Wisconsin Press, 1954); and for early efforts at economic developments, Mira Wilkins, *The Emergence of Multinational Enterprise: American Business Abroad from the Colonial Era to 1914* (Cambridge: Harvard University Press, 1970).

Other useful works include Ralph W. Hidy, *The House of Baring in American Trade and Finance* (Cambridge: Harvard University Press, 1949), which deals with the most important nineteenth-century assembler and provider of foreign capital; Halvdan Koht, *The*

American Spirit in Europe: A Survey of Translantic Influences (Philadelphia: University of Pennsylvania Press, 1949), and Max Silverschmidt, *The United States and Europe, Rivals and Partners* (New York: Harcourt Brace Jovanovich, 1972), which shed light on the interchange of ideas; Marvin Trachtenberg, *The Statue of Liberty* (New York: Viking, 1976), which is stimulating on the interrelations of international political and aesthetic attitudes; and James Reed, *The Missionary Mind and American East Asia Policy, 1911–1915* (Cambridge: Harvard University Press, 1983), which shows how the missionary effort to convert the Chinese ended up converting American church goers to the support of a metaphorical China. Perhaps the best way to sense the persistence of "republican" ideals is to read some of Woodrow Wilson's speeches on relations with Latin America, on the war in Europe, and on his plans for the peace settlement.

Reginald C. Stuart's chapter can be read in the context of "manifest destiny," for which one should read Albert K. Weinberg's classic *Manifest Destiny: A Study of Nationalist Expansion in American History* (Baltimore: The Johns Hopkins University Press, 1935). The most pertinent books for expansionism and Canada are Donald F. Warner, *The Idea of Continental Union: Agitation for the Annexation of Canada to the United States, 1849–1893* (Lexington: University of Kentucky Press, 1960), and Alvin C. Gluek, Jr., *Minnesota and the Manifest Destiny of the Canadian Northwest* (Toronto: University of Toronto Press, 1958).

Carl Berger assesses a long-lived project that includes relevant books by James M. Callahan, Lester B. Shippee, Albert B. Corey, and John E. Brebner in "Internationalism, Continentalism and the Writing of History: Comments on the Carnegie Series on the Relations of Canada and the United States," in R. A. Preston, ed., *The Influence of the United States on Canadian Development* (Durham, N.C: Duke University Press, 1972), pp. 32–54. See also Charles P. Stacey, "The Myth of the Unguarded Frontier, 1815–1871," *American Historical Review* 46 (1950): 1–18; James Snell, "The Eagle and the Butterfly: Some American Attitudes Towards British North America, 1864–1867" (Ph.D. dissertation, Queens University, 1971); and Allen P. Stouffer, "Canadian-American Relations, 1861–1871" (Ph.D. dissertation, Claremont Graduate School, 1971). Other useful essays include J. C. A. Stagg, "James Madison and the

Coercion of Great Britain: Canada, the West Indies, and the War of 1812," *William and Mary Quarterly*, 3d Series, 38 (1981): 3–34; Douglas Frank, "The Canadian Rebellion and the American Public," *Niagara Frontier* 16 (1969): 96–104; James M. Callahan, "Americo-Canadian Relations Concerning Annexation, 1846–1871," *Studies in American History* (Bloomington: Indiana University Studies, 1926), vol. 6, pp. 187–214; Joe Patterson Smith, "American Republican Leadership and the Movement for Annexation of Canada in the Eighteen Sixties," Canadian Historical Association, *Annual Report* (1935), pp. 65–75; and Doris W. Dashew, "The Story of an Illusion: The Plan to Trade the Alabama Claims for Canada," *Civil War History* 15 (1969): 332–48.

Russell F. Weigley's companion essay on the United States and Canada dwells on military factors in maintaining the North American peace and thus points toward a different set of secondary sources. Basic is Richard A. Preston, *The Defense of the Undefended Border* (Montreal: McGill-Queens's University, 1977). An excellent supplement to Preston for the middle of the nineteenth century, especially useful for setting military issues into the context of Canadian political development, is Charles P. Stacey, *Canada and the British Army, 1846–1871: A Study in the Practice of Responsible Government*, rev. ed. (Toronto: University of Toronto Press, 1963). John Mackay Hitsman, *Safeguarding Canada, 1763–1871* (Toronto: University of Toronto Press, 1968), gives a detaileld view of the military situation in the early years; while Preston's *Canada and "Imperial Defense": A Study of the Origins of the British Commonwealth's Defense Organization, 1869–1919* (Durham, N.C.: Duke University Press, 1967), examines how Canadian-United States military relations helped lay the foundation for the dominions' role in the defense of the British Empire and Commonwealth. Roderick C. MacLeod's *The North-West Mounted Police, 1873–1905* (Toronto: University of Toronto Press, 1976), is by far the best study of the role of this quasi-military force as it affected relations with the United States.

For further reading, see Richard H. Kohn, *Eagle and Sword: The Federalists and the Creation of the Military Establishment in America 1783–1802* (New York: The Free Press, 1975), a peerless history of the political issues involved in the creation of the U.S. Army, including the influence of United States-British-Canadian relations; James Ripley Jacobs, *The Beginning of the U.S. Army, 1783–1812*

(Princeton: Princeton University Press, 1947), which concentrates on military organization and problems but also focuses on the problems of the Canadian border; and Charles Winslow Elliott, *Winfield Scott: The Soldier and the Man* (New York: Macmillan, 1937), indispensable because of Scott's role in military events involving the United States and Canada. Two standard overviews are Robin W. Winks, *Canada and the United States: The Civil War Years* (Baltimore: Johns Hopkins University Press, 1960), and George F. G. Stanley, with Harold M. Jackson, *Canada's Soldiers: The Military History of an Unmilitary People*, rev. ed. (Toronto: Macmillan of Canada, 1954).

Among the books and articles on which Michael A. Lutzker most relied are Dwight D. Eisenhower's presidential memoirs, *Mandate for Change, 1953–1956* and *Waging Peace, 1956–1961* (Garden City, N.Y.: Doubleday, 1963), a retrospective account that warrants comparison with the contemporary record, particularly with recently declassified documents, for Eisenhower underplays the uncertainty and improvisation that characterized American policymaking during the Quemoy-Matsu crises. In "The Taiwan Strait Crisis Revisited: Politics and Foreign Policy in Chinese Motives," *Modern China* 2 (1976): 49–103, Allen S. Whiting rejects the thesis that Mao promoted the 1958 crisis for domestic reasons, emphasizing instead an effort to respond to U.S. actions in Asia and the Middle East. In J. H. Kalacki, *The Pattern of Sino-American Crises* (New York: Cambridge University Press, 1975), the author concludes that China and the United States gradually came to understand each other's "signals" even though they could not come to any formal agreements. In Morton H. Halperin and Tang Tsou, "United States Policy Toward the Offshore Islands," *Public Policy* 15 (1966): 119–38, the authors analyze the reasons why changes in U.S. policy toward the islands were not implemented between the first and second crises, finding the explanation in bureaucratic inertia and the president's inability to overcome distractions caused by other issues. Tang Tsou portrays the main players with considerable insight in *The Embroilment over Quemoy: Mao, Chiang, and Dulles*, International Study Paper #2 (Salt Lake City: Institute of International Studies, University of Utah, 1959).

Several other works deserve attention, including Leonard H. D. Gordon, "United States Opposition to Use of Force in the Taiwan

Strait, 1954–1962," *Journal of American History* 72 (1985): 637–60, which appeared after Lutzker's essay was completed and which, its other merits aside, apparently neglects many recently declassified documents. O. Edmund Clubb, "Formosa and the Offshore Islands in American Policy, 1950–1955," *Political Science Quarterly* 74 (1959): 517–31, a work by a long-time Far Eastern expert, is still valuable. Documenting a wider spectrum of criticism of American policy during the 1958 as compared to the 1954–55 crisis is Marian D. Irish, "Public Opinion and American Foreign Policy: The Quemoy Crisis of 1958," *Political Quarterly* (London) 31 (1960): 151–62. Chi Yung Lin, "The Quemoy Matsu Crisis: A Study of American Policy" (Ph.D. dissertation, Southern Illinois University, 1969), is a thorough and carefully detailed study based on the documents available at the time. In Allen S. Whiting, "New Light on Mao: Quemoy 1958: Mao's Miscalculations," *The China Quarterly*, no. 62 (June 1975): 263–70, a leading scholar draws on Mao's post-crisis writings and speeches to conclude that the Chinese leader made a frank admission that he had miscalculated in 1958 both as to his own objectives and his underestimation of the U.S. response.

John Keegan's essay arises from his earlier works, *The Face of Battle* (New York: Viking Press, 1976) and "The Historian and Battle," *International Security* 3 (1978–79): 138–49. His analysis rests on a close study of the behavior of individual soldiers in battle, an approach pioneered by General S. L. A. Marshall in *Men Against Fire* (New York: William Morrow, 1947). A related study that explores the positive appeals of battle is J. Glenn Gray, *The Warriors: Reflections on Men in Battle* (New York: Harcourt, Brace and Co., 1959; reprinted with new author's foreword by Harper and Row, 1970). Similar, more recent studies of the relationship between individual soldiers' "will to combat" and the performance of their armies are John Ellis, *The Sharp End: The Fighting Man in World War II* (New York: Scribners, 1980), and Richard Holmes, *Acts of War: The Behavior of Men in Battle* (New York: The Free Press, 1986). Attention is also given to these issues in the trenchant memoir from the Vietnam War, Philip Caputo, *A Rumor of War* (New York: Holt, Rinehart and Winston, 1977). Recent attempts from the social sciences to assess the staying power of men in battle include William L. Hauser, "The Will to Fight," in Sam Sarkesian, ed., *Combat Effectiveness: Stress, Cohesion, and the Volunteer Military* (Beverly

Hills, Calif.: Sage, 1980), and Anthony Kellett, *Combat Motivation: The Behavior of Soldiers in Battle* (Boston: Kluwer-Nijhoff Publishing, 1982).

The current state of military history, including its attention to the kind of issues raised in Keegan's chapter, can be followed in Peter Karsten, "The 'New' American Military History: A Map of the Territory, Explored and Unexplored," *American Quarterly* 36 (1984): 389–418. Focusing on a particular phase of that history is Marvin R. Cain, "A 'Face of Battle' Needed: An Assessment of Motives and Men in Civil War Historiography," *Civil War History* 18 (1982): 5–27.

Since the horrors of World War I discredited early-twentieth-predictions that the modern abominations of battle and the cost of war generally would make large future wars impossible, few writers other than Keegan in this essay have returned to the subject. A large literature does exist, however, on the alleged demoralization of U.S. forces during the Vietnam War, including Robert D. Heinl, Jr., "Commentary: The Collapse of the Armed Forces," *Armed Forces Journal* 108 (1971): 30–38; Richard Boyle, *The Flower of the Dragon: The Breakdown of the U.S. Army in Vietnam* (San Francisco: Ramparts Press, 1972); "Cincinnatus," *Self-Destruction: The Disintegration and Decay of the United States Army during the Vietnam Era* (New York: W. W. Norton & Co., 1981); and Shelby L. Stanton, *The Rise and Fall of an American Army: U.S. Ground Forces in Vietnam, 1965–1973* (San Rafael, Calif.: Presidio Press, 1985). The inquiring reader will probably also wish to consult Arthur H. Westing, "War as a Human Endeavor: The High-Fatality Wars of the Twentieth Century," *Journal of Peace Research* 19 (1982): 261–70. An analysis of how wars generally end, if not of how to end all wars, is Fred C. Iklé, *Every War Must End* (New York: Columbia University Press, 1971).

Index

Acheson, Dean, 163, 174

Adams, Abigail, 19 n.10, 31

Adams, Charles Francis, 119

Adams, John: on American Revolution, 24, 25, 26; on cultural achievements, 31, 89; as diplomat, x, 1; as pro-British, 33, 34; on title for president, 29–30

Adams, John Quincy, 78, 91, 103, 116

Aiken, Sen. George J., 174

American-British-Canadian relations: annexation, attitudes about, 103–7, 116, 118–20; border disputes, 107–8, 142–45; and British military position in North America, 134–41; and Canadian independence movement, 110–13, 118–20, 142; and trade, 113–18; and Trent affair, 147–48; and U.S. expansionism, 103–4, 108–9, 136; and War of 1812, 139–42

"Americanization" of third world countries, 24, 33–34

"The American Revolution: The Ideology and Psychology of National Liberation" (Burrows and Wallace), 27

Amity and Commerce, Treaty of, 54, 78

Andover, Massachusetts, demographic analysis of settlers in, 26

Andrews, Israel, 115, 116, 117, 118, 120

Angell, Norman, 199

Anti-Americanism, Canadian, 107, 121

Argentina, American influence on education in, 86

Armed Neutrality, 78

Aroostook "War" of 1839, 108, 145

Arts and literature: American competitiveness with Europe, 28–29, 31–32; influence of nineteenth-century American, 87

Asiatic Bank proposal, 53

Astor, John Jacob, 113

Atlantic cable, 87–88

Bagot, Charles, 141
Bailyn, Bernard, 25
Bancroft, George, 24, 105, 117
Banks, Nathaniel, 105
Baring, Alexander, Baron Ashburton, 145
Baring family, 95 n.21
Barlow, Joel, 76, 77–78, 82, 92
Barnum, P. T., 87
Bates, Joshua, 95 n.21
Battlefield experiences. *See* War
Battlefield, medieval, 194–95
Bayonne Proclamation (France, 1808), 55
Beaumez, Bon-Albert Briois de, 53
Bell, Thomas, 43
Bemis, Samuel Flagg, viii, 144
Bennett, James Gordon, 105, 119
Benton, Thomas Hart, 113
Bismarck, Otto von, 149–50
Blainey, Geoffrey, 153
Blake, George, 13–14
Blodget, Samuel, Jr., 69
Boycotts, consumer, 7–8
Bradley, Gen. Omar, xii
Brasher, Abraham, 14, 19 n.12
Brasher, Helen Kortright, 6, 19 n.12
Brega, George W., 120
British Constitutional Act of 1791, 124 n.6
British East India Company, 41, 46, 48, 49, 51
British North America Act, 150
Brown, Benson, and Ives, 46
Brown, Charles Brockden, 11
Brown, Maj.-Gen. Jacob, 140
Bruni, Leonardo, 4
Buchanan, James, 87
Buffon, Georges Louis Leclerc de, 28
Burgin, Elizabeth, 8, 10
Burrows, E. G., 27

Cables, telegraph, 87–88, 90, 91
Calhoun, John C., 107
Canada: border disarmament, 78; independence, 110-n11, 119, 142, 150; military, 151–53; nationalism, 139, 150. *See also* American-British-Canadian relations
Carleton, Guy, Baron Dorchester, 137
Carney, Adm. Robert, 166–67
Caroline affair, 111, 142–44
Cass, Lewis, 107
Chandler, Zachariah, 119
Chesapeake incident, 32
Chiang Kai-shek, 162, 163, 170, 172, 173, 175–79
China, American trade with, 41–43, 47, 49–50, 55, 59, 71–72
China, People's Republic of, and confrontation with U.S. in Quemoy-Matsu crisis, 161–85
Chou En-lai, 169, 170, 174
Christianity, and U.S. foreign diplomacy, 82, 89–90
Churchill, Winston, 167, 177
Citizenship, meaning of, in postrevolutionary America, 1–6, 11
Civil War, and American-British-Canadian relations, 148–50
Clay, Henry, 103
Clayton, John M., 117
Commerce: British military protection of provincial trade, 135–36; U.S. foreign, in Indian and Pacific Oceans, 39–73; U.S. policy and theory of, in late eighteenth century, 76–79. *See also* Expansionism, U.S.; Reciprocity, U.S. policy
Commercial Convention of 1815, 59
Commercial reciprocity, U.S. policy, 81, 85

Common Sense, 26–27

Communism, U.S. policy on control of, 163, 171, 177

Conkling, Roscoe, 120

Constitution of 1787, 134, 136

Constitution, U.S., 2, 78

Consuls, U.S.: in Canadian provincial ports, 114–15, 120; in India-China trade, 50, 52, 59

Continental Army, 134

Cook, Capt. James, 42

Cooper, Sen. John Serman, 174

Cooper, Samuel, 54

Cornwallis, Charles, Lord, 44–45, 48

Corporations, early multinational, 90, 113

Countryman, Edward, 11

Coverture, 11–15

Coxe, Tench, 69

Coxe, William, Jr., 47

Cress, Lawrence, 4

Crowninshield family, 48, 52

Cultural competition, U.S. and Great Britain, 28–29, 31–32

Danish trade, 50–51

Darby, William, 119

Davis, Daniel, 13

Dearborn, Henry, 104

Declaration of Independence, 2

Democratic party, position on defense of Formosa, 182 n.19

Denby, Charles, Jr., 96 n.27

DePauw, Abbé Corneille, 32

Derby, E. H., 105, 118

Derby, Elias Hasket, Jr., 46, 49, 57

Devereux, Capt. James, 57

Dickens, Charles, 15

Douglas, Capt. James, 56

Douglas, Stephen A., 116

Drew, Capt. Andrew, 142

Duane, William, 117

Dulles, John Foster, 164, 165, 166, 168, 174, 175, 176, 179

Dundas, Henry, 58–59

Durfee, Amos, 142

Dutch East India Company, 56, 57

Economics, eighteenth-century theory, 39–40, 76

Eden, Anthony, 166

Education, nineteenth-century U.S. influence on foreign, 83, 86, 89

Edwards, Jonathan, 82

Egan, Patrick, 91

Eisenhower, Dwight D.: and Quemoy-Matsu crisis, 162–80; and use of nuclear weapons, 166, 172, 178, 180

Elgin, Lord, 166

Embargo Act of 1807, 55, 58

Embargoes: British, of Mauritius, 50, 55, 59; by Jefferson administration, 32, 33

Emotions in battle, soldiers', 193–99

Expansionism, U.S.: and American-British-Canadian relations, 103–4, 108–9, 136; commerce and, 81, 84–86, 88–89, 113–18; ideology and, 103–4, 109–13, 121; in North America, 102; post-Civil War, 119; and slavery, 106, 110, 116, 121

Fairfield, Gov. John, 145

Fallen Timbers (Indian war), 137–38

Familial analogy to American independence, 24–27

Fear, in battle, 194–99

Fenians, 105, 151

Field, Cyrus, 87
Fish, Hamilton, 120
Florida Treaty, 80
Foreign commerce. *See* Commerce
Formosa. *See* Taiwan
France, 80; American alliance
    with, 77–78; China trade, 47;
    end of power in India, 48–49;
    Indian trade and U.S. relations,
    49–51, 52–55; Quasi-War, 138–
    39, 140. *See also* French
    Revolution
Franklin, Benjamin, ix, x, 1, 78,
    103
Frederick II of Prussia, vii
Fremont, John Charles, 113
French Revolution, 30, 79, 112;
    and American attitudes toward
    Britain, 30; women's political
    role and, 15–16
Fulbright, Sen. J. William, 174
Fulton, Robert, 83

Galtier-Boissiere, J., 195
George, Sen. Walter, 167
George III, viii, 26
Ghent, Treaty of, 80
Goodpaster, Col. Andrew, 183
    n.21
Gray, Capt. Robert, 55
Great Awakening, 77, 82
Great Britain: Canadian provincial
    loyalty to, 106–7; decline of mil-
    itary power, 148–50; deterrence
    of American annexation of Can-
    ada, 106, 120, 121; military posi-
    tion in North America, 134–41;
    psychological themes in Ameri-
    can independence from, 23–26;
    toleration of American trade in
    India, 44–47; and trade competi-
    tion with U.S. in Indian and Pa-
    cific Oceans, 41–59; U.S.

cultural competition with, 28–
    29, 31–32. *See also* American-
    British-Canadian relations
Great Republic (merchant ship),
    87, 88
Greeley, Horace, 119
Green, John, 42–43
Green, Sen. Theodore, 174,
    175
Green, William, 44
Greenville, Treaty of, 138
Greven, Philip, 26
Grimke, Sarah, 13
Guadalupe Hidalgo, Treaty of,
    84

Hacker, Barton, 8–9
Haliburton, Thomas Chandler,
    117
Hamilton, Alexander, 18 n.3, 28,
    78, 79, 138–39
Hammond, John Hays, 96 n.27
Hartley, David, ix–x, 1
Harvey, Sir John, 145
Hastings, Warren, 44
Head, Sir Francis Bond, 144,
    146
History of the United States (Ban-
    croft), 24
Hoover, Herbert, 96 n.27
Hopkins, Rev. Samuel, 77, 82
Hornby, William, 44
Hull, Gen. William, 107
Humphreys, David, 82
Hutchinson, Thomas, 25

Impressment of seamen, 32–33,
    80
India, American trade with, 41,
    43–59, 68–73
India Act (England, 1784), 44
Indian buffer state, U.S.-British
    conflict over, 134–40

Industrialization, American, 88–89

Jackson, Andrew, 140
Janis, Irving, 178
Japan: American influence on education, nineteenth-century, 86; U.S. trade with, 55–57
Java, U.S. trade with, 58, 59–60
Jay, John, x, 1, 39, 42, 51
Jay, Sarah Livingston, 1–2, 5, 6–7, 15, 17
Jay Treaty of 1794, 51, 58, 59, 64 nn.43, 44, 68 n.66
Jefferson, Thomas: on American accomplishments, 28; and Canada, 103; and foreign trade, 32, 33, 42, 47, 69, 80; and military, 139
Jones, John Paul, 42
Jordan, Winthrop, 26–27
Joy, Benjamin, 52, 65 n.45

Kefauver, Sen. Estes, 166
Kendrick, John, 55–56
Kennedy, John F., 174
Kenyon, Lord, 59
Kettner, James, 3
Knox, Henry, 136
Korean War, 163
Kossuth, Louis, 85

The Ladies of Castille, 17
Lambton, John George, Earl of Durham, 145–46
Langer, Sen. William, 182 n.18
Laurens, Henry, x
Lawson, Capt. Patrick, 62 n.16
Ledyard, John, 42
Lehman, Sen. Herbert, 167, 182 n.18
Leon, Pauline, 15

Lincoln, Abraham, 148, 153
Linn, Lewis, 104
Lippman, Walter, 174
Livingston, Catharine, 6–7
Livingston, Henry, 8
Livingston, Margaret, 3, 6, 11
Livingston, William, 6
London Exhibition, 87
Long, Sen. Russell, 165
Loyalism, 106–7
Lyons, Richard Bickerton Pemell, 147

McCarthy, Sen. Joseph, 178
Macartney, Lord, 43
Macarty, William, 50
Macdonald, John A., 102, 120
McKay, Donald, 87, 88
Mackenzie, William Lyon, 111, 142
Madison, James, 103, 139
Mahan, A. T., 88
Maine-Canada boundary dispute, 108, 145
Manjiro, 86
Mann, Horace, 86
Mansfield, Sen. Mike, 174
Mao Tse-tung, 162, 163, 172
Marcy, William L., 116, 118, 143
Marshall, Gen. S. L. A., 197
Martin v. Commonwealth of Massachusetts, 12–14
Mason, James J., 147
Mauritius (Isle of France), and U.S. trade with India and China, 49–51, 54–55, 59, 71
Maury, Matthew, 85
Mechanical arts, nineteenth-century American successes in, 87
Menken, Ada, 87
Merchant marine, U.S.: and for-

eign diplomacy, 79, 81, 85, 88–
    89; trade in Indian and Pacific
    Oceans, 39–73
Military service: relationship to
    citizenship in postrevolutionary
    America, 1–2, 4–5; and women,
    in French Revolution, 15. *See
    also* U.S. Army
Militia Act of 1868 (Canada),
    152
Mill, Harriet Taylor, 86
Miller, W. J., 52
Mining engineers, worldwide de-
    ployment of American, 96
    n.27
Missionaries, U.S. foreign, 82, 89–
    90, 102, 113
Model Treaty of 1776, 76, 78
Monroe, James, 103, 116
Monroe-Pinckney Treaty of 1806,
    59
Moore, William, 43
Morphy, Paul, 87
Morris, Gouverneur, 69
Morris, Robert, 41–42, 49
Morse, Sen. Wayne, 165, 167, 182
    n.18

Netherlands, trade with Far East,
    56–58
Neutrality, U.S., 112–13
Nixon, Richard M., 174
Non-Intercourse Act of 1809, 55,
    58
Northwest Indians, British rela-
    tions with, 135–38, 139, 140
North West Mounted Police
    (N.W.M.P.), 151
Nuclear weapons and warfare, 198;
    U.S. policy in Quemoy-Matsu
    crisis, 166, 171, 172, 173, 175,
    178, 180

O'Cain, Capt. Joseph, 67 n.59
O'Donnell, John, 46–47
Osborn, Sarah, 10
O'Sullivan, John L., 104, 110

Paine, Charles H., 143
Paine, Thomas, 26–27
Palmerston, Henry John Temple,
    144, 146, 149
Papineau, Louis Joseph, 142
Parsons, Theophilus, 13, 14
Peabody, George, 95 n.21
Peace movement, American nine-
    teenth-century, 86–87
Pearson, Lester, 166
Peel, Sir Robert, 146
Perry, Comdr. Matthew C., 60
Perry, Oliver Hazard, 140, 141
Pethick, William, 96 n.27
Phillips, Vice Adm. W. K., 181
    n.9
Pieczenik, Steven, 32
Pierce, Franklin, 116, 118
Pitkin, Hanna Fenichel, 4
Pitkin, Timothy, 70–71
Pitt, William the Younger, 44
Pocock, J. G. A., 4
Polk, James K., 84, 113
Poor, John, 118
Potter, John, 118
Privateering, 40, 50, 54–55
Protestant Christianity, and U.S.
    foreign diplomacy, 82, 89–90
Provinces, British. *See* American-
    British-Canadian relations
Psychological aspects of American
    independence, 23–36
Psychological aspects of crisis deci-
    sion-making, 178–79
Psychological experience of battle,
    soldiers', 193–99
Pumpelly, Raphael, 96 n.27

Quasi-War, 54, 138–39
Quemoy-Matsu crisis, U.S. policy in, 161–85

Radford, Adm. Arthur, 164, 169, 177
Reciprocity, U.S. policy, 81, 85
Reciprocity Treaty of 1854, 105, 115–16, 118, 146
Religion: belief among soldiers in battle, 197; influence of American missionaries, 82, 89–90; and rebublican ideology, 82
Republicanism, 75–77; and expansionism, 109, 113
Republican Party, anti-Communist policy of (1952), 163, 177
Reston, James, 166, 167, 174
"Restook War" (Aroostook war), 108, 145
Reynal, Abbé, 28
Ridgeway, Gen. Matthew B., 164
Riel, Louis, 105
Riel Rebellion, 1869–70, 151
Roberts, Edmund, 59–60
Robertson, Walter, 169, 176
Rockhill, William W., 96 n.27
Rowson, Susannah, 10
Royster, Charles, 4–5
Rush, Benjamin, 28
Rush, Richard, 141
Rush-Bagot Agreement of 1817, 107, 141
Russell, William H. "Bull Run," 149
Russian-American Company, 67 n.59

Sansom, Joseph, 104
Sarmiento, Domingo Faustino, 86
Schwoerer, Lois G., 2

Science: American competitiveness with Europe, 31; American faith in, 77
Scott, Winfield, 108, 111, 140, 143–46
Second Mysore War (1780–84), 44–45
Second Seminole War (1835–42), 143
Sedgwick, Judge Theodore, 14
Seward, William Henry, 105, 118, 119, 148
Shaw, Maj. Samuel, 43
Sheffield, Lord, 79
Shore, Sir John, 65 n.45
Siam, U.S. trade with, 57, 59–60
Simcoe, Lt. Gov. John Graves, 137
Slavery, and expansionism, 106, 110, 116, 121
Slidell, John, 147
Smith, Adam, 39
Smith, J. Lawrence, 96 n.27
Smith, Maj. Gen. Samuel, 140
Smithson, James, 95 n.21
South America, proposals for British/American invasion of, 33–34
Soviet Union, and Quemoy-Matsu crisis, 165, 168, 172–73
Stacey, C. P., 101, 102
Stewart, William F., 56–57
Stockton, Richard, 21 n.27
Straight, Willard, 96 n.27
Student Volunteer Movement (1886), 89
Stump, Adm. Felix, 183 n.21
Sumner, Charles, 104, 105, 120
Syngman Rhee, 163

Taiwan (Formosa), civil war, and Quemoy-Matsu crisis, 161–85

A *Tale of Two Cities*, 15
Tallyrand-Périgord, Charles Maurice de, 52–53
Taylor, Gen. Maxwell, 176
Telegraph, international, 87–88, 90, 91
Territorial expansion, U.S. *See* Expansionism, U.S.
Third World, 24, 33–34, 198
Thulmeier, Frederick William von, xii
Tocqueville, Alexis de, 84
Trent affair, 147–48
Truman, Harry S., 162–63, 174
Tsou, Tang, 173
Turgot, Anne Robert Jacques, Baron de l'Aulne, 76
Twining, Gen. Nathan, 174–75

United Nations, 164
United States: Anglophobia, 103; citizenship definitions in revolutionary era, 1–17; commerce, eighteenth-century theory and policy, 76–79; import/export statistics, 1795–1802, 68–73; policy in Quemoy-Matsu crisis with China, 161–85; psychological themes in and responses to independence, 23–36; trade in Indian and Pacific Oceans, 39–73; trade with Mauritius, and relations with France, 49–51, 54–55. *See also* American-British-Canadian relations; Expansionism, U.S.
U.S. Army, growth from postrevolutionary era to Civil War, 133–48
U.S. Congress, and U.S. policy in Quemoy-Matsu crisis, 166–67, 174, 175
U.S. Constitution, 2, 78

U.S. Navy: as commerce-protecting instrument, 81; decline of, 88–89; on Great Lakes, 140, 141; role in Quemoy-Matsu crisis, 163, 172, 175, 176

Van Buren, Martin, 111, 112, 142, 143, 145
van Rensselaer, Rensselaer, 111
Vietnam War, drug use in, 197

Walker Tariff, 85
Wallace, Michael, 27
War: primitive, 192–93; psychological experience of, 193–99; subjective experience of, 189–91
War of 1812, 32–33; 112; and Canada, 106, 107, 114; effect on U.S. military development, 139–42; and Pacific and Indian Ocean trade, 57, 59
Warren, Mercy Otis, 9, 17
Washington, George: and bleeding, 28; on foreign commerce, 48; and military, 136, 138; and neutrality, 112; as pro-British, 33, 34; title for, 29–30; and women in war, 8–10
Washington Treaty, of 1871, 102, 120, 150
Wayne, Anthony, 136, 137–38
The Wealth of Nations, 39
Webster-Ashburton Treaty, 145–46
Webster, Daniel, 108, 145
Wellington, Arthur Wellesley, Duke of, 143
Wells, Rachel, 10, 16
Wheaton, Henry, 87
Wiley, Sen. Alexander, 167
Wilkes, Capt. Charles, 113, 147

Wilkinson, Brig. Gen. James, 138, 139
Williams, E. T., 96 n.27
Wilson v. Marryat, 59
Winthrop, John, 75
Wollstonecraft, Mary, 18 n.2
Women: American influence on foreign attitudes about, 83; citizenship and, 1–2, 5; married, and citizenship, 11–14, 16; political action by, 7–11, 15

Women of the Army, 8–10
Women's rights movement, nineteenth-century, 86
Woodward, A. B., 103
World War I, battlefield experience of, 194, 195
World War II, collective experience of, 190–91

Yung Wing, 86

About the Contributors

JAMES A. FIELD, JR., professor of history at Swarthmore College, has also taught at the U.S. Naval War College and has been an historical adviser to both the United States Army and Navy. His best-known book is *America and the Mediterranean World, 1776–1882* (1969). His many other publications include *History of U.S. Naval Operations: Korea* (1962) and the influential *American Historical Review* article, " 'American Imperialism': The Worst Chapter in Almost Any Book" (1978).

JOHN KEEGAN is defence correspondent for the *Daily Telegraph* in London and is a fellow of the Royal Society of Literature. He taught for many years at Britain's Royal Military Academy, Sandhurst. He is the author of *The Face of Battle* (1976) and *Six Armies in Normandy* (1982), as well as many other books and articles.

LINDA K. KERBER, professor of history at the University of Iowa, has written widely in women's history, concentrating on the era of the American Revolution. Her best-known work is *Women of the Republic: Intellect and Ideology in Revolutionary America* (1980). She coedited *Women's America: Refocusing the Past* (1982) and has also written on early nineteenth-century politics and abolitionism.

HAROLD D. LANGLEY is curator of naval history at the Smithsonian Institution and teaches diplomatic history at The Catholic University of America. He was coeditor of *Roosevelt and Churchill: Their Secret Wartime Correspondence* (1975) and author of *Social Reform in the United States Navy, 1798–1862* (1967).

MICHAEL A. LUTZKER, associate professor in the History Department and Program in Archival Management and Historical Editing at New York University, specializes in the study of peace movements and the impact of war on modern societies. Formerly president of the Conference on Peace Research in History, he has written numerous articles and papers on the American peace movement and on the prevention of war.

DAVID F. MUSTO is professor of psychiatry and the history of medicine at Yale University. On the staff of Yale's Child Study Center and the Bush Center in Child Development and Social Policy, his scholarly interests range widely. He has published important works on psychohistory, on the history of narcotics, and on the Adams Family.

REGINALD C. STUART of the University of Prince Edward Island is known for his numerous works on nineteenth-century United States approaches to war, peace, and nationalism. Among them are *The Half-Way Pacifist: Thomas Jefferson's View of War* (1978) and *War and American Thought: From the Revolution to the Monroe Doctrine* (1982).

RUSSELL F. WEIGLEY is professor of history at Temple University. His books include *Towards an American Army: Military Thought from Washington to Marshall* (1962), *History of the United States Army* (1967; 2d ed., 1984); *The Partisan War: The South Carolina Campaign of 1780–1782* (1970); *The American Way of War: A History of United States Military Strategy and Policy* (1973), and *Eisenhower's Lieutenants: The Campaign of France and Germany, 1944–1945* (1981).

About the Editors

JOAN R. CHALLINOR is a Professorial Lecturer in the Department of History at American University, Washington, D.C. Her earlier works include *Kin and Communities: Families in America*, (coedited with Allan J. Lichtman) and "Family Photographs," published in *Your Family History*.

ROBERT L. BEISNER is Professor and Chairman of the Department of History, American University, Washington, D.C. He is the author of *Twelve Against Empire: The Anti-Imperialists, 1898–1900* and *From the Old Diplomacy to the New, 1865–1900*, and has contributed articles to the *Political Science Quarterly*.